Sex and Marriage in
Victorian Poetry

By the same author

Words, Things, and Celebrations (1971)

Gerard Manley Hopkins: The Poet as Victorian (1968)

A Poetry Anthology, with M. K. Danziger (1968)

An Introduction to Literary Criticism, with M. K. Danziger (1962; revised and reissued as *An Introduction to the Study of Literature*, 1965)

The Voices of Matthew Arnold (1961)

SEX AND MARRIAGE IN VICTORIAN POETRY

Wendell Stacy Johnson

Cornell University Press

ITHACA AND LONDON

First published 1975 by Cornell University Press
Published in the United Kingdom by Cornell University Press Ltd., 2-4 Brook Street, London W1Y 1AA.

International Standard Book Number 0-8014-0845-8
Library of Congress Catalog Card Number 74-25370
Printed in the United States of America by York Composition Co., Inc.

To my students

Contents

Preface

Sex and Marriage in Victorian Poetry—the title could indicate a study of nineteenth-century prudery and hypocrisy. That is probably what the words *sex* and *Victorian,* when juxtaposed, suggest to most readers. But this book is about awareness: the Victorian poets' awareness of sexual drives, sexual frustrations, and what we now call sexism. It has to do with sexual relations, inside and outside marriage, as a literary theme with psychological and political implications in the English poetry of some fifty years, from 1830 to 1880. It is concerned with the idea of marriage in this self-consciously transitional period. The major emphasis is on major poets, especially Tennyson and Browning.

My interest in sex as a significant theme in the poetry of that age began with my paper, "The Theme of Marriage in Tennyson," delivered at the 1957 meeting of the Modern Language Association. As the dedication of this volume is meant to show, my students at Smith College, at Hunter College, and in the Graduate School of the City University of New York have influenced my thinking on the subject since then. They have taught me in the classroom, and some of them have taught me in what they wrote after their college years: in particular, Sylvia Plath,

Gloria Steinem, and Kate Millett. I owe a special debt of gratitude to another former student, Gordon Lea of Herbert Lehman College of the City University, who read these pages, sentence by sentence, and helped to improve them.

W. S. J.

New York City

*Sex and Marriage in
Victorian Poetry*

1 | Sexual Attitudes: "Victorian" and Victorian

"The sexual revolution" became, during the middle decades of this self-conscious century, a familiar phrase. Like other vague but pervasive movements about which we now read, it is almost as much the creation of journalists as their discovery. Like other revolutions or versions of revolution in the western world today, it has for different persons very different, even contradictory, meanings. Yet widely used words and phrases, even if imprecise in their implications, both reflect and affect reality in some way. The fact that we now speak and write of sexual matters more freely than our parents and grandparents did is no doubt significant and no doubt related as symptom and impetus to the sexual attitudes and actions of many people. But what does a revolution in thinking about sexuality and in sexual behavior mean? What changes do we believe have occurred, are ocurring, or should occur? What new possibilities challenge the old, the received, the customary?

First, the very possibility of discussing sexual organs and sexual acts, the demand for openness about what were once called the facts of life, may indicate a variety of attitudes, ranging from approval of "sex education" in the schools to tolerance of pornography. In opposition to this demand is an insistence on the private nature of sexual activity and the impropriety, even the iniquity, of making it a subject of public discussion and exploitation. Second, and more significant, the principle that sexual activity is a private concern, that it should not generally be subject to legal or other social constraints, has led to agitation against laws, civil and ecclesiastical, that proscribe extramarital intercourse, homosexuality, birth control, and abortion. Opposed to this agitation, and to the abolition of some or all of these laws, are both those who argue on traditional moral grounds and those who argue for the right of the still conservative majority to prevail on such touchy questions. Third, and yet more significant, the revival of the women's movement represents not only an assertion of women's rights to social equality but also—because sexual stereotyping has so obviously kept women in what was regarded as their place—an attack on sexual role-playing, on the rigid and largely arbitrary "sexualizing" of persons that limits, according to sex, what work they can do and how they can behave.

In each of these instances a new or revolutionary attitude is opposed to a conservative attitude. But a person may be revolutionary in one respect and conservative in another. A man whose response to overpopulation is to favor birth control and abortion as alternatives to the curbing of sexual appetites may object to minimizing social-sexual contrasts between women and men. A woman who struggles to liberate herself from sexual role-playing may be intolerant of pornography that exaggerates sexual polarity so that women and men are virtually reduced to the status of sexual organs, in a process that deliberately degrades women, especially.

Sexually liberated men and women—the sex educator, the pornographer, the campaigner for homosexual rights, the feminist—may have little more in common than the notion each has of freedom from attitudes of the past. Frequently in ordinary speech and in journalistic comment, and now and then in more thoughtful discourse, this past is labeled "Victorian." In reality, the Victorian past had its own conflicts, its own diversity of liberating or revolutionary attitudes challenging conservative values, its own confusion and ferment about sexual candor, sexual freedom, sexual roles. The sexual revolution—or perhaps, more aptly, several sexual revolutions—actually began in the Victorian age.

Critics, scholars, and teachers have tried in various ways to distinguish what can be said about a culturally and intellectually diverse period of nearly seventy years—one full of conflicts, contradictions, and dizzying changes—from the common associations with the word "Victorian," a word still widely used to condemn someone or something.[1]

1. Much of the criticism of Victorian novelists, poets, and prophets in the past seventy-odd years has reflected, and in part has been, a criticism of the whole age. One can divide it into four stages, each lasting between fifteen and twenty years. Until nearly 1920, critics usually referred to the writers and writing of the previous century in tones ranging from the enthusiasm of G. K. Chesterton praising the Victorians for their vigor, to the reverence of earnest books about Browning (or Tennyson or Carlyle) as a great personality and teacher of philosophy, religion, and morals. A reaction came in the late teens and the twenties with debunking studies, often more popular than scholarly, that attacked Victorian prudery, rarely acknowledging how much of their ammunition against all things Victorian, including Victorian writers, came from those very writers' assaults on prudery. Critics in the next stage. which lasted into the forties, were likely to accept the opinion that, by and large, the Victorian period was one of compromise and

The associations remain. They include some vague ideas about imperialism, laissez-faire capitalism, and child labor, about Whiggery and the triumph of the middle-class mind. Perhaps the most frequent popular assumption is that "Victorianism" means sexual hypocrisy, repression, denial of natural impulse.

Private Lives

One can cite examples from Victorian lives as well as Victorian literature to argue against the notion that all Victorians were prudes who insisted on strict conventionality in sexual matters: George Eliot's relation with Lewes (honorable though that relation certainly was, she had to bear

---

confusion, one somehow inimical to art, and that good Victorians were good in spite of being Victorian. In the fourth stage, recognizable by the 1940's, critics have taken another look at the major writers of the period and at the period itself, trying to interpret and judge the contributions of individual writers, neither praising nor condemning them primarily because of the times in which they lived and wrote. Although there are more reasons than one for these shifts in attitude toward Victorian literature, they seem to be associated with sociosexual matters. To the very early modern critics, Victorian novelists and poets were likely to represent moral principle, a sense of stability, commitment to family life, and assurance as to just what men and women are and should be. This assumption was accepted uncritically by the popularizers of the nineteen-twenties, who reacted to it by calling all Victorians smug and sexually hypocritical. The later revisionist stage tended to emphasize the "un-Victorian" sexual freedom championed and acted on by such Victorians as John Stuart Mill and George Eliot. Slowly it became evident that many Victorians were, in many ways, "un-Victorian." From a sexual or any other point of view, it seems difficult to generalize about what is in fact Victorian—difficult but not impossible if we take into account both popular nineteenth-century assumptions and the remarkable idiosyncracy, not to say oddity, of almost every important Victorian writer.

the stigma of a woman living in sin); Rossetti's open affairs with numerous mistresses and with the wife of his best friend, William Morris; Swinburne's flagrant masochism. A slightly more sophisticated view is that the Victorians were, by and large, hypocrites as well as prudes in public. Even quite serious recent studies have tended to emphasize Victorian repressions and, as it were, underground outlets for the sexual urge rather than to indicate the extent to which Victorians were aware of, and sometimes candid about, social-sexual problems.

Steven Marcus' *The Other Victorians: A Study of Sexuality and Pornography in Mid-Nineteenth Century England* suggests in its main title a contrast between the conventional Victorian figure (whose prudery perhaps remains unquestioned) and the "others" represented in underground literature—although he actually shows an essential relation between the pornography and the literary art of the period, especially that of Dickens. Marcus makes an important point in discussing the books about prostitution and sexuality by the physician William Acton: "sexuality itself had come to be regarded as problematical"; but he does not indicate how often sexuality was problematical, a central, conscious preoccupation, for many major Victorian writers. Still, Marcus' book is a genuine contribution to our understanding of an age. The tendency to see Victorian sexuality as secret and vicious, in radical and piquant contrast to the attitudes associated with "Victorianism," is evident in a less serious study, Ronald Pearsall's *The Worm in the Bud*, which suggests that there were plenty of "dirty" doings behind a prim façade. Russell Goldfarb's *Sexual Repression and Victorian Literature* points out a number of sexual strains and implications in the work of major writers—his analyses are by and large sound—but here, too, as the title implies, the author's interest is more in repression than in open expression. A scholarly study of sexual love in Victorian literature is still likely to skirt the more specifically physical and psychologically complex aspects of the subject even when the literature rather clearly presents them. Gerhard Joseph's *Tennysonian Love*, for example, finds two versions of love in Tennyson, which Joseph calls Dantean and Platonic; neither of these philosophic designations need imply sexual activity at all. In fact, almost no recent book or essay which relates the private matter of sex to the public form of literature tries seriously to qualify the familiar stereotype of the prudish and repressed *or* hypocritical Victorian writer.[2]

Although examples of Victorian sexual daring may indicate that the impressive Victorian artists, the great novelists and poets, were not prudes about sex, some of them *were* sometimes prudish—or, at least, willing to bow to popular opinion—and almost all seem to have been inconsistent. This was a period when the subject of sexual functions and the relations of the sexes was very much in question, very much in the minds of thoughtful and nervous men and women. It is certainly not true that all the Victorians feared sex and tried to ignore it, but a great many of them were preoccupied with sexuality. (They were no more preoccupied than we are in the present age, with our relentless sexualizing not only of almost every aspect of adult life but of virtually every experience from infancy onward, our

---

2. *The Other Victorians* (New York, 1966), p. 264; *The Worm in the Bud* (London, 1969); *Sexual Repression and Victorian Literature* (Lewisburg, Pa., 1970); *Tennysonian Love: The Strange Diagonal* (Minneapolis, 1969).

commercializing of the body and its functions, our substitution of the strip-tease and the worked-up sexuality and violence of the movies for spontaneous sexual response.) The frequent Victorian fascination with—and fear of—sex, which we may too easily dismiss as silly or as the hypocrisy of the prurient, is a reaction that forecasts the modern tendency to give sexuality and the emotions that can be attached to sexual relations the importance, the intensity, and even the fearsomeness that once was associated by most people with religion. The ordinary modern person's persistent and sometimes desperate need to find identity in a sexual role, to express power or be assured of value within a bond of erotic love, was predicted by Matthew Arnold in the last verse paragraph of "Dover Beach," which is a *cri de coeur* for such a love to replace both a lost tragic vision and a lost faith. And the often relentless modern exploitation of all sexual acts and sexual characteristics is only an exaggerated reaction to the Victorian fears about how sex could be used. Freud was born in the Victorian age, and so were most of his patients.[3] Despite the bawdiness of Elizabethans and of Restoration wits, it seems unlikely that any earlier times have been, not so intrigued by, but so obsessed by, so compulsive about, human sexuality as the nineteenth and twentieth centuries. This is what the literature and art, both popular and serious, suggest, whether they mask or shout the concern. So the horror of finding sexual meanings everywhere in one age simply becomes the

3. It has fairly often been pointed out how much his time, place, and personal background prejudice Freud's thought on sexuality and especially on the lesser psychic strength of women (with their supposed "penis envy"), and how these prejudices are formalized and fixed by disciples who regard psychoanalytic theory as dogma.

grim insistence on finding it everywhere in the next, and the blushing young woman with covered ankles is—almost inevitably—succeeded by the topless waitress.

There is some truth in the common assertion that Victorian nervousness about sex resulted from the triumph of middle-class evangelical Protestant values in nineteenth-century Britain—from what Alfred Doolittle, in Shaw's *Pygmalion*, calls "middle-class morality." Most Victorian comments on sexual relations, except those in pornographic and didactic literature, refer only to the relations between man and wife. The institution of marriage was of great importance to thoughtful Victorians because it could channel sexual impulses, but also because its existence made possible discussion of, or at least reference to, them; furthermore, Victorian ideas about marriage reflected major concerns of the age: social order and the challenge of new ideas about freedom, traditional religious dogma and the challenge of a new secularism, as well as sex itself. The defense of marriage laws often meant the defense of social structures and of orthodox religion, just as an attack on marriage meant an attack on society and the church—if not, indeed, on the very ideas of order and Christianity.

G. M. Young asserts that Victorians questioned every idea and institution except representative government and the family.[4] But Victorians did question these institutions.

4. *Victorian England* (London, 1936), p. 150. The tendency, which we inherit from the Victorians, to make too sweeping generalizations about whole ages, and especially the Victorian age, is difficult to avoid. To cite a more recent instance, Kate Millett—who knows the period well—seems to accept the familiar assumption that there was a single "Victorian" attitude, at least one firmly held by a massive majority, when she writes, "The Victorian belief in marriage—nearly an article of faith—is an attempt to beautify

The first great Victorian writer and the one who most influenced other Victorian writers, Thomas Carlyle, detested representative government—embodied in Parliament, which Dickens, following Carlyle, calls the "national cinder-heap" (in *Hard Times*)—and, long before Samuel Butler wrote *The Way of All Flesh*, Victorian family life was criticized, and its basis, the sanctity of Christian marriage, was directly attacked. The facts contradict our easy assumption that to be a Victorian was invariably to be prudish and to regard the institution of marriage as sacrosanct, along with the British family and the state.

Private Lives and Public Ideals

For a great many Victorians, in fact, legal marriage was a matter of no great importance. W. J. Reader comments that historians of Victorian England "generally agree with Engels [that] the poor (though emphatically not the 're-

---

the traditional confinement of women at any cost" (*Sexual Politics* [New York, 1970], p. 79). She proceeds, however, in a succinct account of "Mill *versus* Ruskin," on exactly this matter (pp. 88–108), to show that one very important Victorian writer, Mill, spoke out against this "Victorian belief in marriage" as sacred and indissoluble and against the "confinement of women." In fact, other major Victorians spoke out similarly—in particular, Dickens, Meredith, Hardy, and the young Shaw—and belief in marriage as an unquestionable good is anything but an article of faith in, say, Browning and Swinburne. Kate Millett's treatment of Tennyson in this generally impressive if harshly polemical attack on men's "sexual politics" may suffer somewhat from that tendency to assume that a whole age *and* its major spokesmen remain consistent in their beliefs—beliefs about almost anything. The frightened male chauvinism in some of the later, reactionary Tennyson is painfully clear, but *The Princess* includes more uncertainty and more openness to radical change in sexual roles and mores than her study (pp. 76–79) indicates.

spectable' working class) had a very hazy idea of the marriage bond and took their pleasures as they could."[5] The communist Friedrich Engels, incidentally, was as shocked, in his *Condition of the Working-Class in England in 1844*, as any parson would be by the prevalent sexual license. In his three-volume *London Labour and the London Poor*, published in 1851 (a fourth volume, with data on prostitution, came out a year later), Henry Mayhew wrote candidly about the "Marriage and Concubinage of Costermongers"; among them, he estimated, fewer than a tenth of the couples living together were married, and the legitimacy or illegitimacy of children was a matter of little concern. "Poverty" is not a clear-cut term, and exact data on early Victorian poverty are hard to come by, but it seems fair to conclude that between very nearly half—in the "hungry forties"—and a third of the Victorian population was in serious want, and that a large proportion of the poor—vendors, street sweepers, unskilled mine and factory workers—literally could not afford to marry, since getting married required ready money, and could hardly afford to be over-particular about irregular relations, bastard children, or, indeed, prostitution.

When we think of Victorian people, however, we are likely to think of the middle classes. Among other clichés we apply to that age, phrases and ideas that the Victorians themselves invented—such as "an age of transition"—is the notion that the middle class, which had for centuries been rising like some great mass of yeasty dough, now came into its own. There is a good deal of truth in the notion; both aristocrats and the submerged classes were greatly affected

5. *Life in Victorian England* (London, 1964), p. 84.

by the dominance of earnest, evangelical-Protestant attitudes, including "middle-class morality." But as more than one social historian has observed, there were several "middle classes": The lower gentry increasingly intermarried with commercial families and resembled them, while the more skilled and better paid of the workingmen, as well as their families, were likely to absorb middle-class values and aspire to middle-class status—often with success.[6] Income cannot be regarded as an absolute criterion for defining "middle class." Livelihood is only a somewhat better index. In general, to be sure, middle-class men had regular incomes from respectable sources, ordinarily mercantile; but, at least as important, they themselves—and, above all, their women—were expected to lead regular and respectable lives. That is, the men worked regularly, they and their families went regularly to church or chapel, and the members of the family avoided any appearance of irregularity in their personal lives.

One of the reasons we are likely to think of Victorians as middle-class people is that the essayists, novelists, and poets of the period, from whom we may derive our impressions, were, with few exceptions, of that social milieu. (Swinburne was one exception—his father was an admiral, his mother the daughter of an earl—and the status of Tennyson, whose father was disinherited by the poet's upper-

6. G. Kitson Clark, who in defining the Victorian middle class lists such criteria as income, kind of work, education, and church- or chapel-going, admits that while the very conception of a middle class "is too important and significant to be abandoned," it is also "too inadequate and subjective to be used with any comfort." He suggests very tentatively one definition: perhaps people were middle-class who thought they were middle-class (*The Making of Victorian England* [Cambridge, Mass., 1962], pp. 118–119).

class grandfather and who was himself created baron, is ambiguous.) Victorian literature is largely of the middle class, by the middle class, and for the middle class. Attitudes in literature toward sex and marriage are very much conditioned by that fact: a writer may be lyrically pro or polemically con, but he or she is likely to treat sexual relations from the perspective of the bourgeois rather than the aristocrat or the poor worker.

What were middle-class Victorian marriages like? The answers given in fiction and poetry are mostly men's answers. A crucial question would seem to be, what was marriage like for women? To put it differently, what was the social position of middle-class women, in particular of married women? The answer to that question is not easy to give.[7]

Elizabeth Barrett Browning writes of brutish country men who beat their wives, but probably such violence was rare in middle-class marriage. John Stuart Mill writes of restrictive laws that were applied to all classes—"sexist" laws that prevented married women from owning property and prevented divorced women, no matter how plainly their divorce was caused by a cruel or adulterous husband, from seeing their own children—but law and general custom can be different matters. Perhaps the best source of knowledge about Victorian home life and the Victorian married woman is still fictional literature, although fiction may, as Meredith's does, somewhat distort the reality to suit a moral-comic purpose. Another source is the nonfic-

7. O. R. McGregor, in "The Social Position of Women in England, 1850–1914: A Bibliography" (*British Journal of Sociology*, VI [March, 1955]), points out how neglected, surprisingly, the whole subject has been.

tional literature on women written by women: books on how to be a lady, wife, and mother.

The most prolific writer of such books was Mrs. Sarah Ellis (it seems significant that *Mrs.* always appears on the title pages of her works, following a rule of most publishers for women who wrote books). Early in the Victorian period she wrote *The Women of England, Their Social Duties and Domestic Habits*. Duties come first in the text as well as in the title: the importance of duty was a pervasive idea in nineteenth-century England. Mrs. Ellis' conception of women's obligations is particularly severe. Her recurrent theme, in fact, is the necessity of woman's sacrificing herself. The familiar nineteenth-century belief that women are inferior to men in strength and intellect but superior in moral character—that they are at best Christlike by virtue of self-sacrifice—is here made quite explicit. Mrs. Ellis does not pretend to deal with matters of the highest moral and religious moment: her subject is "the minor morals of domestic life." But the adjective *minor* reflects only womanly and authorial modesty, for when she moralizes—as she does almost constantly—her tone is very serious. To "my sisters," she writes, "You have deep responsibilities; you have urgent claims; a nation's moral wealth is in your keeping."

According to Mrs. Ellis, a Victorian middle-class girl or unmarried woman—evidently an unmarried woman had a status not greatly different from that of a girl until well into middle age, unless she was an heiress—obeyed her parents, learned to sew, play the piano or sing or draw, learned to cook if her family was relatively poor and visited the very poor if her family was relatively rich. A married woman obeyed her husband, bore children, managed a household as economically as possible given her husband's social standing and its demands, and visited friends of whom her husband approved.

This work on the Victorian woman both points to the ideal and chides the actual; from time to time, it criticizes English women for falling short of some attainments, especially intellectual ones, that the author expected of them. It combines "Victorian" piety and a presumably proper sense of woman's rightful place in the home with an insistence that women, who have the leisure to be unselfishly useful in a generally selfish commercial society (as men do not) should take advantage of their leisure to cultivate their minds—for the sake, apparently, of their sons and husbands. If Victorian women are contemptible, intellectually, the author asserts, they are so not by constitution, but as a result of both social limitations and their own laziness. Mrs. Ellis herself was anything but lazy. She wrote prodigiously: books of etiquette, children's stories, novels, accounts of travel, moral tales. She was, in fact, a precursor of the "new woman" who was to support herself by her own labor— even though she wrote tracts that were to some extent designed to bolster the old conceptions of a woman's place and duties.

But this was inevitable. Lacking the genius of a George Eliot, of a Charlotte or Emily Brontë, even of an Elizabeth Barrett Browning or an Anna Jameson, Sarah Ellis could be successful as an author only by producing what was acceptable to most of the middle-class English reading public. What she wrote almost had to be conventionally moral if not moralistic.

The Women of England covers a wide range of categories, including education; dress; conversation; and "Domestic Habits—Consideration and Kindness," to which four chapters are devoted. As this last, obviously important, category indicates, the book never loses sight of the single controlling idea that a woman's life is and should be a life of selflessness. For a woman, social duties and domestic habits amount to the same thing.

This first book-length work of Sarah Ellis' was followed by two others that provide little more than variations on its theme: *The Wives of England, Their Relative Duties, Domestic Influence, and Social Obligations,* and *The Mothers of England, Their Influence and Responsibility,* both published in 1843. Each was reissued several times, until as late as 1860. Again, the titles are revealing. Wives and mothers are to exert influence on husbands and children. The titles reflect another familiar idea, often repeated in the nineteenth century: that women should wield power and have an impact on the world, not directly through the vote or social action, but indirectly through their ennobling influence upon men. This is not so much their right as their social obligation. So "influence" becomes synonymous with "duties," "obligations," and "responsibility."

As is often true with idealizing works of propaganda, Mrs. Ellis' books unintentionally reveal something of the reality behind the ideal. They suggest that a well-conducted Victorian woman who was lucky enough to marry a decent rich man might lead a pleasant if severely limited existence. (She might be luckier yet if he was *indecent* in one Victorian sense, if he had relations with other women and ignored her, so that she was not obligated to go through a dozen or more pregnancies.) Without ever mentioning such a possibility, the books also suggest to a modern reader what a martyr's life a woman might lead with a husband who was not even, say, a heartless tyrant but simply stupid.

Sarah Ellis' books were in demand partly because they served as guides to etiquette for socially mobile wives and husbands and partly because they gave a sense of the *status quo* that many Victorians, moving into the solid middle class and often baffled in the process, craved. But if his exact position in society was unclear to a tradesman's son now rich and well-connected, it was beginning to be unclear as well to an even moderately intelligent woman. Referring to such books as those of Mrs. Ellis, Ray Strachey speaks of "a breath of change in the air which called forth . . . a definite statement of the whole position. It was as if it were felt necessary to put into words and to teach in the most deliberate manner the duty of female submissiveness which before had been entirely taken for granted."[8]

Public Conflicts

A very important element in the concern about sexuality and the questioning of marriage was the Victorian movement for women's rights, the true beginning of a woman's liberation campaign, although its roots went back to the lonely work of Mary Wollstonecraft, whose *Vindication of the Rights of Women* (1792) applied some radical Romantic ideas about individual potentiality to her own sex. From the second decade of the nineteenth century until its end there was almost constant agitation for women's rights to higher education and to some degree of control over their own lives and—this was the key demand, perhaps ini-

8. *The Cause: A Short History of the Woman's Movement in Great Britain* (London, 1928), p. 46.

tially more significant than the demand for the franchise—for far-reaching reforms in the institution of marriage.

Many of the philosophic radicals of the century, Benthamites and Utilitarians, were opposed to such reforms. James Mill, for one, found it easy to dismiss the issue on the familiar ground that women were represented by their husbands (or fathers or sons) and that marriage therefore protected them adequately. As an answer to the elder Mill, William Thompson published, in 1825, his *Appeal of One Half the Human Race, Women, Against the Pretensions of the Other Half, Men, to Retain Them in Political and Thence in Civil and Domestic Slavery*. The work is in effect an attack on contemporary marriage. Thompson writes, "The ex-parte marriage code, absurdly called the marriage contract, partakes no more of the nature of contracts than state codes or any other codes of law made without the consent of those whose happiness they affect."[9] Thompson was an Owenite socialist, a follower of Robert Owen, the reformer who advocated the abolition of private property as well as of all forms of capitalism.

Although the writing and thought of the French Auguste Comte and Claude de Saint-Simon had some currency, Owen's was the most widely heard radical voice in early Victorian England that addressed itself to thoroughgoing change, including change in the laws governing marriage.[10]

9. London, 1825, p. 12.

10. On radical socialism, feminism, and the early Victorian attacks on marriage, see John Killham's comprehensive study *Tennyson and "The Princess": Reflections of an Age* (London, 1958), especially the two chapters on "The Feminist Controversy in England Prior to *The Princess*" (pp. 120–141). See also *Sexual Politics*, pp. 61–88, for a brief account of nineteenth-century feminism, both British and American; on how feminism affected

He was frequently accused of advocating free love and trying to undermine any kind of marriage—of attacking the
home and family—and the ambiguity of some statements he
made encouraged such accusations. In any event, Owen
makes his argument against marriage as it existed quite clear
and goes beyond even the reformist idea of divorce for
cause, in his *Lectures on the Marriages of the Priesthood of
the Old Immoral World* (1835). This is a broadside against
old religion and the established order, which are to be
changed before the relations of the sexes can be free and au-
thentic. Marriage, Owen argues, is based on lies and leads to
lies; here he anticipates the language of Meredith and of
Browning. He asserts that marriage, religion, and private
property—a trinity of evils—are the great causes of crime
and of immorality among most of mankind. And his conclusion is that the "marriage of the priesthood" must be
utterly abolished.

This attack by Owen, and others who followed, inspired
counterattacks and now and then defenses of his ideas, in a
flurry of pamphleteering. From the 1830's on, for five or
more decades, the questions of women's rights, marriage,
and divorce were bruited in polemical form—before they
appeared in the novels of Eliot, Meredith, and Hardy as
literary issues.

The climax, in polemic literature, to the agitation for
women's rights came with John Stuart Mill's book on *The
Subjection of Women* (1869)—and that book does not
raise the question of divorce.[11] *The Subjection of Women*

English fiction of the period 1837–1873, see Patricia Thomson's
The Victorian Heroine: A Changing Ideal (Oxford, 1956).

11. "I do not think that the conditions of the dissolubility of
marriage can be properly determined until women have an equal

is, however, the first statement by a major Victorian intellectual that defines and defends the right of women to be regarded as independent human beings—human beings who should be able to vote, to own property, to receive a liberal education. The implicit attack on the submissiveness of wives, and thus on the moral and legal solidity of marriage, horrified many people at the end of the sixties. Yet Mill, who had moved for woman's suffrage in 1867 and had carried nearly a third of the sitting members of the House of Commons on the issue, attracted now fairly widespread and certainly significant support (although nothing approaching majority support). Mill's work has had, in the long run, by far the greatest influence of any Victorian book on our thinking about the legal and political rights of women. It suggests, at least, the most serious questions about mid-Victorian marriage laws and marriages.

Many Victorian men and women were hostile to such questioning. But the anxious desire to assert the ideal of marriage and to reiterate its traditional symbolic function, if not in fact its sacredness, a desire apparently felt by a good many sensitive Victorians, was not only a consequence of unreflecting conservatism. The literary tradition in which marriage means a harmonizing of opposed forces—of ambition and duty, of power and love, of cosmic nature and limited humanity—a tradition most beautifully represented by Shakespeare's last romances, appeals to a poet's imagination. Blake, whose *Marriage of Heaven and Hell* envisions an ultimate uniting of reason and energy (but not

voice in determining them," Mill wrote (*The Letters of John Stuart Mill*, ed. Hugh S. R. Elliot [London, 1910], II, 212). On Mill's tactics in regard to this question, see Michael St. John Packe, *The Life of John Stuart Mill* (New York, 1954), pp. 492–503.

at all a denial of difference) uses the metaphor. So does Coleridge, in "The Ancient Mariner"; the man chosen to hear about a saving reconciliation between man and nature, between the mariner and the apparently alien life of albatross and sea snakes, is a wedding guest who must be made to understand the true, sacred, reconciling principle of marriage. For Victorian writers, too, the idea of marriage can have great power.[12] It can take on symbolic meaning, as it does for Tennyson, although it may be difficult to express concretely in novels and in novelistic verse.

The subject of marriage, then, involving sexual relations and the nineteenth-century "woman question," as well as ideas about social reconciliation and the future of the race, is one that Victorian writers can hardly avoid. Often it is more than a topical subject: it is a theme, a complex and problematic theme central to much of human experience and not only a temporarily, sociologically "relevant" matter. In distinguishing what is true of the significant literature this age produced—significant, that is, *as* literature— from what we think of as "Victorian" attitudes toward the relations of the sexes, it may be worthwhile to look closely at some versions of this theme, and especially at versions written by major artists in the five decades—roughly, between 1830 and 1880—before the full tide of feminism with its idea of the "new woman" was felt, before Ibsen and Shaw.

12. The symbolism may be social and political, as in Disraeli's *Sybil*, where the joining of the heroine and Egremont represents the healing of a rift between "the Two Englands," between the Saxon working class and the Norman gentry—although the point is badly compromised by the late discovery that Sibyl is really an heiress.

Mid-Victorian disagreements on the subject of sex and marriage often anticipate our own conflicts: whether human sexuality should be openly recognized and represented; whether purely private choice should be allowed in sexual matters or social and specifically legal restraints be applied; whether, above all, the social-sexual roles of women and men, in or out of marriage, truly express or distort their human natures.

In Victorian prose and poetry, too, there is a deeper conflict, one that underlies these and that appears as well in much of the literature on sexuality of our own times: the conflict between the idea that sexual identity is simply biological, that sexual activity is an individually chosen mode of gratification and expression, merely one aspect of social behavior, and the idea that sexual identity and sexual activity are awesome, demonic, implying the deeply mythic and mysterious. This is the conflict between what we might call the newer, the secular, attitude and the traditional ones, both the sacramental attitude of religion and the idealizing attitude of romance. Grasping the implications of this conflict in its various manifestations is helpful for understanding the Victorian world and our own—our own divisions, indecisions, and attempts at or fears of sexual revolution. Perhaps more important, it can be helpful for understanding some of the most impressive literature of the last century—even that which seems to us limited or flawed—for understanding how complex it is, how rich, how relevant to us, not only as moderns, as radicals or conservatives, as women or men, but as human beings.

2 | Sexual Attitudes: Secular, Sacramental, and Ideal

In *The Prisoner of Sex* (1971) Norman Mailer attacks not so much the arguments as the implicit attitude of several women writers. Mailer, who is more than candid about sexual organs and acts—*compulsive* is perhaps a better word, as his title suggests—seems in his fiction to be a purist, even in a sense a puritan, in his attitude toward sex. In *Deer Park* (1955) the rare perfect sexual climax is a mystical experience that makes lesser sexual experiences appear frustrating and disgusting; in various later comments Mailer disparages homosexuality and (like D. H. Lawrence) condemns masturbation with a zeal that can almost be called religious. And his response to such writers as Kate Millett and Germaine Greer is that of the religious zealot. Perhaps the most revealing anecdote in *The Prisoner of Sex* is Mailer's account of telling Gloria Steinem that, having spoken publicly of women at their worst as "low sloppy beasts," he might have added that women at their best are goddesses. He fails to understand that the second remark is more offensive than the first. An exalting of Woman to divine status reminds one of the Victorian Coventry Patmore; and the whole notion of women as either bestial or divine, which psychiatrists call the "madonna-harlot syndrome," is intensely Victorian—its best exemplars are Rossetti and Tennyson—as well as modern. Mailer's language insistently yokes sex with religion. The final sentences in his antifeminist polemic, insisting that he is not opposed to women's political equality but only to the diminishing or denying of women's sacred sexuality, ring true. His objection is to the political treatment of a religious subject: he is attacking the secularizing of sex. Even more than Lawrence, Mailer expresses a perhaps heretical but still religious sense of sex. In some respects a remarkably "poetic" writer—personal, explosive, apocalyptic—he is in this way a descendant of Patmore and Rossetti as well as of Lawrence.

The objects of his attack are also descendants of certain Victorian writers. Kate Millett, who is Mailer's major target, virtually acknowledges the fact in writing about Mill and Ruskin. Her analysis of sexual relations in literature—marital and extramarital—with its emphasis on not sacramental or symbolic but social meanings, on the psychological *and* political subjection of women as a class, derives in large part from the age of Robert Owen and John Stuart Mill, of George Eliot and George Meredith.

Again, the conflict is not so much between discipline and freedom or even between men's dominance and women's liberation as between a virtually religious attitude toward sexuality and a rational, secular attitude. The religious attitude, as the references to Lawrence and Mailer imply, need not mean literally taking marriage as one of the Christian sacraments, although it is closely related to Christian tradition—even when that tradition is distorted to carry what Denis de Rougemont regards as the heretical implications of idealized romantic love.[1] There are two versions of

1. *Love in the Western World* (rev. ed.; New York, 1956). The

the traditional and antisecular conception of love, one truly
sacramental and orthodox, the other idealist and thus in a
sense heretical. The orthodox insists that, like any other
sacrament, marriage has a physical and historical reality as
well as a sacred meaning and is therefore, paradoxically,
subject to imperfection; to deny this earthly limitation
would be in effect to deny the Incarnation (for every

---

idealizing of sexuality, an idealizing that tends to emphasize the
ecstatic time- and body-transcending quality of "romantic" emotion
and that tends to ignore or deny the validity of the ordinary
affections characteristic of marriage, is associated by Rougemont
not only with the courtly love of romance but also with the
Manichean heresy, the belief in a conflict between the wholly evil
flesh and the divine spirit. The thesis of his work, which finds the
direct source for courtly love and later romance in heretical beliefs,
has been challenged by other scholars. M. C. D'Arcy, for one, in
The Mind and Heart of Love (London, 1946), questions the neat
distinction between *eros*, or boundless desire, and *agape*, or
Christian love. Father D'Arcy does, however, agree with Rougemont that the result, direct or indirect, of Manichean gnosticism is
opposed both to Christianity and to the marriage sacrament: "Most
critics can see that a purely naturalistic outlook . . . is anti-
Christian, but not so many grasp the truth that a too spiritual ideal
which despises the body and this earth is also anti-Christian. . . .
Human love in the Gnostic system is either consumed away in
pride or else it is self-destructive; it never finds a happy marriage"
(p. 51). In *Love and Death in the American Novel* (rev. ed.;
New York, 1966), Leslie Fiedler comments, "It is wrong, I think,
to believe with Denis de Rougemont . . . that the troubadors were
secret sharers in the Albigensian heresy; they were heretics of
another order—not secret but *unconscious* self-castrators. For surely
their exaggerated worship of the lady unmanned them successfully
enough to have pleased any of the world-denying Cathars among
the Albigensians" (p. 49). The theme of Fiedler's work, one
relevant to both the tradition of romance and the subject of this
book, is "the failure . . . to deal with adult heterosexual love and
[a] consequent obsession with death, incest, and innocent homosexuality" (p. 12).

sacrament is an expression of the Incarnation). Sexual idealism, the glorifying of romantic love toward which many Victorian and modern writers are drawn, is antisacramental, can often be antisexual, and in its most extreme form reaches a climax which is death. Insistence not upon the limited sacredness of an earthly sacrament (the water of baptism can be polluted and cold while efficacious, and a marriage can be sexually and psychologically imperfect while sacred) but rather upon the absolute transcendence of mystical experience in the sexual act may lead to disgust with, and rejection of, earthly sexuality.[2] Still, the two attitudes, the sacramental or religious and the idealizing or romantic, are often intermixed; and both imply opposition, if not hostility, to the secular attitude.

The secular attitude, which regards sex as a biological and social reality but not necessarily a demonic force or a sacred and profoundly mysterious matter, may also lead in its extreme form to distaste for the awkward fact of sexual identity and the messiness, physical and psychological, of sexual relations. There is something problematic in this as in the opposite extreme, some lack, some incompleteness hinted at by the mystical intensity of a Coventry Patmore and by the cool rationality of a John Stuart Mill—although both these writers valued marriage in their different ways. Of the two, Mill seems the less limited, the more open to dialogue and debate.

The fact that Victorian conflicts about sex usually had to do, at least explicitly, with marriage—virtually no one defended prostitution or homosexuality, and few writers openly championed absolute "free love"—need not obscure

2. So it seems sometimes to do, oddly, in Mailer.

the basic similarities between the problems of our century and those of the nineteenth century, when there was the first widespread questioning of marriage as a sacrament, along with a widely articulated belief that women were an exploited group. Not only Victorian pamphlets and polemics, but also more lasting works of literature, novels and poems, reflect those questions and reveal the roots of these problems.

Not, of course, that sex and marriage were less important themes in earlier art and literature, from Homer's story of Helen and Sophocles' of Oedipus to Chaucer's "marriage group" and Shakespeare's *Antony* and *The Tempest*—to say nothing of English stage comedy with its wry comments on marriage yet invariable conclusion with the promise of a wedding, or the English novel with its similar ending. In the nineteenth century, however, marriage is not so often the means of concluding a story either happily or tragically. Rather, it may be an institution and an experience to be analyzed, questioned, perhaps redefined, and an idea that has deep social as well as symbolic implications.[3] Sex and marriage now make up an important theme in a new way, as the sanctions given to sexual relations by religion—those implied in *The Tempest*—and the sanctions given by the tradition of romance—typified by the tale of Tristram and Iseult—are challenged by antiromantic secularism.

We have observed that marriage as an experience, often

3. Walter Houghton's section on love, the woman, and marriage in *The Victorian Frame of Mind* (New Haven, 1957) indicates the complexity of the matter—a greater complexity than is suggested by his general comment on "Victorian love" as limited to marriage, and as an "object . . . scarcely mortal" (p. 341); see, for instance, his discussion (pp. 381–385) of reactions against loveless marriage.

one in sharp contrast to the ideal, provides a subject which allows the Victorian secularist writer to deal directly or by implication with a number of profoundly troubling elements of his age. First, there is the tension (often the conflict) between the conventional demands of society, embodied in law, and the needs or, at least, the desires of the individual. Second, the questions of marriage and divorce lead at once to the question of women's rights, of women's role in society, and, by implication, of the rights and roles of other restricted and exploited persons. Such issues, in turn, involve—again—the worrisome matter of sexuality, of the use and abuse of sexual energy to manifest power or affection, and the question of inhibiting or even denying the sexual drive, as if to deny man's identity as a sexual animal, part of a fierce and amoral physical nature. Finally, the idea of marriage as not only the harmonious relating of opposites but also the fullest kind of physical and mental communion between persons raises the question whether such a communion is possible; this is the question that haunts so much of post-Romantic literature.

Law and freedom, the place of woman in society, the nature of sexuality and of man's animal nature itself, the psycho-sexual isolation of the individual—these are some of these problems that most mattered to thoughtful Victorians. Some of these are approached directly by Mill, who attacks the first two and at least implies concern about the third in both *The Subjection of Women* (1869) and his short essay on marriage, probably written in 1832.[4] This essay was written for Harriet Taylor, the married woman whom Mill loved. Not intended for publication, it seems much

---

4. See F. A. Hayek, *John Stuart Mill and Harriet Taylor* (London, 1951), pp. 58–78.

more daring than the later book: it insists that "the arguments . . . in favour of the indissolubility of marriage, are as nothing in comparison with the far more potent arguments for leaving this like the other relations voluntarily contracted by human beings, to depend for its continuance upon the wishes of the contracting parties." Mill's primary interest in the subject of marriage and divorce has to do, already, with the effect of both on women. The institution of indissoluble marriage no longer acts as a protection for women and children; "the strongest of all arguments [for divorce] is that by no other means can the condition & character of women become what it ought to be."[5] The burden of Mill's commentary on marriage is the necessity for women to be equal to men in education and in legal status. On the nature of sexuality, Mill is perhaps less radically open, more unrealistically high-minded. He regards "the law of marriage as it now exists" as one "made *by* sensualists, and *for* sensualists and *to bind* sensualists," and he asserts that, for the "highest natures," the passionate relation between the sexes is purely one of admiration and love.[6] There is, here, no hint of lust or of sheer animal desire in true marriage. But there is an assumption that a lasting union of two persons is possible.

Secularism and the Novel

Mill's interest in marriage and divorce was of course directly related to his interest in the married Harriet Taylor. Like Mill, George Eliot loved—but unlike Mill, she lived with—a married person who could not obtain a divorce. Her insistence that George Henry Lewes was her husband,

5. Hayek, p. 74.
6. Hayek, p. 60.

not legally but really, implies a criticism of the marriage and divorce laws that is not made so explicit as Mill's but remains just as earnest. The unhappy marriage of Dorothea Brooke in *Middlemarch* and her decision as a widow to give up the Casaubon fortune in order to marry Will Ladislaw make a clear moral point. Even so fine a spirit as Dorothea— and she is certainly one of Mill's "highest natures"—can suffer from a false and, at last, a degrading, union. Again, harsh law—the marriage law and the legal right of Casaubon to affect his widow's life from the grave—is opposed to the freedom of the noble individual. Again, it is the woman who is exploited and restricted. If George Eliot does not fully explore, she does subtly suggest the reality, and the frigid absence, of sexual forces. And in the unhappily married Dorothea she embodies the deadening sense of isolation which only a bond with a kindred spirit, with Will Ladislaw, can alleviate. Certainly the idea of marriage is central to this novel, to its theme and its structure. The marriage of Lydgate and Rosamond is parallel to that of Dorothea and Casaubon. And Dorothea's false marriage, to which abstract idealism led, is finally canceled out by a true marriage which arises from the experience of human reality.

The Subjection of Women was published in 1869 and *Middlemarch* in 1871. Although Mill's essay on marriage and divorce dates from the early 1830's and George Eliot's union with Lewes began in the early 1850's, we are likely to associate criticism of the marriage laws and agitation for women's rights—leading to the idea of the "new woman"— with the later decades of the century. In these decades a disturbing current of thought and feeling on such matters came more often to the surface. True, it seems clear from Thackeray's pictures of disastrous marriage in *Vanity Fair* and Dickens' poignant story of Lady Dedlock in *Bleak House*—to choose only two examples—that marriage could represent a complex problem at the heart of the mid-Victorian novel, not only a way to end it, as the marriages of major characters usually were for Richardson, Fielding, and Jane Austen. But the fullest and most critical treatment of this subject in fiction came in the seventies, eighties, and nineties, with the work of such writers as Thomas Hardy and George Meredith.

For Hardy the institution of marriage is one of several social manifestations that frustrate and sometimes destroy individuals. Wife-selling and adultery in *The Mayor of Casterbridge*, seduction and the tragic wedding-night confession in *Tess of the D'Urbervilles* suggest the terrible importance that Hardy can give the marriage bond. And in *Jude the Obscure* the two impossible marriages of Jude and Sue, along with Sue's disillusioned refusal to remarry after her divorce and her consequent suffering from the intolerance of others, make up a telling revelation of how hypocritical the conventions of marriage can be.[7]

7. On Hardy's attitudes toward marriage and divorce, see H. C. Duffin, *Thomas Hardy* (New York, 1937), especially pp. 240 and 243; Pierre d'Exideuil, *The Human Pair in the Work of Thomas Hardy* (London, 1930); and J. Hillis Miller, *Thomas Hardy: Distance and Desire* (Cambridge, Mass., 1970), especially his chapter on erotic desire and disillusionment, "Falling in Love." William J. Hyde points out, in "Theoretic and Practical Unconventionality in *Jude the Obscure*," *Nineteenth-Century Fiction*, XX (Sept., 1965), 155–164, that Hardy's Sue Bridehead refers specifically, not to Mill's *Subjection of Women*, but to his essay *On Liberty*. Another Victorian novelist who is interested in the problems of marriage, divorce, and woman's place in society is George Gissing. For instance, his very late novel *The Odd*

It is, however, Meredith for whose fiction marriage is consistently a major theme, if not *the* major theme. Meredith's later novels—*The Egoist, Diana of the Crossways, One of Our Conquerors, Lord Ormont and His Aminta,* and *The Amazing Marriage*—have in common the subject of a hollow marriage either contemplated or unfortunately made. Four of the five concern liaisons based on pride or foolishness that threaten to trap the woman or the wife. Clara Middleton, in *The Egoist,* and Diana Merion, in *Diana of the Crossways,* are the most memorable in a series of women on whom a socially desirable marriage to a proud and wealthy man is pressed, with predictably unhappy results. But each Meredith heroine refuses finally, even when caught in the legal toils of a bad marriage, to be degraded into a possession. Clara escapes from her egoist wooer and from the image of herself as a "dainty rogue in porcelain" that belongs in a stifling world of willow-pattern china; she escapes with Vernon Whitford to the mountains and fresh air that represent personal freedom. Diana also escapes at last from a false conception of herself: she is finally seen not as a weak hunted animal but as the huntress strong and chaste. Aminta, too, breaks away from her proud and selfish Ormont, and Carinthia Jane of

---

Women, published in 1893, is about late-Victorian single women: they were "odd" because men outnumbered women, and many inevitably remained single. But Gissing's women are odd in other senses as well. There are overtones of lesbianism in the novel, and his people are certainly neurotic; they become social derelicts or alcoholics. Though the effect may be melodramatic, Gissing does nevertheless point up the fact that a Victorian woman without a dowry might well face, at best, the dreary and frustrated life of a poor companion or a governess.

The Amazing Marriage leaves her proud and arrogant Fleetwood. The novel of Meredith's "marriage group" that does not quite follow this pattern is *One of Our Conquerors*, in which Victor Radnor and Natalia defy convention and live as man and wife, although Victor is already married to an older woman. Here again the results are disastrous—their illegitimate daughter is rejected by her fiancé, and both parents suffer—but the contrast is clearly made between a false, merely legal marriage and the marriage of true minds.

Because Victorian novelists were often preoccupied with immediate social questions, it is hardly surprising that their novels should be concerned with marriage, with its effect on women, and with the place of women in society. From the 1857 parliamentary act creating a divorce court (but by no means making divorce easily obtainable) to the 1882 Married Woman's Property Act, and of course afterward, these matters were more and more widely debated. Writers of prose fiction, from Meredith in the 1870's to Shaw at the end of the century, almost inevitably took part in the debate.

Less generally recognized, but no less significant, is how often and how early in the period the subject of contemporary marriage was an important one for the Victorian poet. Among recent critics, only John Killham—writing of Tennyson—has touched on this point.

In the middle decades of the last century, there appeared a number of long poems treating of love and marriage in a new way. Not only were the points of view a departure from the traditional ones: the poets sought to communicate them by providing stories and characters, as if they were really writing little novels in verse: moreover, these verse-narratives were clearly intended to leave the reader to reflect upon a social question—the position of women in life.[8]

The novelistic poems Killham cites, along with Tennyson's *The Princess*, are Elizabeth Browning's *Aurora Leigh*, Clough's *The Bothie of Tober-na-Vuolich*, and Patmore's *The Angel in the House*. One can add that along with these long novelistic works (he might have included Browning's *The Ring and the Book*, which Henry James calls a novel in verse), there were a number of shorter poems on sex and marriage—by Browning, for example, and, most notably, by Meredith.

In fact, Meredith's poetry, like his fiction, is very largely concerned with such matters, displaying a striking range of explicitness about physical relations, of attitudes toward sexual love, and of emphasis on various subsidiary or related topics.

Sex and the Secular: Meredith's Poetry

"Love in the Valley" is perhaps the most light-hearted of Meredith's poems about wooing. The beloved, here, is associated with a number of flowers, white, red, and variegated, often with the pure white lily. Probably most readers now find a distinct, even intense, sexual quality in these verses, but it is deliberately restrained. Indeed, the speaker's emotional response to his chaste mistress is ambivalent: his "love that so cleaves would fain keep her changeless; / Fain would fling the net, and fain have her free." As in the novels, especially *Diana of the Crossways*, the wooing and sexual winning of a girl are considered a way, not only of

8. *Tennyson and "The Princess": Reflections of an Age* (London, 1958), p. 1.

changing her, of destroying her virginity, but actually of
trapping her, of destroying her freedom. And although the
man, the speaker, does desire her, he also wants her to remain white and chaste—so she seems "sweeter unpossessed."[9]

Although there is something sentimental about "Love in
the Valley," something of the "Victorian" feeling that a
woman must be either an angel or a fallen creature, a lily
or a sick, corrupted rose, the other poems of Meredith on
the close relations of men and women acknowledge the
sexual impulse and rarely pull back from it in this way.[10]
These include "Earth and a Wedded Woman," which
makes a parallel between the dry earth with its need for
rain and the waiting wife, in need of her husband (the
sexual meaning is clear enough, but it is odd and interesting
that the coming of a rainstorm somehow reconciles the
woman to waiting for her husband, still at war); "The
Rape of Aurora"; "The Song of Courtesy," about the
traditional folk-tale situation of the knight pledged to
marry the loathly hag; and the remarkable "Margaret's
Bridal Eve," with its evocation—*"red rose and white in the
garden"*—of sexual flower imagery that echoes Tennyson's
in *Maud*, and its almost explicitly sexual refrain, *"There's a
rose that's ready for clipping."* Again and again, the poet
uses his metaphor of man's wedding the spirit of nature: the
human, thinking, animal must be married to the elemental

9. *The Works of George Meredith* (New York, 1910), XXV,
81; all quotations of Meredith's verse are from this edition
(Volumes XXIV, XXV, or XXVI).

10. See Delmar Bogner, "The Sexual Side of Meredith's Poetry,"
Victorian Poetry, VIII (1970), 107–125, especially pp. 121–122; this
essay emphasizes Meredith's sexual imagery in works other than
Modern Love.

world in order to understand his environment and himself. This metaphor, which occurs early and late in Meredith—from "By the Rosanna" in 1861 to "Wind on the Lyre" in 1892 and "Earth and Man" in 1893— recalls the Romantic poets' symbolic allusions to marriage, Blake's in *The Marriage of Heaven and Hell* and Coleridge's in "The Ancient Mariner." This is true especially of these lines from "South-West Wind in the Woodland":

> For every elemental power
> Is kindred to our hearts, and once
> Acknowledged, wedded, once embraced,
> Once taken to the unfettered sense,
> Once clasped into the naked life,
> The union is eternal.   [XXIV, 45]

The metaphor suggests, too, great symbolic meanings that are implicit in other Victorian passages and poems about marriage by Arnold, Tennyson, and Browning, for whom the wedding of man and woman can signify the union of the self and the world of potentiality, or of the human and the natural, or of active passion and receptive intelligence. But it is a metaphor, not a sacramental image.

Meredith shows in other short poems (as well as in *Modern Love*) his awareness of how the actual marriages of men and women can fail. In "Archduchess Anne," "A Preaching from a Spanish Ballad," and "The Nuptials of Attila" the marriages all end in disaster. "The Hueless Love" and "Union in Disseverance" indicate that there can be platonic affection but no passionate union of man and woman. In his later poems, as in his novels, Meredith stresses the point that men must recognize the rights, the independence, the intelligence of women if they are to succeed not simply in possessing their wives but in being truly married to them.

The most striking example is "A Ballad of Fair Ladies in Revolt" (composed in 1876, according to G. M. Trevelyan), a lively, odd, and curiously effective poem that might well serve almost a hundred years after its conception as a rallying song for women's liberation. Although in some ways surprisingly like Tennyson's *Princess*, this work is more consistent in its attitude, and it carries the implications of that poem further. This is not a poem of disillusionment about the possibility of a successful modern marriage, for the woman speaker says to the men she encounters, "You have us if you wed our cause." Yet she knows that marriages are often, in fact, matters more of conflict than of harmony, and that women can be disillusioned. Of simple young girls she says, "When they know men they know the state of war: / But now they . . . / . . . deem you hold the half of happy pairs." She knows, too, that women are obliged to use their beauty, as they themselves are used; but the woman who so uses herself and is so used, though she seems to walk "in union" by a husband's side, is in reality "a poor slave." Answering the philistine male speaker who "speaks the popular voice," she insists that women's wrongs are not rare and characteristic only of the past, but are evident all about them, here and now; to his smug assertion that women now are sheltered, as if in Eden, she answers,

> We are somewhat tired of Eden, is our plea.
> We have thirsted long; this apple suits our drouth:
>   'Tis good for men to halve, think we.

This witty turn is both a reply to the ages-old misogyny

that blames Eve for the fall of mankind and a neat suggestion that in abrogating to himself the right to knowledge, to the hard life of experience, the man is defining the woman as his creature and himself as God. Finally, she is asked why women want to go out into the world's ways instead of being sheltered at home: "What seek you?" (This sounds startlingly like the more modern question, "What do they want?") She responds, referring to those world's ways, the streets of Victorian England,

> —We hear women's shrieks on them . . .
> . . . And that roar,
> "What seek you?" is of tyrants in all days.
> Sir, get you something of our purity,
> And we will of your strength: we ask no more.

After the dialogue, the male speaker's more sensitive male companion, persuaded by the other speaker, goes off with the women; the commentator—not far removed, surely, from Meredith himself—asks,

> Have women nursed some dream since Helen sailed,
> Over the sea of blood the blushing star,
> That beauty, whom frail man as Goddess hailed,
> When not possessing her (for such is he!),
> Might in a wondering season seen afar
> Be tamed to say not "I," but we?

The end of this poem, then, does insist upon the ideal of marriage, of harmony in equality, between man and woman. It is consistent with the burden of Meredith's novels of the seventies and later, which often give some hope for the marriage of true minds even while they reveal the emptiness of merely legal marriages. The darkest view

of marriage, perhaps, came earlier, in Meredith's best-
known poetic work, *Modern Love*.[11]

Just as Hardy's stories and his Victorian poems such as
"Revulsion" and "Neutral Tones" emphasize unhappy marriage and human disillusionment, the isolated state of most
human beings, so the poems (versions of sonnets) in *Modern Love* echo the movement from early love to bitterness,
from passion to poison.[12] The poet himself had moved
from the mood of "Love in the Valley," possibly inspired
by his first wife as he saw her in 1849, to this dark vision
of marriage produced following her death in 1861, only
four years after she had deserted him with her lover Henry
Wallis. Two points are worth making initially about this
series of fifty sixteen-line verses. First, the title suggests that

11. But in one of the poems already cited about disastrous
marriages these curious lines occur:

> Love is winged for two,
> In the worst he weathers,
> When their hearts are tied;
> But if they divide,
> O too true!
> Cracks a globe, and feathers, feathers,
> Feathers all the ground bestrew
>
> I was breast of morning sea,
> Rosy plume on forest dun,
> I the laugh in rainy fleeces,
> While with me
> She made one.
> Now must we pick up our pieces,
> For that then so winged were we.   [XXVI, 30]

12. Hardy's poems were mostly published after the Victorian
era, but it seems clear that a good many are Victorian in date of
composition, and they reflect something perhaps of Meredith's—
and indeed Browning's—awareness of how poignant dead love and
dead marriages can be.

it is in the modern world that married love can go so sour, can become so painful, because it is transient if not illusory. No reason is clearly given in the poetry: there is no indication that modern men and women are more likely to be ill-matched than earlier couples were. But the situation appears to be peculiarly "modern" in the sense that the self-conscious husband and wife analyze their feelings and suffer from a keen apprehension of reality, with their "deep questioning, which probes to endless dole." They are both fully aware of their own feelings and earnest about an ideal of love in marriage, an ideal now dead and to be mourned. Second, although adultery enters into the story, as both husband and wife turn to others for sexual and emotional release, it is evident that this is a symptom and not the cause of their marriage's having failed. The belief, usually ascribed to the Tennyson of the *Idylls,* that infidelity both undermines marriage and poisons human life is not at all present here. In fact, the infidelities, painful as the wife's can be to the husband, are revealed as being in a way, entirely honest, as gestures that recognize and result from the fact of a dead marriage.

Law and custom versus freedom, the role of woman, the compelling force of sexuality, the experience of isolation within the marriage bond—*Modern Love* touches on all these. Marriage is called "this wedded lie." The man and wife are "falcons in a snare." Even though the husband tries to recognize the woman's feelings, her suffering, and not to blame her, he cannot resist this comment when she leaves him so that he can seek out his mistress:

> Their sense is with their senses all mix'd in,
> Destroyed by subtleties these women are!
> More brain, O Lord, more brain!

One might read these lines by the creator of brainy Clara Middleton and Diana Merion as a dramatic outburst in a largely fictional series of poems; but, like much Victorian semidramatic, semipersonal verse, this passage invites further speculation. *Modern Love* was published seventeen years before *The Egoist*. And it would seem that here man's ancient temptation to project his emotions into woman and then blame her for them is given some expression. Still, on the subjects of sexuality and, finally, the psychological isolation of each person, the speaker—the husband—tries to be fair if not generous. He avows his own masculine sexual drive and, in his reflections on a simple country couple's marriage—"They have the secret of the bull and lamb"—as in his more direct "What are we first? First, animals," he implies a recognition of sexual needs that includes the woman. His marriage gone sour is termed ironically, at last, "the union of this ever-diverse pair." In the most familiar lines of *Modern Love*, he declares that in such domestic tragedy as this, "No villain need be! Passions spin the plot: / We are betray'd by what is false within." What is false within is man's, and woman's, own limited nature: egoistic and yet other-seeking, longing for freedom and yet jealously possessive, but above all earnest, self-analytical, and therefore dissatisfied. This is "modern love."[13]

13. Meredith sometimes, in his poetry, imagines a true modern marriage of sensitive, intelligent people, but it seems to be a very difficult matter. In one of his more obscure poems, "The Sage Enamoured and the Honest Lady," he writes of generous "gratitude" in relations between the sexes:

> And let it have survived
> Their conflict, comes the peace between the pair,
> Unknown to thousands, husbanded and wived:

Meredith is fascinated by the intense power of sexuality that links men and women not only with animals but also with the elemental forces of inanimate nature; at moments this fascination may suggest D. H. Lawrence's sense of sex as elemental and demonic. But Meredith is a rationalist at heart, and his understanding of how women, and men as well, can be trapped and made miserable by the social, largely arbitrary rules of marriage shows a basically secular attitude, one not at all sacramental or idealizing, religious or—in the popular sense—romantic.[14]

Secularism in Elizabeth Barrett Browning

Elizabeth Barrett Browning's comments on marriage are by no means alien to the spirit of Meredith's work; they

---

> Unknown to passion, generous for prey:
> Unknown to love, too blissful in a truce.

This is his vision of what marriage should be:

>   they, mate and mate
> Fair feminine and masculine shall join
> Upon an upper plane, still common mould.
>   .   .   .   .   .
> Then shall those noblest of the earth and sun
> Inmix unlike to waves on savage sea.
> But not till Nature's laws and man's are one
> Can marriage of the man and woman be.

A question these last lines raise is whether "Nature's laws" are biological, psychological, ethical, or what.

14. The ambiguity of the word *romantic* makes it almost as difficult to use as *nature*. In these pages, *romantic*, not capitalized, implies both a relationship with romances, especially those that transmit woman-worship, and the idealizing and sentimentalizing of sexual love, as in popular songs—in other words, something like the everyday sense of the adjective. *Romantic*, capitalized, refers to the Romantic movement in western philosophy, art, and literature.

represent an awareness of how immoral the marriage contract can be. Although the popular story of her elopement and happy marriage may make that comparison seem surprising, her better verse is far enough removed from the sentimentality of the *Sonnets from the Portuguese* to support it. *Aurora Leigh,* in particular, has some clear insights into the brutality and suffering that could and can pass as normal married life.

As Alethea Hayter remarks, in *Mrs. Browning,* her "general expectation of happy marriages was low."

She had seen too many instances of mistakes and disillusions, treacheries and tyrannies, in . . . marriages. Men and women were equally to blame—men for duplicity, for trying to make women commit themselves by acknowledging their love first, for tyrannizing the moment such a confession had been made, for ungenerously regretting their loss of freedom; women for boasting of their conquests, for fickleness and calculation, for marrying for convenience without love. She spoke with horror of "marriages where illusion is lost on both sides."

To friends she wrote, "*Marriage in the abstract* has always seemed to me the most profoundly indecent of all ideas—and I could never make out how women, mothers and daughters, could talk of it as setting up in trade"; and "You do not think . . . that *marriage* as it exists on all sides of us, is a better, happier, holier condition . . . than a single life. You do not deny it to be an *abomination* . . . and not marriage in the right sense at all [even though marriage] is the happiest condition, *when attained*—and highest too."[15] Here is the contrast, so often made by Victorian writers,

15. Alethea Hayter, *Mrs. Browning: A Poet's Work and Its Setting* (London, 1962), pp. 188–189; these pages include comments on "the degrading of women" in marriage.

by Mill, Meredith, and the later Robert Browning, between the familiar practice of marriage and the ideal widely acclaimed but rarely achieved.

For us today, some of the most interesting verse passages of Elizabeth Barrett Browning are her serious reflections on modern love and marriage in *Aurora Leigh*. This novel in verse, as it was called when it appeared in 1856 (and the comment anticipates James's upon *The Ring and the Book*), deals with a range of interrelated social questions: the place of an independent woman in Victorian society and the problems of poverty and prostitution, of social equality and individual fulfillment, especially fulfillment in women's lives.[16] The plot is fantastic. Aurora Leigh refuses her cousin Romney's offer of marriage in order to lead a single life, and a successful one, as a poet. Romney plans, as a social gesture, to marry a poor girl, Marian Erle. But she is melodramatically abducted on their wedding eve, drugged, raped, and virtually imprisoned in a house of prostitution. She escapes and has an illegitimate child. Aurora, improbably, finds Marian in Paris and protects her. Meanwhile Romney, who was to marry the wicked Lady Waldemar, loses in a fire both his home and his eyesight. In spite—in a sense, because—of these disasters, Aurora and Romney ultimately marry, and their marriage provides a happy ending of a sort. The conclusion may suggest that of Tennyson's *Princess;* a proud, strong-minded woman is reconciled to an idealistic wounded man (with his schemes for radical changes in society, Romney is a philanthropic, almost Owenite figure). Aurora remains at the end the stronger and wiser of the two, even though her superiority is that

16. See Hayter, pp. 159–174.

of the sensitive, intuitive, and therefore "feminine" mind over the mind that addresses itself to large ideas of reform, the mind concerned more with social justice than with individual love.

It is the ideas of *Aurora Leigh* that are interesting—although there are a few passages that have a certain poetic vitality—for the plot often creaks and the characters are mostly unbelievable. Ending with a marriage, the poem seems to make a final hopeful comment on the possibility of a fruitful relation between the sexes, a marriage of feminine intuition and masculine intellect. But the cruelty of the villainous Lady Waldemar, suffering from unrequited love and making others suffer too, and above all the cruel aspects of society revealed in the experiences of Marian Erle remain in our minds as lurid yet perhaps essentially true glimpses of the real world that this one remarkable marriage cannot change. The hostile reactions of the clergy, the rich, and the poor to Romney's socialist ideas, especially to his defense of married women as human beings with their own rights, and the nature of marriage in a world where it is considered right and proper for the ordinary husband to kick and beat his submissive wife, are not altered by the final marriage.

If it seems odd to compare Elizabeth Barrett Browning with George Meredith, it may also seem odd to emphasize her secularism so much. We may think of her as the strong-minded and pious wife who gradually converted her husband to an apparently conventional Christianity; this is the aspect that Betty Miller's biography of Browning stresses.[17] But of course she was also a social reformer who was

17. *Robert Browning* (New York, 1953).

keenly aware of the wrongs done people subjected to political bondage (including women); she was the close friend and correspondent of the redoubtable Anna Jameson, the very model of a mid-Victorian independent woman, who left her husband to support herself by writing books on art and travel; and her religious background, like her husband's, was a theologically liberal Protestantism for which the sacraments had little if any meaning.[18] Clearly, because of her ideas on the relations of the sexes and on women's roles—if not at all on trinitarian Christianity— she can be considered a secularist, one for whom marriage was a social arrangement, often an evil one.

Secularism and Skepticism in Matthew Arnold

Matthew Arnold's distaste for such dissenting Protestantism as that of the Barretts and the Brownings may suggest Anglican zeal. Yet, in spite of his consistent religious interests, Arnold is a kind of secularist. "A kind" because, like many other Victorians, he wanted to keep many of the forms of Christianity while discarding much Christian belief. On sexual relations, his point of view appears to be not only secular—in the sense that no mythic or deeply religious sanction is given to such relations; he is also skeptical about the possibility of any satisfactory and lasting romantic love, in or out of marriage.

To be sure, Arnold is not much concerned with a conflict between Victorian marriage laws—or conventions— and individual freedom, for his poetry tends to conceive of human life as fated, not free; he has nothing to say on the

18. See Hayter. On Mrs. Anna Jameson, see Clara Thomas, *Love and Work Enough: The Life of Anna Jameson* (Toronto, 1967).

place of women in modern society (except in the essays, where he approves of women's colleges that teach Greek); and the sexual drive is present in his poems only in symbolic and implicit ways. Arnold is, however, interested in the experience of isolation and the attempt, almost always doomed, to break through that isolation so that two persons can be united, can indeed be spiritually married.

One of the earliest poetic expressions of Arnold's interest in isolation and the gesture of love—in the theme of marriage, in fact—is "The Forsaken Merman." Published in 1849, the same year as Meredith's "Love in the Valley," this fantastic work of symbolism in the form of monologue both dramatizes and gives mythic distance to a poignant sense of regret for a marriage, a union of opposites, that has, perhaps inevitably, failed. It is a poem about the isolation that results from divorce: the divorce of an ideal free self from an actual society, of beauty and energy from duty and order, of nature from humankind—and of husband from wife. For, here, the husband is a natural being of the sea and the wife a human creature of the land. The sea is a place of color, of spontaneous sexual life, and of birth, a place where children are born; in its green caverns the merman has a "red gold throne," the little mermaiden's hair gleams "golden," the ceiling is amber, the floor is pearl, and all around "the sea-snakes coil and twine." The land is white and gray, a place of work with spindle and wheel, of formal worship, and of death; in the "white-walled town" graves stand next to the "little grey church," and the "wind blows coldly." Yet the merman's human wife has returned to the town on land at Easter time, to save her human soul, and has left grieving the king of the sea and their children alone. The result of her leaving, of this divorce, is in fact a mutual grief and sense of loss, as the merman understands. The Easter-time resurrection of Margaret, the wife, her return from the depths to the life of work and worship, suggests an echo of the Christian Resurrection. But it is also a dying to the life of nature—a life sexually fruitful and emotionally free but one that she cannot sustain.[19]

The moving quality of "The Forsaken Merman" derives only partly from its musical and expressive form; the voice of the speaker who addresses his half-human children carries the rhythm of the waves in irregularly flowing lines that anticipate those of "Dover Beach." It is the result, as well, of simple and affecting language that reveals profound feeling. This feeling is intense regret for the loss, the ultimate impossibility to man, of natural passion. This poem, which is about man and nature, society and self, even obliquely perhaps about Hebraism and Hellenism, represents as well Arnold's version of an experience more often treated by Tennyson and Browning: the conflict between the moral, religious, and legal demands men make upon themselves as social beings and the spontaneity of true, free love.

But Arnold is inclined to see fate, the gods, or ineluctable time and change, rather than law or religion, as the enemy of lasting love. Again and again, his poetry mourns the cooling and death of passion. In "A Memory Picture" he seems to be denying the assertion of Wordsworth (as he does in many poems)—the Wordsworth of "Tintern

19. See my *Voices of Matthew Arnold* (New Haven, 1961), pp. 84–91.

Abbey" and the Immortality Ode—that memory binds past to present, man to nature, and the mortal mind to immortality. Here the speaker muses on his loved Marguerite and cries in the refrain, "Quick, thy tablets, Memory!" Time, however, which governs men, mocks that refrain. "Time's current strong / Leaves us fixed to nothing long." That very fact brings some grim comfort to the speaker in "A Modern Sappho," a woman bereft of love who does not—as such a woman would in Tennyson—long for death, but only waits her turn.

> I shall suffer—but they will outlive their affection;
>> I shall weep—but their love will be cooling; and he,
> As he drifts to fatigue, discontent, and dejection,
>> Will be brought, thou poor heart, how much nearer
>> to thee![20]

For the most part, and certainly in the poems grouped under the title "Switzerland" that are concerned with the speaker's hopeless love for his Marguerite—"A Memory Picture" is the first of these—Arnold expresses deep regret that love cools to "fatigue, discontent, and dejection." No doubt his feelings are mixed; there is something like relief along with haunting sadness in these poems about love, poems that are not so much love lyrics as antilove lyrics. The second of them, "Meeting," already suggests how negative the speaker's attitude will be toward his affair with Marguerite: he addresses the "guiding powers who join and part," and it is clear that the function of parting, not joining or marrying, is the major one of these abstract

<hr />

20. *The Poems of Matthew Arnold*, ed. Kenneth Allott (London, 1965), p. 110; all quotations of Arnold's verse are from this edition, to which page numbers in the text refer.

powers. This is the burden of the next poem, called "Parting": "a sea rolls between us— / Our different past," the speaker declares, but that sea of divorce seems to be more than a matter of different backgrounds. In fact, the next poem, the first entitled "Isolation" ("To Marguerite") makes a philosophic generalization about human life: "Thou hast been, shalt be, art, alone." It continues,

> Or, if not quite alone, yet they
> Which touch thee are unmating things—
> Ocean and clouds and night and day;
> Lorn autumns and triumphant springs;
> And life, and others' joy and pain,
> And love, if love, of happier men.
>
> Of happier men—for they, at least,
> Have *dreamed* two human hearts might blend
> In one, and were through faith released
> From isolation without end
> Prolonged; nor knew, although not less
> Alone than thou, their loneliness.[21]

The dream that two hearts may "blend / In one" is the ideal of marriage later expressed by Tennyson in *The Princess*, where the married couple is to be a "single pure and perfect animal, / The two-celled heart beating, with one full stroke, / Life"; and by Patmore in *The Victories of Love*, where marriage means that "benevolence, desire . . . become the pulses of one heart."

Arnold, then, denies what other poets before and after assert, but he is enough a Victorian to find the denial deeply painful. The most celebrated of the lyrics in the "Switzerland" sequence begins,

21. P. 122.

> Yes! in the sea of life enisled,
> With echoing straits between us thrown,
> Dotting the shoreless watery wild,
> We mortal millions live *alone.*

These lines are filled with not only regret but something close to despair, as they develop the image of islands, declare that surely since once men were all "Parts of a single continent" they could communicate, could be at one, and finally ask,

> Who ordered, that their longing's fire
> Should be, as soon as kindled, cooled?
> Who renders vain their deep desire?—
> A God, a God their severance ruled!
> And bade between their shores to be
> The unplumbed, salt, estranging sea.[22]

The answer, asserting that fate or unalterable law—virtual synonyms, in Arnold's poetry, for *God*—decrees men's isolation. It has been read as the poet's rationalizing of the failure of his own love affairs; but throughout the poems on Marguerite—and in the rest of Arnold's poetry as well—the deep and consistent sense of personal isolation appears, whether or not it is accepted in this way. The latter part of Arnold's career can even be defined as a slow and often painful movement from a nearly despairing isolation to the conviction that men must somehow overcome this feeling through such means as culture, religion, social institutions— perhaps including the institution of marriage.

Now, however, the hope for union has to be at best postponed to an imagined heaven. In "A Farewell," after

22. Pp. 124–125.

dwelling on how women long for men who have the strength and consistency which he lacks, the speaker suggests,

> Yet we shall one day gain, life past,
> Clear prospect o'er our being's whole;
> Shall see ourselves, and learn at last
> Our true affinities of soul.

As Kenneth Allott points out, the last phrase may refer to Goethe's doctrine (in *Die Wahlverwandtschaften*) of "elective affinities," the inevitable and mutual attraction of two persons. But unlike Goethe, Arnold projects the ultimate understanding of these "true affinities" into an afterlife (in which he does not literally believe). It seems appropriate that the speaker addresses his beloved Marguerite late in the sequence as "my sister"; he is explicitly denying the possibility of marriage for them—and perhaps the possibility of true and lasting marriage in the modern world. He declares that after death,

> we shall know our friends!—though much
> Will have been lost—the help in strife,
> The thousand sweet, still joys of such
> As hand in hand face earthly life.

What will have been lost is the happy experience of marriage.[23]

23. Pp. 127–128. The idea recurs in Arnold, especially in the "Switzerland" poems, as one expression of his haunting sense of human isolation:
> Like driftwood spars, which meet and pass
> Upon the boundless ocean-plain,
> So on the sea of life, alas!
> man meets man—meets, and quits again.
>   ["The Terrace at Berne," *Poems*, p. 481]

Understandably, Arnold omitted several of the "Switzer-land" poems from the 1852 volume of his collected verse, published just after his wedding to Frances Lucy Wightman. Several poems in the sequence called "Faded Leaves," about the poet's courtship and his fiancée, were also omitted from the volume, probably as being too personal and immediate. In general, these poems are less memorable than those in the "Switzerland" group. The most interesting are those that express the most doubt, the least assurance about the lover's being loved.

The second of these five poems is "Too Late" (the first, "The River," was not published in full until 1958). Although it admits the possibility that two lives may be united, using the metaphor of Aristophanes in Plato's *Symposium*—"the twin soul which halves their own"—its emphasis is, as the title suggests, on circumstances that prevent the joining of soul mates. It is not specified what these circumstances are; if the poem is literally autobiographical, it may simply refer to Justice Wightman's forbidding his daughter to see Arnold, but in themselves the lines are more likely to mean that a woman has become engaged or even married before meeting her true love.

"Separation" is not much more hopeful: "Dead be the past and its phantoms to me!" Two other poems of the group, "On the Rhine" and "Longing," are more concerned with "despair" and "hopeless longing" than with the promise of love fulfilled. Three poems, probably written about the same time as these, apparently reflect the poet's feelings about the woman who was to be his wife. "Calais Sands" represents his hope for reunion and reconciliation. "Urania" (originally entitled "Excuse," a poem that has sometimes been supposed to be about Marguerite

instead of Lucy Wightman) is an exculpation of his beloved's coldness. "Euphrosyne" expresses his fear that he
has lost her. The last of these poems, "Euphrosyne" (entitled "Indifference" in the 1852 volume), makes quite clear
Arnold's frequent tendency to regard sexual love as a
weakness and a source of pain, of frustration. The quatrains
on fidelity—on troth, or truth—read,

> Truth—what is truth? Two bleeding hearts,
> Wounded by men, by fortune tried,
> Outwearied with their lonely parts,
> Vow to beat hence forth side by side.
>
> The world to them was stern and drear,
> Their lot was but to weep and moan.
> Ah, let them keep their faith sincere,
> For neither could subsist alone!
>
> But souls whom some benignant breath
> Hath charmed at birth from gloom and care,
> These ask no love, these plight no faith,
> For they are happy as they are.[24]

These lines throw a curious light on "Dover Beach," which
Allott believes was written soon after they were.

The most impressive new poem in Arnold's *Empedocles*
volume of 1852 that deals with love and marriage is "Tristram and Iseult." In this first modern version of the great
love story—preceding Wagner as well as Tennyson and
Swinburne—Arnold characteristically dramatizes, not the
taking of the love potion or the passionate embraces of the
two lovers, but their death scene. The contrast with Tennyson is especially striking: in *The Idylls of the King*, Iseult

24. P. 239.

of Ireland is simply an adultress, and Tristram is a treacherous knight who is struck dead by the bloody Mark in a moment's climax to his own bloody and lecherous career. For Tennyson, the passion of the two lovers is associated with blood lust and falsehood. For Arnold, the inevitable death of that passion—and of Tristram and Iseult—gives deep pathos to their story. In the first section, "Tristram," the dying knight waits for his beloved to arrive and dreams of their past; his speeches alternate with the narrator's comments (the first two sections are a curious combination of dramatic and narrative forms), which finally describe the coming of Iseult. The second section, "Iseult of Ireland," shows the lovers' final meeting and their death together; but this is hardly a Wagnerian *Liebestod*, and the scene ends with a cool passage that refers to the figure of the huntsman on the arras in their death room:

> thou wilt rouse no sleepers here!
> For these thou seest are unmoved;
> Cold, cold as those who lived and loved
> A thousand years ago.[25]

The third and last section, "Iseult of Brittany," is concerned with the time after this death. The surviving Iseult, the wife, sits under the hollies with her children and tells them the story of how Vivien enchanted Merlin. Here is an example of Arnold's surprising and remarkably effective endings which comment obliquely on the meaning of the poem by shifting to an apparently quite different subject. But this section has, as well, a passage that exemplifies Arnold's tendency to make his point in rather prosy verse; in the passage (omitted from several editions) Arnold again re-

25. P. 215.

flects—paradoxically, with some heat—on how futile and ephemeral such a passion as Tristram's and Iseult's is:

> I swear, it angers me to see
> How this fool passion gulls men potently;
> Being, in truth, but a diseased unrest,
> And an unnatural overheat at best.
> How they are full of languor and distress
> Not having it; which when they do possess,
> They straightway are burnt up with fume and care,
> And spend their lives in posting here and there
> Where this plague drives them.[26]

This is clear enough, but the last lines of the poem, about Vivien and Merlin, are much more impressive:

> Nine times she waved the fluttering wimple round,
> And made a little plot of magic ground.
> And in that daisied circle, as men say,
> Is Merlin prisoner till the judgment-day;
> But she herself whither she will can rove—
> For she was passing weary of his love.[27]

The subject of Tristram and the two Iseults offers a number of possibilities for dealing with free love, marriage, and infidelity. But Arnold seems to be interested in it because it provides the occasion to observe how, in time, passion turns to weariness, how love fails. For him, it is not only marriage law but the very law of nature—in which all change, all die—that frustrates love.

Yet in opposition to this deep feeling that passion is unnatural and short-lived, that every man is essentially isolated—a feeling that can be borne only with some sort of

26. P. 221.
27. P. 224

stoic resignation—Arnold more and more frequently poses
the also urgent sense of need for communion between persons (in love, in marriage) and among persons (in a society). The need for love is deep; Arnold is not persuaded
that its fulfillment is an immediate possibility. This is the
need that Arnold's most widely known lyric, "Dover
Beach," celebrates.

Allott suggests that "Tristram and Iseult" reflects Arnold's own loves—with Marguerite as Iseult of Ireland and
his wife as Iseult of Brittany—and that "Dover Beach" was
written, at least in part, during a visit to Dover soon after
Arnold's marriage.[28] If this is so, both poems may be read
as having very personal significance. The first dramatizes
a poet's disillusionment with youthful passion but perhaps,
in the figure of innocent Iseult—the wife of Tristram's de-
clining years—and her fair children, also implies a hope for
marriage that is fruitful. "Dover Beach," instead of contrasting fresh and colorful nature with the cooling and
death of love and life, reacts against philosophic or religious
faith in a moral, purposive universe and, reacting to another
and a greater disillusionment, falls back upon the need for
human love.

> Ah, love, let us be true
> To one another! for the world, which seems
> To lie before us like a land of dreams,
> So various, so beautiful, so new,
> Hath really neither joy, nor love, nor light,
> Nor certitude, nor peace, nor help for pain.[29]

Essentially, then, in spite of its beauty of diction and its

28. Pp. 196, 240.
29. P. 242.

haunting rhythm suggesting the fascination of an oceanic image that it seems in so many words to deny, "Dover Beach" is a poem of disillusionment. But it also presents what one finds rarely in Arnold's verse, an emphasis, not on the transitory nature of sexual love, but on man's need for such love.

In "The Buried Life," too, the bond between man and woman is profoundly important. Yet it may be less an intrinsically valuable experience or a promise for the future of the race than a means of escaping from unbearable isolation. This poem, one of Arnold's most interesting in conception, has to do with more than man's isolation from other men or even his isolation from all of nature. The subject is man's isolation as a conscious being from his own essential self. The way to escape from this terrible sense of being cut off from oneself is, perhaps, an extension of the way suggested in "Dover Beach" to assuage the pain of being alienated from the natural order. The poem begins rather like one of the lyrics on Marguerite, then asks,

> Alas! is even love too weak
> To unlock the heart, and let it speak?
> Are even lovers powerless to reveal
> To one another what indeed they feel?

The answer, as far as the speaker and the woman he addresses are concerned, might seem to be No. But he proceeds, discoursing on man's ignorance of his own deepest feelings and tendencies, to imagine a positive answer instead.

> Only—but this is rare—
> When a beloved hand is laid in ours,
> When, jaded with the rush and glare

Of the interminable hours,
Our eyes can in another's eyes read clear,
When our world-deafened ear
Is by the tones of a loved voice caressed—
A bolt is shot back somewhere in our breast,
And a lost pulse of feeling stirs again.
The eye sinks inward, and the heart lies plain,
And what we mean, we say, and what we would, we
      know.
A man becomes aware of his life's flow,
And hears its winding murmur; and he sees
The meadows where it glides, the sun, the breeze.

                         .   .   .   .   .

And then he thinks he knows
The hills where his life rose,
And the sea where it goes.[30]

Two points: this experience "is rare"; and the result of it,
when "another's eyes" are "read clear" and a "loved voice"
is heard, is that "The eye sinks inward." The rare moment
of true love is not essentially one of union, of marriage: it
is a means of pursuing self-knowledge.

In Arnold's poetry, then, even in these attempts to rally
the spirit and assert the need for an intimate bond of sexual
love—in effect, of marriage—there is always some doubt.
Arnold's lyrics about love are mostly denials that it can last.
His choice of the romance of Tristram and Iseult as the
source for a major poetic effort may imply some affinity for
the quasi-religious tradition of passionate romantic love.
But Arnold's lovers are shown when their passion has
waned and when they themselves are dying calmly. Even
the happily married princely couple in "The Church of

30. Pp. 272, 275.

Brou" are most movingly described in calm death. And almost the best that can be said for love in "Dover Beach" and "The Buried Life" is that it has its—possibly momentary—uses.

Sex and the Sacramental: Hopkins

Arnold was in temperament the most catholic of secularists. He was always attracted to the ideal of the universal, in religion as in other areas. Profoundly aware of, and disturbed by, the flux of human life—the time and change that chill men's and women's passions—he could admire the temper and the faith of a Newman. If one can hardly imagine his being converted, as his younger brother Thomas was, to Newman's religion, neither can one imagine his wholeheartedly embracing a secularism that ignores or scoffs at the poetry and the traditions of that faith.

Gerard Manley Hopkins, who was for a time Thomas Arnold's colleague at University College, Dublin, represents a different temperament but not a total contrast. More than an admirer of Newman, he was largely Newman's own convert. Matthew Arnold and Hopkins are the two great Victorian poets produced by Oxford, and their various careers might be said to typify two strains, not only in Victorian Oxford, but also in Victorian intellectual life: the partly skeptical, searching, and synthesizing mind of liberalism, influenced by the Noetics, and the partly fideistic, conscientious, and authority-seeking spirit of religious conservatism, influenced by Newman. One method, perhaps curious, of distinguishing the two strains is to consider the attitudes toward physical nature of this post-Romantic generation. Although he venerates Wordsworth, Arnold is unable to find sacramental meaning in nature; his "Dover

Beach" is testimony of this inability. Hopkins is a sacramental poet, for whom all nature has a sacredness as intense
as it was for the poet of the Immortality Ode, but a sacredness with a firmer ground. This means that, among many
other objects and events, sexual identity and sexual acts are
for Hopkins sacramental.

A fair number of Hopkins' poems are charged with sexual quality. It would be disingenuous to deny that the feeling is largely homosexual; the poems themselves, not only
a few suggestive letters, carry this feeling. But the point is
accidental and probably less important than the fact that
physical sexuality, the church-blessed marriage of the flesh,
can be a sacred or a creature-hallowing experience in this
poet's Catholic imagination.

There are two occasional marriage poems by Hopkins,
"At the Wedding March" (1879) and the fragmentary
"Epithalamion" (1888?). The first is fairly conventional,
the second extraordinarily fanciful. The wording in the
earlier poem is sometimes ambiguous; the first clause, "God
with honour hang your head, / Groom," suggests that the
bridegroom is both hanging his head, embarrassed by a
godly modesty, and hung, as it were, by God with a wreath
of honor. (The poem has a good deal of such plurisigna-
tion, with the words *kind* and *divined* both carrying double
meanings.) Oddly, perhaps, the husband, not the wife, is
described as being properly embarrassed. In any event, the
clear and deeply felt celebration of God's "wedlock, his
wonder wedlock" is as enthusiastic as, say, Coventry Patmore's, even if more succinct and powerful.

The "Epithalamion" of Hopkins was not completed, unhappily, because it might have proved to be one of the

poet's most striking longer pieces.[31] It begins with a "make-believe" scene; the speaker and reader imagine themselves "leafwhelmed" in a valley, a "dean," that is described in boisterously vivid language. To this place comes a "listless stranger" who hears the sound of boys bathing in the valley stream and then finds a pool for himself, into which, stripping off his clothes, he plunges. The pool is evoked in curious words, as he

>   sees it is the best
> There; sweetest, freshest, shadowiest;
> Fairyland; silk-beech; scrolled ash, packed sycamore,
>   wild wychelm, hornbeam fretty overstood
> By. Rafts and rafts of flake leaves light, dealt so, painted
>   on the air,
> Hang as still as hawk or hawkmoth, as the stars or as
>   the angels there,
> Like the things that never knew the earth, never off
>   roots
> Rose. Here he feasts: lovely all is!

This bather is himself lovingly described, with his "looplocks / Forward falling," as he undresses and then swims in the "kindcold element." But all this description of place and movement is only a way of leading up to the poet's "sacred matter," and at least he asks,

> What is . . . . the delightful dean?
> Wedlock. What the water? Spousal love.

31. *The Poems of Gerard Manley Hopkins*, ed. W. H. Gardner and N. H. Mackenzie (4th ed.; London, 1967), pp. 197–199. See Norman White, "The Setting of Hopkins' 'Epithalamion,'" *Victorian Poetry*, X (1972), 83–86.

The conceit is extreme; it appears to make the river an image of the bride in this poem where the only actual human figures are male, boys heard and a man seen.

Both these poems celebrate the joy of marriage as an earthly, physical, and at the same time sacred bond. Like Patmore, again, Hopkins regards the marriage sacrament as a religious mystery. Yet he has none of Patmore's awareness that earthly marriage can pose problems, that it can, in fact, be less than perfect.

Sex and the Sacramental: Patmore

The difference between Hopkins and Patmore may result in large part from Patmore's having actually experienced marriage, as of course Meredith, the Brownings, and Arnold did. Still, if Meredith's *Modern Love* is a psychologically vivid account of modern man and woman trapped by the secular contract of marriage, Patmore's nuptial poems, collected as *The Angel in the House*, are lyric versions of how man and woman—not especially "modern"—are fulfilled or mostly fulfilled in the spiritual harmony of marriage. For Patmore marriage is not only a contract; it is, again, a sacrament, and a sacrament that virtually replaces the eucharist in this extraordinary poet's imagination as the central expression of divine love in human life.

Frederick Page remarks that *The Angel* proper, including "The Betrothal" and "The Espousals," is about "an ideally perfect marriage," while the later part of that work, the two books called *The Victories of Love*, is about "an unideal marriage heroically made perfect."[32] *The Angel*

32. *The Poems of Coventry Patmore*, ed. Frederick Page

contrasts with *Modern Love,* but *The Victories of Love* provides a less extreme and more interesting contrast, because the problem it presents is a version of Meredith's—a lack in marriage, a lack of perfectly joyous love, preys upon the minds of wife and husband—but the outcome in the two poems is strikingly different. *The Angel* is the bland story of Felix Vaughan's love for his Honoria, and it begins with Felix's announcement of the subject that is his only poetic inspiration: not the epic matter of King Arthur or the fall of Jerusalem, but "my Wife, / And love, that grows from one to all." The story is told in lyrics that proceed from the early love of boy for girl through their wooing, his proposal and her acceptance, to a happy wedding. The smooth stream of this love's course—the lovers' problems make hardly more than ripples—is anticipated by the central figures' names, Felix and Honoria: happiness and honor are inevitably to be joined. In this respect, as J. C. Reid suggests, *The Victories of Love* is more like a novel than *The Angel* is.[33] And, like a "romantic" novel, it raises doubts and difficulties about the love of man and woman only to resolve them at the end. The conclusion of the work, a section entitled "The Wedding Sermon," serves to sum up Patmore's view of marriage. It seems appropriate that this conclusion should be a sermon delivered by a wise old priest; here Patmore, who as he wrote was close to conversion to Roman Catholicism, finds the full significance of marriage to be religious. We are told to

---

(London, 1949), p. viii; all quotations of Patmore's verse are from this edition, to which page numbers refer.

33. *The Mind and Art of Coventry Patmore* (London, 1957), p. 265.

> fathom well the depths of life
> In loves of husband and of wife,
> Child, Mother, Father; simple keys
> To what cold faith calls mysteries.[34]

"The love of marriage" is the closest thing on earth to divine love. Echoing Tennyson's *Princess* (which was being revised while this verse was being written), the speaker declares that in true marriage,

> benevolence, desire,
> Elsewhere ill-join'd or found apart,
> Become the pulses of one heart,
> Which now contracts, and now dilates,
> And, both to the height exalting, mates
> Self-seeking to self-sacrifice.

Such a marriage, here undeniably sexual, symbolizes Christ's marriage to the Church.[35]

In Patmore's idea of marriage, law is not at all opposed to personal freedom or love. Instead, marriage is both a sacred *and* a legal bond; and marriage laws are good and necessary, imposing obligations more to be trusted, as conducing to man's happiness, than the often false impulses of youthful desire.

> The bond of law
> Does oftener marriage-love evoke,
> Than love, which does not wear the yoke

34. *Poems*, pp. 322–323.

35. *Poems*, p. 323. On Patmore's tendency to replace the sacrament of the Eucharist with that of marriage—quite literally, with sexual intercourse—see Hoxie Neale Fairchild, *Religious Trends in English Poetry*, IV (New York, 1957), 317–344, especially IV, 337–338.

> Of legal vows, submits to be
> Self-rein'd from ruinous liberty.
> Lovely is love; but age well knows
> 'Twas law which kept the lover's vows
> Inviolate through the year or years
> Of worship piec'd with frantic fears,
> When she who lay within his breast
> Seem'd of all women perhaps the best,
> But not the whole, of womankind,
> Or love, in his yet wayward mind,
> Had ghastly doubts its precious life
> Was pledged for aye to the wrong wife.

As for the role of a woman in marriage, in one sense—the spiritual—it is at least equal to a man's:

> Who tries to mend his wife succeeds
> As he who knows not what he needs.
> He much affronts a worth as high
> As his, and that equality
> Of spirits in which abide the grace
> And joy of her subjected place.[36]

But even though the woman's "deep wit," which is more a matter of feeling than one of Meredithian brain, may be wiser than the man's, hers remains, socially and legally, the "subjected place." Patmore never suggests that this is not as it should be; indeed, he indicates that the "subjection of women," which Mill was to attack, is normal and right.[37]

36. *Poems*, pp. 327–328, 329.
37. "The pasha-like Patmore, who snorted derisively at Mrs. Browning's *Aurora Leigh*, rejected scornfully all 'liberal' notions that men and women are inherently equal. The man delights in ennobling his weak, slightly irrational wife, just as God takes pleasure in strengthening the irresolute and fallible soul by bestowing on it

Sexuality of a quite literal sort is present in Patmore, and his giving sexual desire a form, a limit, and a symbolic and religious significance does not amount to a "Victorian" denial of this desire or its importance.

Finally, as for that terrible sense of isolation that many Victorians—such men as Carlyle, Tennyson, and Arnold —feel and fear, all of Patmore's verse, from the mild "Tamerton Church-Tower, or, First Love" to the partly mystical odes of *The Unknown Eros,* insists that man is not alone, that because each person is a creature of divine Love, he or

---

the immeasurable privilege of his love" (John J. Dunn, "Love and Eroticism: Coventry Patmore's Mystical Imagery," *Victorian Poetry,* VII [1969], 210). This essay is illuminating on Patmore's *The Unknown Eros,* a series of odes on sexual love, published between 1866 and 1879, which refer to Cupid as the unknown god and also to conjugal love as a virtually unused subject for lyric poetry (see Patmore's *Mystical Poems of Nuptial Love,* ed. Terence Connolly [Boston, 1938], especially p. 149). The sequence is about mystical religious experience as much as about marital relations; the sexual bond of man and wife symbolizes the communion of the soul with God, and one thesis is that the fullest realization of marital bliss comes, not on earth, but ultimately in heaven. The odes treat a variety of subjects, social and political as well as erotic and religious, but a quasi-mystical conception of marriage is the recurrent theme that gives the poems whatever consistency and unity they have as a group. It may not be always a very attractive conception, however. As Dunn points out, writing of *The Unknown Eros,* "to many readers, an arrogant and patronizing lover relishing the piquancy of a kittenish rebellion against his tyranny is not a satisfying image of the relationship between God and the soul. . . . Somehow in all of this talk . . . one hears the jolly bullying of a Victorian husband who has generously decided to tolerate, within limits, the whims of his properly submissive wife" (pp. 214–215). Finally, Dunn stresses that, for Patmore, sexual love must involve pain—in a way that, surprisingly, links him to Swinburne.

she has access to the secondary and symbolic love which is marriage.[38]

Sex, Sacramental or Ideal: Clough

Most thoughtful Victorians were unable to share the faith of a Patmore, a Hopkins, or a Newman. Yet relatively few were willing to commit themselves to a thoroughgoing secularism. The profoundly Victorian mingling of conscientious doubt with a yearning for fixed belief, for a true and complete conversion to some faith that could give value to men's lives and to all human history, is nowhere better exemplified than in the work of Arthur Hugh Clough. And Clough's treatment of sexual matters gives one clear focus to this problem of mixed feelings: he represents the sacramental sense of marriage as an earthly, animal reality that is consistent with and symbolizes a divine reality as well as the tendency to make a radical separation of the sexual real and the spiritual ideal.

Clough, more than any other Victorian poet, has been the victim of his own myth, of our tendency to read every poetic utterance as unambiguously self-revealing and

38. Although the view is in a sense traditional, Patmore's erotic presentation of it shocked some of his contemporaries and appeared inappropriate to others, including Newman. J. C. Reid writes of the "direct sexual symbolism" in the *Unknown Eros* odes, as in the lines,

> the whole
> Unfathomable and immense
> Triumphing tide comes at the last to reach
> And burst in wind-kiss'd splendours on the deaf'ning beach,
> Where forms of children in first innocence
> Laugh and fling pebbles on the rainbow'd crest
> Of its untired unrest.

See Reid's *The Mind and Art of Coventry Patmore*, pp. 286 ff.

to find everywhere the expression of a supposedly failed mind and spirit, one wrecked by the conflict between conscience and impulse or between the need for faith and the need for honesty. In fact, Clough is one of the few successful Victorian ironists in verse. (Arnold's irony, powerful but unsubtle, is limited to his prose criticism, while Tennyson and Hopkins are virtually, and Swinburne is totally, devoid of that tone; only Browning can be compared to Clough in this respect.) He shows in fictional and dramatic forms, as well as in verbally ironic ways, the conflicts that typify his age and, to a great extent, our own. So, significantly, the poet who does not want his wife to lose her individuality and who, at the same time, is wholly conscious of his own sexual drives is sensitive enough to the world he lives in to reveal how men both idealize women while they exploit them and feel a terrible sexual urge with which they find it painfully difficult to cope.[39]

One of Clough's most remarkable evocations of sexuality, in which the subject is dealt with quite directly, is "Natura Naturans." This witty and serious poem yokes the elemental energy of an evolving nature with the sexual energy of a loving couple—it suggests the verse of Meredith—and it concludes,

39. Clough's sensitiveness to the position of women, his awareness of their need to act independently, was influenced, no doubt, by his close and sympathetic relationship with his sister Anne Jemima Clough, one of the Victorian leaders in women's education. She was active in the North of England Council for Promoting the Higher Education of Women and became the first principal of Newnham College. See the life by the poet's daughter, Blanche Athena Clough, *A Memoir of Anne Jemima Clough* (London, 1897).

> Such sweet preluding sense of old
>   Led on in Eden's sinless place
> The hour when bodies human first
>   Combined the primal prime embrace,
> Such genial heat the blissful seat
>   In man and woman owned unblamed,
> When, naked both, its garden paths
>   They walked unconscious, unashamed.[40]

The ending raises some questions: is Eden sinless because it is innocent of sexual consummation (one traditional view)? And how ironic are the rhymed words *unblamed, unashamed*, with their apparent implication that modern love, far from Eden, does involve blame and shame?

Clough has, too, passages and poems that can certainly be read as unironically conventional. His voice seems to express an especially conventional man's point of view when he writes of "the golden bliss of, Woo'd, and won, and wed," in his early topical poem (of 1845) "The Silver Wedding"—and even, perhaps, when his heroine Elspie, the simple Scottish girl, speaks of marriage as a bridge in the 1848 *Bothie of Tober-na-Vuolich* (entitled then *The Bothie of Tober-na-Fuosich*). Developing an image that both Clough and Arnold use to signify the joining of islands and isolated beings, she says to her lover, Philip,

> Sometimes I find myself dreaming at nights about arches
>   and bridges,—
> Sometimes I dream of a great invisible hand coming
>   down, and

40. Arthur Hugh Clough, *Poems*, ed. H. F. Lowry, A. L. P. Norrington, and F. L. Mulhauser (Oxford, 1951), p. 38; all quotations of Clough's verse are from this edition, to which page numbers refer, and are by permission of the Oxford University Press, Oxford.

Dropping the great key-stone in the middle: there in
    my dreaming,
There I felt the great key-stone coming in, and through
    it
Feel the other part—all the other stones of the archway,
Joined into mine with a strange happy sense of com-
    pleteness.[41]

Yet the language here is charged with remarkably uncon-
ventional feeling, the sexual feeling of a young woman.
And although this passage is one of several that predict a
true union, a marriage that bridges differences and joins
man and woman, it does not imply for Elspie and Philip a
sweet and simple happy ending. It does not imply their
living happily ever after. For this democratic youth and
unpretentious maiden—she will not have servants and be a
fine lady—the living-out of marriage is to involve problems,
to be less than perfect.

Clough the narrator is not only aware of that likelihood
but aware also that marriage has a physical, explicitly sexual
aspect that can raise problems. The most remarkable part
of this book-length poem—more like a pastoral tale, perhaps,
than a novel—is a fanciful commentary on just that aspect,
a comment not so much ironic (in any usual sense of the
term) as oblique and witty. The corpulent Hobbes, who
early in this verse tale—and early in Philip's wooing of
Elspie—says that the young man will "study the question of
sex in the Bothie," sends to the married couple a letter full
of fanciful biblical allusions with a postscript that draws on
the story of Jacob, Rachel, and Leah (in Genesis 29 : 1–30).

41. *Poems*, p. 159.

Listen to wisdom—*Which things*—you perhaps didn't know, my dear fellow,

I have reflected; *Which things are an allegory, Philip.*

For this Rachel-and-Leah is marriage; which, I have seen it,

Lo, and have known it, is always, and must be, bigamy only,

Even in noblest kind a duality, compound, and complex,

One part heavenly-ideal, the other vulgar and earthy:

For this Rachel-and-Leah is marriage, and Laban, their father,

Circumstance, chance, the world, our uncle and hard task-master.

Rachel we found as we fled from the daughters of Heth by the desert;

Rachel we met at the well; we came, we saw, we kissed her;

Rachel we serve-for, long years,—that seem as a few days only,

E'en for the love we have to her,—and win her at last of Laban.

Is it not Rachel we take in our joy from the hand of her father?

Is it not Rachel we lead in the mystical veil from the altar?

Rachel we dream-of at night: in the morning, behold, it is Leah.

"Nay, it is custom," saith Laban, the Leah indeed is the elder.

Happy and wise who consents to redouble his service to Laban,

So, fulfilling her week, he may add to the elder the younger,

Not repudiates Leah, but wins the Rachel unto her!

> Neither hate thou thy Leah, my Jacob, she also is
>   worthy;
> So, many days shall thy Rachel have joy, and survive
>   her sister;
> Yea, and her children—*Which things are an allegory,*
>   Philip,
> Aye, and by Origen's head with a vengeance truly, a
>   long one![42]

The burden of this allegory may remind one of Patmore's reflection that no wife is altogether "heavenly-ideal." Yet here the emphasis is not on how love must be restricted by law but rather on the necessity of taking bitter with better, the "vulgar and earthy" in marriage—including the physical aspect of sexuality—along with the "heavenly-ideal." At least the Victorian tendency to separate soul's beauty from body's beauty is not here a matter of conflict, and the poet's spokesman recognizes—as the later Tennyson cannot always recognize—that if there are two, true marriage embraces them both.

A later work of Clough's, *Amours de Voyage*, does not end with a marriage, and the fact is significant. The "fear of sex" that Walter Houghton finds in these verses, the fear or anxiety that Hobbes's idea of marriage as bigamy is designed to allay, seems clear and compelling in the letters of young Claude to his friend Eustace.[43]

> And as I walk on my way, I behold them consorting
>   and coupling;

42. *Poems*, pp. 173–174.

43. Even more than the "fear of sex," Houghton comments, Clough revealed a "deep distaste for the unreal and distorted vision of life that love creates" (*The Poetry of Clough* [New Haven, 1963], p. 410). Houghton goes on to comment on the poet's doubts about the wisdom of marriage for the artist or the literary man.

> Faithful it seemeth, and fond, very fond, very probably
> faithful,
> All as I go on my way, with a pleasure sincere and
> unmingled.
>
> . . . . .
>
>   could we eliminate only
> This vile hungering impulse, this demon within us of
> craving,
> Life were beatitude, living a perfect divine satisfaction.[44]

Claude's turning away from love and marriage at the end of *Amours de Voyage* involves not only the rejection of the sexual urge but also a sense that the life of the clear-headed intellectual is incompatible with the wedded life. Again, there may well be irony here; but the portrait of Claude reveals a real problem.

In Clough's *Dipsychus*—clearly a work full of ironies—the mock hero's first sexual temptation is made explicit, and Dipsychus rejects it with an invocation of

> mothers, and of sisters, and chaste wives,
> And angel woman-faces we have seen,
> And angel woman-spirits we have guessed.[45]

But the more serious temptation comes after he has spoken of ideal and sacred marriage with its "matrimonial sanctities" and when the Spirit, the voice of worldy wisdom, proposes a judicious marriage, a good match according to the world's standards. This, too, is rejected, but not so decisively. Dipsychus wants to believe that "a new Adam and a second Eve" might in a garden without the serpent solve

44. *Poems,* pp. 204–205.
45. *Poems,* p. 229.

"the vext conundrums of our life." He wants to believe that "heart can beat true to heart." But, like Arnold, he considers such love "rare, so doubtful, so exceptional," that perhaps the tempting Spirit's advice—to make a "good" marriage—is not bad. The problem of Dipsychus, then, is to reconcile ideality and the real world. The issues of man's sexual nature and of marriage provide specific and important ways to focus on this problem. Yet neither at the end of *Dipsychus* nor in any of the later poems do Clough's characters formulate such a reconciling and ultimately sacramental view of sexual relations as Hobbes does at the end of *The Bothie*. Clough rarely if ever dramatizes a strictly secular attitude; the extremes in his poetry are the merging of spirit and sexuality in *The Bothie* and the idealistic and antisexual divorce of the two by the divided and perplexed young Dipsychus.

Katharine Chorley writes of Clough as "the uncommitted mind." Although her phrase is accurate in some respects, the poet does not, as an ironist, need to be committed; Clough does reveal the dilemmas of an age for which physical, sexual love cannot always seem to retain its old sanctions, its sacramental quality, so that the mind is torn between a commitment to spiritless sexuality and one to sexless spirituality.

Fleshly and Ideal in Rossetti

Dante Gabriel Rossetti, probably like most Victorians, wanted it both ways—and he seems in his poetry and painting rarely to compromise between the extremes of the spiritual and the sexual. In *The House of Life*, Oswald Doughty has suggested in his study *A Victorian Romantic*

(London, 1960), he appears, perhaps deliberately, to confuse the figure of the dark sensual mistress with that of the pale dead wife; but, if Doughty is right, this is a matter of strategy, of masking the autobiographical. Actually, the tension between the two figures is at the center of the work. Here and in almost all his verse Rossetti is a poet of the fleshly and the ideal, but his Leah and Rachel are two, not one.

Rossetti, who was at various times close to both Meredith and Patmore, expresses an attitude that is less than rationally secular about sex and more than sacramental. He alternates in his poetic portraits between the image of the sexual woman, seductive and seduced—Lilith, Astarte, Venus—and that of the pure and spiritual being—the Virgin Mary, the courtly lady, the blessed damozel. The contrast between these two types, "Body's Beauty" and "Soul's Beauty," as they are called in two sonnets of *The House of Life*, is more extreme than the contrast between Meredith's proud passionate woman and Patmore's Angel in the House. Clearly, in "Jenny," Rossetti does not simply and heartlessly echo the popular Victorian transformation of the myth of Man's Fall into that of woman's fall, with the woman either a pre-Adamic angel or a ruined creature, either better or worse than a man (in Mailer's words, either a goddess or a beast). Yet the tendency, the madonna-harlot syndrome, is there. And, like Tennyson in *Maud* and the later *Idylls*, he presents the contrast so insistently as to make true earthly marriage seem all but impossible—impossible, that is, for either the wholly fleshly animal being, because marriage is a spiritual state, or for the purely spiritual being, because earthly marriage is, precisely, earthly.

In his study *Rossetti and the Fair Lady*, David Sonstroem

lists and discusses four fantasies, one or more of which can
be found in virtually all of Rossetti's poems and paintings:
the saving lady, or Beatrice; the *femme fatale*, or Lilith; the
fallen woman, or Mary Magdalene; and the victim, or
Ophelia. The first and last of these are related because they
are pure, often ethereal. The other types are, for worse or
better, carnal and often voluptuous. As Sonstroem and a
number of other critics have observed, Rossetti consistently
transformed the women in his own life into just such literary types as these, seeing events and people *sub specie lit-
terarum*.[46] Even though it may be difficult to know which
real woman, or if only one, is represented in any particular
literary work as a Beatrice, Lilith, Mary Magdalene, or
Ophelia, the pervasiveness of this sexual "typing" of real
people is clear.

Both fallen woman and heavenly damozel suggest someone quite different from the ordinary maid or wife.
Throughout Rossetti's poetry, in "The Blessed Damozel"
but also *The House of Life*, sexual love is associated with a

---

46. Middletown, Conn., 1970, pp. 3–4. Rosalie Glynn Grylls writes
of the young Rossetti, "He begins to see the woman under a
literary light—Beatrice or a Magdalen or a Proserpine—and then
develops a sense of responsibility towards the image" (*Portrait of
Rossetti* [London, 1964], pp. 52–53). The first woman he saw in
this way was his sister Christina, whom he painted as the Virgin
Mary in two of his earliest oils. Christina Rossetti, the most talented
woman poet of the period, was certainly a virgin, but she under-
stood sexual passion even though she rejected marriage. (That is,
she rejected two suitors.) This is evident not only in her lyrics but
also in her longer narrative poems, *The Prince's Progress* and
Goblin Market; the latter, a brilliant merging of religious and
sexual language, is about the desire for "forbidden fruit," to use
the poet's own phrase, and has distinctly sexual, perhaps ultimately
homosexual, implications.

fall or with death, and true marriages, it seems, are to be realized only in death, only in heaven. Love is often incomplete in life, as in "stillborn Love," but is to be consummated after life and outside time:

> But lo! what wedded souls now hand in hand
> Together tread at last the immortal strand
>   With eyes where burning memory lights love home?[47]

Even though Robert Buchanan's famous, or infamous, 1871 attack in the *Contemporary Review* accuses him of fleshliness, Rossetti retains in his poetry enough of the original Pre-Raphaelite otherworldliness to transform sexual love repeatedly into purely spiritual, unincarnate marriage. Of course, the influence of Dante and the need for a Beatrice are evident throughout his life. And, even in "Jenny" (where the most sexually interesting object is the girl's golden hair) and in the supposedly sensual parts of *The House of Life*, Rossetti never approaches the fleshliness, the sexual intensity, the explicit evocation of intercourse, that Patmore presents in his religious, quasi-mystical, and allegorical odes.

From the point of view expounded by Denis de Rougemont, one might argue that Rossetti's poetry is closely related, as was the poetry of his great namesake and that of the early Italian poets he translated, to the tradition of the troubadors. One might, indeed, argue that Rossetti follows a tradition of courtly love that praises fair ladies and disdains ordinary marriage, a tradition of romantic love linked to death that is best represented by the story of Tristram

47. *The Poetical Works of Dante Gabriel Rosetti*, ed. W. M. Rossetti (London, 1911), p. 204. Other citations of Rossetti's poetry refer to this edition.

and Iseult. This is certainly more true of him than of, say, his close friend William Morris, who was absorbed in the matter of romance.[48] But probably the best Victorian and early modern exemplar of the antisacramental myth of sexual love, a myth totally opposed to marriage, is another of Rossetti's close associates, Algernon Charles Swinburne.

Against Marriage: Swinburne

Swinburne is a poet whose intense idealism about sexual passion—an idealism expressed as much in his evocations of pain as in his visions of earth goddesses—makes him in verse, as in fact, an opponent of marriage. It might be supposed

48. The sexual love and marriage represented in the poetry of Morris are for the most part distant, dimly perceived, projected out of time into a trancelike heaven or backward in time to a past scene that is as flat and fixed as one in a tapestry. *The Earthly Paradise*, as Paul Thompson observes, was written by Morris in a period darkened for him "by the crisis of emptiness in his marriage," and it includes the elements of mistaken marriage and of love that can lead only to death. (See *The Work of William Morris* [New York, 1962].) In fact, the title of Morris' later work *Love Is Enough* might be thought to be ironic, as Philip Henderson comments (*William Morris* [London, 1967]), except that Morris is not at all given to irony. In this poem, a king and would-be lover returns home after seeking his beloved, "to find his throne usurped and his people disaffected—much as Morris had returned from Iceland to find Rossetti in his place" (Henderson, p. 128). Yet there is less reflection or generalizing upon modern marriage, the nature of sexual love, or the bonds between the sexes in Morris than in Rossetti. Morris makes virtually no comment upon marriage as a "wedded lie" or a sacred mystery. When sexual love is happily consummated in his romances, it is treated as entirely natural and is associated with delight in the physical nature of trees, earth, and sky; it sometimes becomes part of a social pattern, but for Morris marriage is a sacrament only in the sense that the whole immanent physical world is sacred.

that Swinburne the (sometimes) revolutionary spirit, attacking arbitrary powers and laws, established rule and established religion, would be a complete secularist in sexual matters. But religious language and emotion are everywhere in Swinburne, and his imagined and relatively direct responses to sexuality reflect anything but the cool rational considerations given it by Mill or even Meredith. Swinburne's idealism, however, is not at all a bland belief that sexual relations can be consistently satisfactory or sexual rapture lasting. Quite the contrary: his poetry suggests that sexual consummation is fully achieved in a virtually mystical, perhaps humanly impossible, experience of oneness that transcends the sexual individuality of male and female, of person and person, as it transcends the dialectic of time, the illusion of seasonal change.

Again, as with Clough, we had better be careful not to "read in"—not to project the fairly little that is known and the great deal that is conjectured about Swinburne's sexual life into his poetry. He explained some of that poetry —such supposedly shocking verses as "Anactoria" and "Dolores"—by pointing out that it evokes attitudes and moods and does not make direct personal statements. Here is a recurrent problem in Victorian poetry, which is often dramatic and at the same time partially or ambiguously self-dramatizing. But if Arnold can declare that he is not the self-destroying Empedocles and if Tennyson can be defended as a dramatist, not an advocate of war, in *Maud*, the case is somewhat more doubtful with Swinburne. At least his preoccupations with erotic love and death are consistent, and there are enough lyric expressions of it to let us speak of his essential imaginative idea.

The early verse dramas suggest, already, the poet's preoccupation with what John Rosenberg calls "the underlying theme of almost all of Swinburne's major poetry," that is, "the association of love with death."[49] *Chastelard* (1865), the initial play of the Mary Stuart trilogy, is the most striking of these plays (although the association appears in even the undergraduate dramas *The Queen Mother* and *Rosamund*). Chastelard is the first in a series of Swinburnean men whose erotic passions make them suffer, even die, at the hands of powerful beloved women. He seems perversely to long for the Queen to order his execution, and his longing is expressed in extravagantly sexual, voluptuous language: he wants to kiss the Queen's throat as the axe will kiss his own. In *Atalanta in Calydon*, however, Swinburne's first really major effort and the work that brought him fame (it was published some months before *Chastelard*), we find a more complex, more profoundly imagined vision of love and death.

Because *Atalanta* is an extraordinarily complex work of art, it invites a number of partial readings, indeed of misreadings. It has been taken as simply an imitation of Attic tragedy, a collection of rich verbal effects and *jeux d'esprit,* a Shelleyan-Promethean hurling of defiance against the Christian God. It is all these. It is also the dramatizing of sexual attraction and response. And, perhaps most important, it is a drama of doubleness, of division, in which love is opposed to strife, the human to the divine, and life to death, and in which every one of these dualities is imaginatively dissolved—love *is* strife, the human *is* the divine, life *is* death—even though the painful dichotomy remains in man's actual tragic experience. The work is filled with such

49. *Swinburne: Selected Poetry and Prose* (New York, 1968), p. xv.

words as *twin* and *twain*. There are some fanciful triads, too, perhaps in mocking reference to Christian tradition (Artemis is called *threefold*), but again and again it is doubleness that the poetry stresses. The doubleness is first of all associated with seasonal time, spring and winter, warm and cold. But it comes to be a more profound dichotomy, for this is the drama of people who, being mortal, seem painfully divided between soul and body, between life and death, while they seek the impossible ideal which still glimmers as the ultimate, the divine truth of Unity, a unity that means death for the individual. This experience of painful, perhaps illusory, doubleness, together with the need for oneness, is expressed through action as well as imagery and diction, and is expressed finally as sexual experience and sexual need.

One aspect of this apparent, painful doubleness that shatters the unity of truth is the way in which the major human actors in the play merge into the divine or at least the more than human. Atalanta herself is the earliest and best example. She is not only the favorite of Artemis: she is a version of that divine chaste huntress, and she seems to her admirer Meleager virtually a goddess herself. Her earthly sexuality may be in doubt—the Chief Huntsman at the very beginning of the drama calls her a "maiden rose," and the wise Oeneus later refers to her as "Virgin, not like the natural flower of things / That grows and bears and brings forth fruit and dies"—and all the speakers except the obtuse Toxeus and Plexippus regard Atalanta as someone or something disturbingly more than an ordinary maiden.[50]

50. To Althea, she is a "strange woman," "adorable, detestable." See *The Collected Poetical Works of Algernon Charles Swinburne*

The other main characters, Althea and Meleager, also come
at last to seem mythic, virtually preterhuman; and this is
one explanation for their perplexing psychological motiva-
tions, for the mother killing her dearly beloved son and the
son blessing his maternal executioner.

The reversals, ironies, and mergings of apparently opposite sexual qualities are also striking. Several critics have
commented upon how the women in the drama, Atalanta
the bold huntress and Althea the vengeful sister and
mother, are distinctly masculine according to conventional
typing, while the men, the mild and sweetly articulate
Meleager and the even milder Oeneus, seem in the same
sense almost feminine. The brutally and stupidly male
types, Toxeus and Plexippus, make these points several
times in taunting both Atalanta and Meleager. Toxeus asks,
"Except she give her blood before the gods, / What profit
shall a maid be among men?" (IV, 280).[51] His question suggests both that women properly are sacrificial victims and
that, in giving their blood with the loss of virginity, they
are the sexual victims of men. This is the way things are
and should be. Plexippus taunts Meleager with his and Atalanta's apparent reversal of sex roles:

> Why, if she ride among us for a man,
> Sit thou for her and spin; a man grown girl
> Is worth a woman weaponed; sit thou here.   [IV, 280]

(London, 1904), IV, 307. All other quotations of poetry are from
this edition and are identified by volume and page numbers in
the text.

51. The resemblance of Toxeus and Plexippus to coarse and
unsympathetic male speakers in Meredith as well as Tennyson
hints at an interest in women's rights, an interest Swinburne hardly
pursues in later verse.

Later Plexippus expresses male indignation about the strong and independent woman, an indignation that leads—when he and his brother try to seize the boar's hide that Meleager has given Atalanta and are killed in the ensuing battle—to the inevitable tragic disaster. About Atalanta he asks,

> shall she live
> A flower-bud of the flower-bed, or sweet fruit
> For kisses and the honey-making mouth,
> And play the shield for strong men and the spear?
> Then shall the heifer and her mate lock horns,
> And the bride overbear the groom, and men
> Gods.   [IV, 281]

The theme is familiar; it is present in earlier literature (for instance, in Chaucer's Wife of Bath's prologue) as a comic idea, but in Victorian and later literature it becomes quite serious. Of course, Plexippus is too obtuse and crude—like the comparable father of the prince in Tennyson's *The Princess*—to be considered to have a serious idea at all; but his sister Althea, the mother of Meleager, is another matter, and earlier in the drama, less brutally but still in a conventional vein, this remarkable woman raises the same question. Cautious and skeptical, putting no faith in the gods yet fearing any breach of law and order, she declares that no man can prosper

> through laws torn up,
> Violated rule and a new face of things.
> A woman armed makes war upon herself,
> Unwomanlike, and treads down use and wont
> And the sweet common honour that she hath,
> Love, and the cry of children, and the hand
> Trothplight and mutual mouth of marriages.   [IV, 265]

Paradoxically, Althea herself (who later declares she wishes she had never married) is a strong and dominating woman. But she fears disordered sexual relations even as she might seem in some respects to exemplify them.

Althea is also fearful of sexual love, of any passion that may threaten the calm and fragile scheme of things.

> Love is one thing, an evil thing, and turns
> Choice words and wisdom into fire and air.
> And in the end shall no joy come, but grief,
> Sharp words and soul's division and fresh tears.
>
> [IV, 265]

The later, celebrated, chorus that begins, "We have seen thee, O Love, thou art fair; thou art goodly, O Love," does not contradict this attitude. It proceeds to sing of the power personified in Aphrodite as "an evil blossom," one that—and now Swinburne is following the epic and tragic precedents—brings not peace but destruction.

Love often appears to be destructive, disastrous, in *Atalanta*. Yet it is inevitable, and in its several manifestations it represents a tragic but necessary attempt to break through the illusory doubleness of life and death, human and divine, and specifically of male and female; for sexual differentiation is perhaps the very first, most basic, manifestation of that "heart's division" through which Swinburne's voices again and again, in dramatic and lyric forms, try to pierce in order to achieve a sense of the unity of all life.[52]

It might appear that Swinburne would, like Patmore and like Tennyson in *The Princess*, glorify marriage as an ap-

52. See Richard Mathews, "Heart's Love and Heart's Division: The Quest for Unity in *Atalanta in Calydon*," *Victorian Poetry*, IX (1971), 35–48.

proximation of this unity, of two hearts beating as one. But a striking characteristic of Swinburne's poetry, which helps to explain his kaleidoscopic imagery, his constantly shifting use of symbolic language, is that it is never satisfied with approximations. Certainly the most articulate speakers in *Atalanta*—including, ultimately, the fairly conventional Althea—either reject or disregard marriage as an expression of love.

This is true not simply because marriage can involve pain and frustration, although, in the words of one chorus, the gods have

> Put moans into the bridal measure
>   And on the bridal wools a stain;
> And circled pain about with pleasure,
>   And girdled pleasure about with pain;
> And strewed one marriage-bed with tears and fire
> For extreme loathing and supreme desire.   [IV, 285]

They do so, more significantly, because marriage as an institution, whether a secular and merely legal one or a sacramental and therefore religious bond, insists upon the individuality, if not the rights, of separate parties, upon sexual differentiation. Very often in Swinburne's poetry the ideal of sexual union seems to be not marriage but merger, a total and mystical oneness that is, so to speak, self-consuming.

In *Atalanta*, there is no expression of passionate love that is directed toward marriage. Meleager specifically and repeatedly says that he regards Atalanta, not as a nubile maiden, but as a goddess whom he worships,

> Most fair and fearful, feminine, a god,
> Faultless; whom I that love not, being unlike,
> Fear, and give honour, and choose from all the gods.
>   [IV, 269]

Meleager's love for his mother, Althea, is also at last a kind of worship. The apparently incestuous intensity of relations between mother and son has been commented on a number of times, and it has been suggested that Althea's anxiety about the coming of Atalanta to Calydon and even her causing her son's death are the result of maternal sexual jealousy. But Althea says only that there is some cursed fatality that Atalanta will bring; and her clear motive for letting Meleager die is the family piety of one who is as much a sister of the men her son has slain as a loving mother. Perhaps a more perplexing motive is that of Meleager himself when, destroyed by Althea, he hails her as he dies.

> Thou, too, the bitter mother and mother-plague
> Of this my weary body—thou too, queen,
> The source and end, the sower and the scythe,
> The rain that ripens and the drought that slays,
> The sand that swallows and the spring that feeds,
> To make me and unmake me—thou, I say,
> Althea, since my father's ploughshare, drawn
> Through fatal seedland and of a female field,
> Furrowed thy body, whence a wheaten ear
> Strong from the sun and fragrant from the rains
> I sprang and cleft the closure of thy womb,
> Mother, I dying with unforgetful tongue
> Hail thee as holy and worship thee as just
> Who art unjust and unholy.   [IV, 330]

In this extraordinary passage the mother is associated, not only with the earth, but also with divine force, with that which is feared and must be worshiped.

For Meleager, then, love—whether erotic or filial—*is* worship. And this worship is expressed by the gesture of sacrifice, of giving: giving the symbol of triumph in battle, the boar's skin, to Atalanta (perhaps, as one or two critics have suggested, it is also the symbol of male potency) and giving his own life back to Althea. In the ultimate resignation to death there is a combination of intensely sexual and religious language, along with a deliberate use of paradox that may well remind us of other poets, Dylan Thomas, for one, and especially of Hopkins, many of whose lines in *The Wreck of the Deutschland* seem to echo parts of *Atalanta*.[53] The fire that burns throughout the work, in both literal and metaphorical images, now becomes a divine destructive force as well as life itself. It also takes on a distinct sexual meaning: Meleager is a firebrand by name and destiny, although his protective mother has kept the symbolic brand that represents him unlit in order to extend his life; now that this brand *is* lit, now that he comes to life, so to speak, in a passionate way—whatever one makes of the boar, the modern reader can hardly fail to find a sexual overtone in the burning brand—Meleager is both passionately living for the first time and, for the first time, passionately dying.

The virtual identification of love with both worship and death or self-immolation in *Atalanta in Calydon* sets a pattern that much of Swinburne's poetry tends from now on to follow. This pattern represents a speaker or central character who has the painful experience of a frustrated woman-

53. Hopkins' address, not to a goddess-like mother, but to God the Father, may for instance, echo Swinburne: Hopkins' God has "almost unmade me"; Swinburne's goddess seems "to make me and unmake me." Renée Overholzer argues that the *Deutschland* is a direct reaction to and against *Atalanta*. On Swinburne's importance for Hopkins, see Elisabeth W. Schneider, *The Dragon in the Gate* (Berkeley, 1968).

worship, an erotic love for some queen or goddess that is likely to be sexually unconsummated. As John Rosenberg remarks, "there are scarcely any lovers in Swinburne's poetry. There is much passion but little conjunction; emotion is felt but not communicated and not returned. Swinburne has mistakenly acquired the reputation of an erotic poet; he is rather the poet of love's impossibility."[54] The result of love's impossibility, of frustration, is the lover's return to a maternal force—if not actually a mother figure, an abstraction like "mother Night" or, very often indeed, the maternal sea. This matrix is both life giver and destroyer, a womb that is also a tomb. And some form of imagined death, whether the burning death in *Atalanta* or the plunge into watery depths in "The Lake of Gaube," represents the true consummation of passion, the return to primal unity.

There are, of course, variations on the pattern. In "Laus Veneris" and several other poems the goddess Venus seems to merge in her own figure the two aspects of woman, the erotically enticing and the maternally destructive. At least so it seems to the divided and still largely Christian mind of the knight, in "Laus Veneris," who is in her thrall, the knight for whom love of Venus is not only a kind of death-in-life but also the assurance of ultimate punishment by God.[55]

"Laus Veneris," like *Atalanta*, is a dramatic work. In direct lyric modes one can often trace the pattern of love

54. *Selected Poetry and Prose*, p. xxiv.
55. On the knight's point of view as distinct from the poet's, see Julian Baird, "Swinburne, Sade, and Blake: the Pleasure-Pain Paradox," *Victorian Poetry*, IX (1971), 49–75, especially pp. 63–74.

and death even more clearly. "The Triumph of Time," which may echo Shelley's "Epipsychidion" in its language but also suggests the situation of Tennyson's "Locksley Hall," dwells on the frustrating sense of doubleness, of separation, involved in love. *Twain* is a key word for the lover, who declares that "time shall not sever us wholly in twain" and imagines that he and his beloved might have been

> Twain halves of a perfect heart, made fast
> Soul to soul while the years fell past;
> Had you loved me once, as you have not loved.   [I, 35]

This is the very desire expressed in the marriage poetry of Patmore ("the [two] pulses of one heart") and of Tennyson ("the two-celled heart beating, with one stroke"), the desire denied by Arnold ("men . . . *dreamed* two human hearts might blend in one"). But doubleness and division are human realities and set man as a lover apart from the oneness of the matrix, "the sweet sea": "I would we twain were even as she, lost in the night and the light." The climax of this poem is the speaker's utterance of what might well be called a death wish:

> I will go back to the great sweet mother,
>   Mother and lover of men, the sea.
> I will go down to her, I and none other,
>   Close with her, kiss her and mix her with me;
> Cling to her, strive with her, hold her fast:
> O fair white mother, in days long past
> Born without sister, born without brother,
>   Set free my soul as thy soul is free.
>
> O fair green-girdled mother of mine,
>   Sea, that are clothed with the sun and the rain,

Thy sweet hard kisses are strong like wine,
  Thy large embraces are keen like pain.
Save me and hide me with all thy waves,
Find me one grave of thy thousand graves,
Those pure cold populous graves of thine
  Wrought without hand in a world without stain.

                                              [I, 42–43]

In defending his first series of *Poems and Ballads* (1866), Swinburne writes that "the book is dramatic, many-faced, multifarious; and no utterance of enjoyment or despair, belief or unbelief, can properly be assumed as the assertion of its author's personal feeling or faith."[56] One might argue that this collection is less "many-faced" than other Victorian volumes of poetry and that a good deal of personal belief and disbelief or, at least, very personal emotion does shine through its dramatic masks. Still, there is enough dramatizing of real and mythic sources to provide oblique versions of Swinburne's basic patterns and themes. "Anactoria," for one, loosely based on the ode by Swinburne's favorite woman writer, Sappho—he praises her at length in "On the Cliff"—has a special point of view. Yet even here the evocation of sadism as a lover's attempt to break through the frustrating fact of division and difference, the yoking of eroticism with death, and the final phrase of the poem, "the insuperable sea," are clearly related to what is said in more seemingly personal verses. Other familiar dramatic poems in this and the succeeding volume, *Songs before Sunrise* (1871), repeat the motif of the goddess both erotic and maternal who is associated with both life and death:

56. *The Complete Works of Algernon Charles Swinburne*, ed. Edmund Gosse and T. J. Wise, Bonchurch Edition (London, 1925), VI, 354.

"The Hymn to Proserpine," "The Garden of Proserpine," and "Hertha," to name a few. Yet other poems, such as the notorious "Faustine" and "Dolores," emphasize the fatal aspect of the beloved and dominating woman. And the more or less explicit linking of love with destruction is everywhere; in the spiritual autobiography "Thalasius" it is represented by an encounter with the god of love who declares, "my name is death." But of all the earlier poems based on ancient sources or poems otherwise mythological, the most curious exploration of sexual ideas, one that both goes beyond the pattern and illuminates the meaning of that pattern, is "Hermaphroditus" (in the 1866 *Poems and Ballads*).

It seems appropriate that Swinburne should write of the mythical young boy united with the nymph who loved him. The story is an acting-out of Aristophanes' conceit, in Plato's *Symposium*, about love as the "desire and pursuit of the whole," and thus an imagined merging of the sexual "twain," a triumph over doubleness, over sexual and personal division. Yet it results not in fulfillment but in "barren hours," in the "waste wedlock of a sterile kiss." Swinburne's virtual merging of opposites—male and female, love and cruelty, life and death—results, that is, in an oceanic and wholly self-contained universe and not at all in a harmonious relating or a partial union of still distinct persons and elements.

In the profound sterility which is oneness, not in fruitfulness and the dialectic of sex, of time, Swinburne finds truth. The references to marriage in his verse, often disillusioned, harsh, even bitter, as well as his private expressions of hostility toward the institution, may have derived in large part from his own frustrated passion for his cousin.

But they are much more than reflections of one unhappy love affair. Rosenberg observes that "the lovers in 'At a Month's End' seem not only lost to each other but eclipsed by the larger motions of nature around them."[57] And this is the sense that radically differentiates the poem from a number of poems by Browning on the dying away of passionate love, poems it otherwise closely resembles. The controlling idea is that of an elemental force and reality that can alternatively be called Love, Life, or—perhaps most appropriately, from an individual human being's point of view—Death. Paradoxically, the worst death, the dreariest sterility, sometimes seems to Swinburne to be that of ordinary conventional life and its sexual productiveness.

Such an attitude is repeatedly suggested in Swinburne's verse, as, for instance, in these lines from "Dolores":

> No thorns go as deep as a rose's,
>   And love is more cruel than lust.
> Time turns the old days to derision,
>   Our loves into corpses or wives;
> And marriage and death and division
>   Make barren our lives.   [I, 159]

Marriage is directly linked with "division" here, because it is something less than fusion or unity. Furthermore, marriage represents for Swinburne the quintessential social lie, the pretense made by rulers and rules that men's tragic doubleness can be resolved in easy conventional ways. It seems especially significant, in this connection, that his most ambitious extended narrative on the subject of erotic passion is a version of the Tristram story, which Denis de

57. *Selected Poetry and Prose*, p. xxix.

Rougemont regards as the archetypical version of the myth of romantic love and death.

Tristram of Lyonesse tells a tale already told by Arnold and by Richard Wagner, a tale that allows Swinburne to emphasize adultery and the literally "barren" life of the married woman. Tristram's marriage to the "other Iseult," in Swinburne's version, is not only a failure but is a "Maiden Marriage" (this is the title of his Part IV), one that is unconsummated. The "white-handed Iseult, maid and wife"—who is unlike the same character in Arnold's poem, who has children—curses Tristram and "his harlot," vowing revenge on them. But her frustration is less significant than that felt by the lovers themselves, a frustration that can be ended only in the peace of death. The whole work ends,

> Nor where they sleep shall moon or sunlight shine
> Nor man look down for ever: none shall say
> Here once, or here, Tristram and Iseult lay:
> But peace they have that none may gain who love,
> And rest about them that no love can give,
> And over them, while death and life shall be,
> The light and sound and darkness of the sea.   [IV, 151]

Again, the last word is *sea*. Again, the only true consummation of erotic passion is in death, a return to the unity of that great symbolic matrix.

It has been persuasively argued that Swinburne follows Blake in opposing a sort of pantheism to what he conceives of as the dualities of Christian theism, the dualities of soul and body, or heaven and earth, or eternity and time.[58] This argument might seem to contradict the assertion that he

58. By Julian Baird, in "Swinburne, Sade, and Blake."

belongs in the tradition of the dualistic Manicheans, of
those Cathars who condemned the sacrament of marriage
because it sullies spiritual love with fleshliness, and even in
the tradition of the courtly troubadors who eschewed marriage as a dull misrepresentation of passion. But Denis de
Rougemont himself, who outlines that tradition (and almost certainly exaggerates the clear direct relations between heresy and romance) comments, "Catharist dualism
issues in eschatological monism, whereas . . . Christian or-
thodoxy . . . becomes ultimately dualistic, even though,
contrary to Manichaeism, it professes the idea of a single
creation, accomplished entirely at the hands of the Deity,
and one that began by being entirely good."[59] "Eschatological monism" is a phrase that applies to Swinburne's
poetry in a special sense: over and over, it seems that the
end of passion, the end of conflict, indeed the end of all
things, is not only a death but a merging into the night, the
sea, the one. Swinburne's supposed advocacy of the flesh
and of fleshly vices is really an insistence on the unity of
life and an insistence that is ultimately anything but fleshly:
it denies a dualism of body and spirit in order to assert that
the body is really no single body but an abstraction, one
which might as well be called spirit. Swinburne is the poetic spokesman for Carlyle's "Natural Supernaturalism,"[60]

59. *Love in the Western World*, p. 76.
60. Swinburne was influenced by Carlyle's transcendentalism and
by the imagery that expresses it—the imagery of temporal and
illusory clothing that may be discarded, imagery that occurs constantly in Swinburne's poetry along with the desire to plunge
naked into the depths of sea or lake. One might well argue that
Carlyle extends his inherited Scotch Calvinism, with its quasi-
Manichean stress on the total depravity of the fallen natural world,
into an actual rejection of the reality of this nature, of this "illu-

which is a kind of pantheism; nature is supernatural in that it is one, timeless, in some sense divine.

In many respects Swinburne's treatment of love and sexuality is strikingly unique. No other Victorian writer deals so openly with such aspects as homosexuality, masochism, and sadism. Yet it would be misleading to assert that Swinburne is atypical or a freak. His way of coping with sex, his sexual idealism or tendency to regard sexual passion as a virtually mystical passion for oneness—a passion can mean the destruction of a limited individual existence—is closely related to the responses of other artists, Victorian and modern, from Tennyson to Henry Miller and Norman Mailer, who either sublimate sexuality in pseudo religion or sublimate religion in pseudo sexuality, and for whom sexual experience is not the gratification of appetite or the demonstrating of erotic love for a specific person or the expression of a philoprogenitive urge.

Problems

In the work of each of these Victorian poets, sexual love takes on great significance.[61] For a secularist like Meredith

---

sion" of time and space. If Carlyle's specific views on love and marriage had any impact on Swinburne, they would be the views of *Sartor Resartus*, in which erotic love is "a discerning of the Infinite in the finite" and not those of the later, more bitter, indeed paranoid essays such as the infamous "Nigger Question," in which Carlyle makes an exact parallel between marriage and slavery— leaving little doubt as to which sex is slave and which master— in the process of extolling slavery as a necessary institution.

61. It has some importance, too, for other poets of the age: for the remarkable William Barnes in such dialect poems as "The Wife a-Lost" and "The Bachelor," for one instance. Charles Kingsley, for another, wrote several staunchly Protestant attacks in verse on celibacy. Walter Houghton comments that Kingsley was

the intimate relation of man and woman seems to express
not only natural energy but also social realities and problems: the problem of reconciling order with urgent individual, sexual, impulse; of defining the place of women in a
new society so that they are neither brutalized nor denied
the sexual role of the "other"; of expressing and accepting
sexuality in a humane manner that avoids the cruel exploitation of persons with which sensitive mid-Victorian men
and women were familiar; the haunting problem of people's
isolation in the cold modern world and their need for communication with others, their need for love in some lasting
form—lasting beyond the time of early intense sexual attraction. For Meredith, sexuality is a phenomenon biological, social, and psychological. For a sacramentalist like Patmore the sexual relation is symbolic. In the sacrament of
marriage it represents the mysterious relation of God to
man—more specifically, that of Christ to his bride the
Church. If the symbolism raises problems—the subordina-
tion of wife to husband, as of human to divine, seems

---

convinced he was saved from debauchery by marriage (*The
Victorian Frame of Mind*, pp. 375–377). And A. Dwight Culler
makes the fascinating suggestion that Kingsley's antipathy to Newman, the "score" he had to settle, was "a sexual one"; that is,
Newman's example of celibacy had so appealed to the younger man
that it stood in the way of Kingsley's marriage and "seduced
him"—so Kingsley thought—"into an unnatural view" of sex.
Culler points out that Kingsley's famous attack is couched in sexual terms: Newman is supposed to threaten "the brute male force
of the wicked world that marries and is given in marriage."
Kingsley goes so far as to attack the traditional Christian language
of Christ as the bridegroom of the soul; unlike the Tennyson of
In Memoriam, he is horrified by the "repulsive" idea that a male
figure can be the husband of the male as well as the female soul.
See Culler's edition of *Apologia pro Vita Sua* (Boston, 1956),
pp. ix–xi.

clearly implicit—all other significance, biological, social, and psychological, must nevertheless be subordinated to this sacramental meaning. For such an idealist as Swinburne, the fulfillment of sexuality is not a mysterious relation of the human to the divine, of the many to the One, but a mystical union. If his poetry implies social and psychological questions—the question of sexual role-playing, for instance, or why dominant women and submissive men cannot be recognized by society—these are subsidiary to the ultimate idea of the one force, perhaps pantheistic, in which all energies, especially the sexual, must merge.

Possibly none of these points of view can be satisfactory for thoughtful Victorians or for modern men and women. The poets cited so far, who were after all artists rather than theologians or social theorists, do not articulate attitudes that are altogether clear and simple. Certainly, for the distinctly "major" poets, whose work is in most respects even more complex, the subject of sexuality is anything but simple, is indeed profoundly problematic.

The theme of sex, marital and extramarital, implies, then, a range of problems—freedom and order, women's roles, sexual exploitation, isolation in the modern world, the need to give a mythic, a religious, or an idealistic meaning to intense biological and psychological urges. It implies these problems—and more—in the work of Tennyson.

3 | Marriage and Divorce in Tennyson

More than any other Victorian poet, Tennyson has suffered from the Victorian and modern fondness for seeing eras, and especially his era, as all of a piece. This is largely, no doubt, because he is thought of, and with some justice, as the quintessential Victorian, the spokesman for his period.[1] He may serve that purpose because, far from having a consistent body of ideas and attitudes, he is uncertain about crucial questions and he accepts, even embraces and insists upon, contradictions within himself. He also changes. It has become all too easy to think of the young Romantic Alfred Tennyson as speaking the mind of the laureate or even of the older Alfred, Lord Tennyson. For example, so wide-ranging and distinguished a critic of the age as Walter Houghton appears to suggest that the Tennyson of *The Princess*, a remarkably liberal poem about woman's role in society and one with positively radical implications, is quite consistent with the Tennyson of the later *Idylls,* which express reactionary attitudes toward woman and a profound fear of sexuality.[2]

1. See Valerie Pitt, *Tennyson Laureate* (London, 1962), pp. 247ff.
2. "Love," in *The Victorian Frame of Mind* (New Haven, 1957), especially pp. 348–349 and 368–372.

Perhaps the simplest way to describe Tennyson's chang- ing response to sexuality and marriage *is* to observe the changes in his conception of woman—not women, but the abstraction *woman*. In his early poetry the woman is often the speaker or central character; and she is likely to be as- sociated with delicate flowers, with inwardness, with sub- jective, sometimes morbid, states of mind. In fact, as Lionel Stevenson suggests, following an idea of Jung's, Tennyson's image of the "high-born maiden" may symbolize the brood- ing soul.[3] In "The Palace of Art" the explicitly personified Soul is feminine; and such figures as the Lady of Shalott and Mariana have been interpreted as more subtle projec- tions of the poet's spirit. By the time of *Maud*, however (the few women mentioned in *In Memoriam* are hardly symbolic), the symbolic woman has become more com- plex: she is associated with both lily and rose, as both a chaste subject and a sexual object, and she tends increas- ingly to become an objectification of man's own dangerous sexual urge, not of the self or soul, but of the appealing and yet frightening "other." In the *Idylls*, although there is a contrast of women—Enid the True and Vivien the False—the dominant woman and the one most ruthlessly allegorized at the end, Guinevere, seems to personify Sense in "the world-wide war of Sense and Soul, typified in in- dividuals."[4] Tennyson has moved from a vision of woman as Soul in a world of selfish sensuality to a vision of woman

3. "The 'High-Born Maiden' Symbol in Tennyson," *PMLA*, LXIII (1948), 234–243.

4. Quoted from Hallam Tennyson, *Alfred Lord Tennyson: A Memoir* (London, 1899), p. 529; this source is hereafter cited in the text as *Memoir*.

as Sense, the enemy of Soul. On the way, understandably, the idea of marriage as an earthly sexual bond has suffered.

Of course, the simplest way of outlining a poet's development of a particular subject can hardly do justice to all his poems. Actually, with his deep concern about the relations between the sexes, Tennyson can at various times represent both idealizing and disillusioned attitudes toward marriage and toward woman as wife. Although the young man of "Locksley Hall" whose Amy has married for money is as bitter as Meredith in *Modern Love,* the speakers in "The Miller's Daughter" and "The Gardener's Daughter" pay tributes to wives and to marriages as blissful as Patmore's in *The Angel in the House.* Marriage, for Tennyson, signifies both the troth, absolute truth in sexual love, and the grim reality of a commercial contract which, because it amounts to a lie, is as sterile as it is hypocritical. The urged defined in "The Palace of Art" to strive for moral, social goals, and the morbid tendency to withdraw into himself—these two poles of the poet's temperament—are expressed repeatedly in the opposed themes of true marriage and isolation, of union leading to birth and sterility leading to death.

Tennyson is concerned with the conflict between conventional bonds and the demands of "free love," with the place of woman in modern marriage and modern society, with the powerful and often frightening nature of sexuality, and especially with the terrible sense of personal isolation.[5] All these matters are, for him, summed up in the

5. It is tempting to associate these concerns with events in the poet's life. On the unhappy marriage of Tennyson's parents, and on his long-delayed marriage to Emily Sellwood, see Jerome

symbolic meaning of marriage as the reconciliation of law and spontaniety, of man and woman, of spirit and flesh, of the individual and the evolving race. In spite of Tennyson's reference to this consistent symbolism in poetry early and late, however, it seems more and more difficult in the poetry of his middle and later periods for him to realize the higher significance of marriage. He moves from a conception of marriage as a mode of salvation, although the institution is often perverted, to doubt and cynicism about actual marriages, and to distaste for the physical, sexual reality involved in the marriage bond—distaste for what is unideally of the earth, distaste often focused on the fleshliness of women. The implications of this movement for Tennyson's imagination and his poetic art are deeply significant.

Early Poems: Isolation

The figure of the delicate young lady, unmarried or bereft of love, appears again and again in the poet's early verse. Sometimes she seems merely to provide the occasion for graceful writing, and the maiden is as decorative as nubile; "Lilian" and "Madeline" are perhaps literary counterparts of popular Victorian prints of wide-eyed young women with elegant names. Tennyson sometimes, on the other hand, characterizes his ladies, as he does in "Isabel," an early poem about the ideal wife. This "stately flower of female fortitude, / Of perfect wifehood and pure lowlihead" (the implication may well be that wifehood and humility are synonymous) has "the laws of marriage character'd in gold / Upon the blanched tables of her heart."[6] All

---

Hamilton Buckley, *Tennyson: The Growth of a Poet* (Cambridge, Mass., 1961).

6. *The Poems of Tennyson*, ed. Christopher Ricks (London,

of this seems fairly commonplace, not to say banal. But the "queen of marriage, a most perfect wife" is described in curious imagery—"a clear stream flowing with a muddy one"—that hints at something other than the ordinary and the sentimental (and very possibly reflects the young poet's knowledge of how difficult and unhappy his own mother's lot as a wife had been), suggesting something less than a harmonious union with a sympathetic mate. And the best-known early poems about young ladies, "Mariana," "The Lady of Shalott," and "Oenone," all have to do with loneliness, with the longing for death, with the failure of love and marriage.

Each of these three women has been chosen—from Shakespeare, Arthurian legend, Greek mythology—to represent isolation, a frustrated need for love, an anticipation of death. In each poem a refrain or repeated phrase emphasizes these themes. Mariana, whose "life is dreary," cries, "He cometh not, . . . I am aweary, aweary, / I would that I were dead!" Her final lines discard all hope that her betrothed will appear:

> "He will not come," she said;
> She wept, "I am aweary, aweary,
> O God, that I were dead!"   [p. 190]

The Lady of Shalott does not speak, but the insistent refrain rhymes in the ballad, "Camelot" and "Shalott," establish the contrast between the capital city and her world.

1969), Longmans Edition, p. 184. All quotations of Tennyson's poetry are from this edition, to which page numbers refer. The text is identical with that of the Eversley Edition, ed. Hallam Tennyson (London, 1908–1913), except for a few corrections in punctuation,

Camelot is the center of a society, the place of "knight and burgher, lord and dame"; Shalott is literally isolated, an island surrounded by lilies, where the fairy lady lives alone, seeing life only in a mirror. Thus society and active life are opposed to loneliness and morbid withdrawal. Yet the two names rhyme. And another rhyming name is substituted twice for these: "Lancelot" takes the place of "Camelot" in the first stanza of Part III, and of "Shalott" three stanzas later. The actual and active Lancelot is associated with the city and the court of Arthur, but his mirrored image is effective in the lonely maiden's bower.

It is possible to read this fantastic ballad as a more or less unconsciously symbolic account of the poet's own fears. Such a reading can be supported by reference to "The Palace of Art," where the speaker's soul—an aesthetic soul— is isolated in a gothic building, from which she looks out, and then escapes, into the world of people. In both poems a lone woman's looking out a window is the turning point and, in a sense, the crucial moral action, since it leads to her abandoning a self-contained and intensely self-conscious existence, to the abandoning of Romantic egoism and self-centered art in favor of social commitment. According to such a reading, "The Lady of Shalott" implies Tennyson's early and almost Keats-like fear that leaving the Romantic bower and venturing into the world of society will destroy the lyric muse, the poetic soul. The Lady sings her last song as she floats toward Camelot.

> For ere she reach'd upon the tide
> The first house by the water-side,
> Singing in her song she died,
>   The Lady of Shalott. [p. 360]

Still, "The Palace of Art" is an allegory and "The Lady of Shalott" a fantasy, at most a symbolic poem. And for our purposes the most striking fact about this fantasy is that here, as in the later version—"Lancelot and Elaine," in the *Idylls*—the isolated maiden sees but cannot be united with the other, the woman cannot be joined with the man, and the subjective artist with the objective world; so her going into that world means, not marriage, not love fulfilled, but death. This is her "curse." Versions of this curse appear to be visited on a great many other characters in the poetry of Tennyson.

"Oenone" is concerned with a more general curse, one affecting two societies. The focus is on the speaker's suffering: the curse of Paris' sexual drive, which is to destroy a civilization, results specifically now in the suffering of one woman, a wife who has been destroyed by it. It is characteristic of Tennyson to tell the familiar story of the judgment of Paris from the point of view of the lonely woman who first suffers from that curse; one can hardly imagine any other writer doing just this. Like Mariana's, Oenone's story is about a failure of marriage, and, like Mariana, she speaks of both lost love and her own death. She is also like the Lady of Shalott in being wholly desolate, divorced from love (we remember that Shakespeare's Mariana will at last, in the dark comedy *Measure for Measure*, be married). She is without husband or child:

> never child be born of me,
> Unblest, to vex me with his father's eyes!
>
> . . . . .
>   whereso'er I am by night and day,
> All earth and air seem only burning fire.   [p. 397]

This reference to a child unborn and the last ominous statement as well are to be echoed, in the *Idylls*, by Arthur speaking to Guinevere: "Well is it that no child is born of thee. / The children born of thee are sword and fire." Oenone suggests what is to become a major theme in *The Princess* and at the end of *In Memoriam*, as well as in the *Idylls*. For Tennyson the failure of marriage is the failure of the most basic social relationship, the relationship on which the family and thus the entire social fabric seems to rest; for Tennyson childlessness means sterility and death. The ideal of marriage signifies not only reconciliation of male and female, action and passivity, self and other, but also fruitfulness, new birth, promise for the future.

The complaints of the three ladies are echoed in other poems: in the refrain of "Mariana in the South"—"to be alone, / To live forgotten, and love forlorn"—and, indeed, in the words of several men. The voice of the young man in "Locksley Hall" is less lyric and more bitter, as he expresses the Victorian rebel's reaction to custom and law: "cursed be the social lies"; But in one superb instance, in "Tithonus," a man sums up the lyrical ladies' sense of loss and longing for death.

Throughout his poems of 1830 to 1842, the poems written during Tennyson's "ten years' silence," there persist the themes of lost love, isolation, and the half-fearful, half-longing anticipation of death. The last two of the so-called early sonnets epitomize these themes: "If I were loved, as I desire to be," and "The Bridesmaid," which ends, "My life is sick of single sleep: / O happy bridesmaid, make a happy bride!" But from this period come also the idyllic pictures of marriage in "Circumstance"—a brief lyric about "two lovers whispering by an orchard wall, / Two lives bound fast in one with golden ease"—in "The Miller's Daughter," and in "The Gardener's Daughter." Among the *English Idyls* of 1842, "Dora" includes both the themes of the fulfillment of marriage in a child and the sadness of a lonely maiden.

"Dora" is a story of alienation, marriage, and reconciliation through the saving child. When Farmer Allen's disinherited son dies, his baby reconciles the grandfather to both his daughter-in-law and the memory of William. For William's cousin Dora, whom he refused to wed, the story must, however, end with a bittersweet flavor: she lives "unmarried till her death." In the growing child there may be promise for the future, but the final note is Dora's; it reminds us of the loneliness and looking toward death of Tennyson's other lovelorn women.

The idea of marriage and of its issue can represent hope for harmony and continuity, a hope that offsets Tennyson's melancholy sense of loneliness and death. Presenting the themes of marriage and isolation, the poet alternates between two moods, two visions, two voices, one asserting the continuance of life—the message of his early lines "Nothing Will Die"—and the other brooding on the death of the isolated individual—the burden of the complementary and contrasting lines "All Things Will Die."

References to doubleness of mind appear in phrases and passages again and again. In "The Lotos-Eaters," for example, the attraction of a morbid mood, of life in death, in a womblike, tomblike world, is celebrated by the mariners' "Chroric Song." These entranced mariners are as isolated from society as the fairy Lady of Shalott is before she looks out her window to the larger world. In their enchanted land, or rather on their magic island (again, they are literally isolated, islanded), they sing,

> Dear is the memory of our wedded lives,
> And dear the last embraces of our wives
> And their warm tears; but all hath suffer'd change;
> For surely now our household hearths are cold,
> Our sons inherit us, our looks are strange,
> And we should come like ghosts to trouble joy.   [p. 434]

These lines anticipate the tale of Enoch Arden. In fact, however, they present a rationalization: the lotos-eaters have been tempted and have succumbed to the longing for peace, for escape from society and its responsibilities. They have chosen death instead of marriage.

Tennyson's early poems, then, express both lyrically and dramatically what have been called idealizing and disillusioned attitudes toward sexual love, toward marriage, and really toward earthly human life. The two moods, the two attitudes, are antithetical. Certainly, Tennyson's development indicates that one implies and tends to lead to the other—idealizing illusion to bitter disillusion. For the moment, we are concerned with the alternating moods. Perhaps the clearest embodiment of these two moods—one concerned with physical continuty, life, the future, and the other obsessed with spiritual isolation and death—is "The Two Voices." In this poem the turning point, the saving vision, again involves the ideal union of the sexes and the figure of the child.

"The Two Voices": Marriage as Conversion

The explicit subject of "The Two Voices" is suicide. This poem is, apparently, the young poet's "To be or not to

be." Yet it is not strictly a monologue, for it dramatizes both
depression and optimism. The two voices of the title are
those of despair and hope. In fact, however, there are not
two voices but three. For the speaker, in his own voice, replies first to the counsel of death and then to that of life.
Like many of Arnold's most personal lyrics, this semidramatic work presents hope for meaningful life, but also the
deepest anxieties in the disembodied and mysterious speech
of a voice that is not clearly the poet's or the speaker's own.
Because the speaker chooses finally to head the voice of joy
and hope, the poem does not end with the irresolution of
Tennyson's other early semidramatic poem on life and
death, "Supposed Confessions of a Second-Rate Sensitive
Mind," with its exclamations.

> O weary life! O weary death!
> O spirit and heart made desolate!
> O damned vacillating state!   [p. 202]

Yet it does not have a simply happy ending or what might
be called a total conversion. The voice urging suicide domi-
nates the first three-quarters of "The Two Voices." Its responses to the speaker's reasons for living, although life is
misery, seem persuasive: man has no duty to live; he can
gain no final knowledge in this life; his existence will soon
be forgotten; he has nothing to gain from suffering and
nothing to lose from inevitable and all-consuming death.
Even after the brief cryptic words of the life-affirming
voice are heard and heeded, even at the end of the poem,
that first morbid voice is remembered.

Still, the message of "The Two Voices" is "Rejoice! Rejoice!" The final argument is not an argument at all but the
Wordsworthian imperative, arrived at hardly by rational

means or even reflection. The voice of life does say that "something is or seems, / That touches me with mystic gleams," and does argue, pseudopsychologically, that it is "life, not death, for which we pant." But even after hearing that argument, the speaker sits "as one forlorn." His capacity to rejoice derives from neither "mystic gleams" nor psychological generalizations; it is the result of an intuitive response to something outside the self-conscious speaker. Like the Lady of Shalott and like the poet's personified soul in "The Palace of Art," he looks out a window.

The fact that this is essentially a poem of threes, not twos, a poem of synthesis, not of unresolved doubleness, is suggested by its very form: it is composed entirely in triplets. And as there are really three voices, so there are, in the vision seen outside the speaker's window, three figures: man, wife, and child. The last, scornful, remark of the suicidal voice is just, "Behold, it is the Sabbath morn." The promising association of "the dawning east" on this Sunday (and every Sunday is a memorial of Easter) need not be spelled out.

What seems most striking is the introduction next of a domestic triad.

> One walk'd between his wife and child,
> With measured footfall firm and mild,
> And now and then he gravely smiled.
>
> The prudent partner of his blood
> Lean'd on him, faithful, gentle, good,
> Wearing the rose of womanhood.
>
> And in their double love secure,
> The little maiden walk'd demure,
> Pacing with downward eyelids pure.

These three made unity so sweet,
My frozen heart began to beat,
Remembering its ancient heat.

I blest them, and they wander'd on;
I spoke, but answer came there none;
The dull and bitter voice was gone.   [p. 540]

The first three of these tercets have been regretted by sympathetic critics.[7] And some of the diction is regrettable. The adjectives, especially, suggest a sweet and simple life more sentimentalized than realized. The wife who is "prudent," "faithful, gentle, good," and the maiden who is both "demure" and "pure" remind one of Coventry Patmore's most watery-sugary verse. The husband's gravity, firmness, and mildness smack of the pomposity that we must finally ascribe to Tennyson's Arthur. Partly for these reasons, this passage, which is crucial to the poem, is also crucially important for an understanding of Tennyson's later and greater work, of its power and its limitation. It includes the vision, the imagery, and also the flat diction, the flawed tone, of the later lyrics from *In Memoriam* and the later Arthurian *Idylls*. Here is the idea of marriage, the blood union of firm manhood and gentle womanhood. Here is the image of the rose, "the rose of womanhood," which persists for Tennyson—not only in *Maud* but also in *The Princess* and the *Idylls*—as the image of woman as a sexual being.[8] And here is the figure of the unifying child, the

7. As Masao Miyoshi puts it, "the passage is an object of derision to twentieth-century readers and is a sore point even for otherwise sympathetic students" (*The Divided Self: A Perspective on the Literature of the Victorians* [New York, 1969], p. 120).

8. On this sexual flower imagery, see E. D. H. Johnson, "The Lily and the Rose: Symbolic Meaning in Tennyson's *Maud*,"

living reconciliation of opposites, the two-in-one synthesis of male thesis and female antithesis. But here also is the problem of tone. The lines seem insipid because these three people embody a simple and sweet ideal; they are not real people with any complexity or dimension, people who might exist in any particular time and place. Here is the abstract ideal, not the fully imagined reality, of marriage.

Yet a glimpse of this ideal triad does convert the speaker from his isolation and his preoccupation with death. It leads him to a version of the "Everlasting Yea"—a "Yea" perhaps as vague, as impossible of flesh-and-blood realization as Carlyle's. It represents the speaker's hope for getting out of himself into relation with the world: he blesses the family of three, and although he is not quite like the ancient mariner blessing superficially alien but vivid and appealing creatures, his is another moral act that is self-redeeming. (One might argue that Tennyson's three figures stand in illuminating contrast to Coleridge's sea serpents, being superficially attractive yet lacking all vividness.) Only now can the other voice be heard, the voice of hope—hope that

> no tongue can prove
> That every cloud, that spreads above
> And veileth love, itself is love. [p. 54]

Wordsworthian joy in nature, in the dawn, in the grass and flower, in the cloud, may follow from the vision and the voice. But this conversion to hope and even joy is not

---

PMLA, LXIV (1949), 1222–1227. In this as in other respects Tennyson's precocious comic play "The Devil and the Lady"— written when he was fourteen and never completed—anticipates the serious later verse: the lady's husband sees her as "chaste," like the "virgin lily," while her first would-be lover sees her as a "rosebud." The play also involves male transvestism and adultery.

Wordsworthian, because its source is not an experience of nature but, rather, an idea of human society. This idea, opposed to isolation and death, is the idea of marriage as the type and the continuing demonstration of a harmonizing, synthesizing force of love in the universe. This idea is more fully explored in *The Princess*.

The Princess: Marriage as Ideal

The Princess (1847) is appropriately subtitled *a Medley* —appropriately, because of its use of musical forms and because it includes a variety of themes. It deals with Tory and radical attitudes toward social change, with the recurrent Tennysonian motif of shadow and substance, or appearance and reality, with the place of woman in modern life, and finally with the nature of sexuality and the ideal of marriage as not only a joining of the sexes but also a temperamental modifying of each sex. The problem it raises is whether this ideal is realizable.

John Killham demonstrates how the poem uses the old form of a fantastic tale to reflect on the current debate about the "woman question." In effect, *The Princess* argues against extreme positions, both ancient and modern, regarding the relations of the sexes, against the reactionary idea that women are inferior to men, incapable of higher education or of any independence, but equally against the radical idea that independent women, to obtain their rights, must abandon the institution of marriage. "Whether the marriage-relationship could survive the fulfilment of women's aspirations is the real point at issue."[9] On this point

9. John Killham, *Tennyson and "The Princess": Reflections of an Age* (London, 1958), p. 65.

Tennyson seems to be at least hopeful. His poem is a sympathetic and fairly enlightened plea, not for the exercise of mastery by men or for things as they were, but for an ideal that is to be projected into the future and worked for in the present.

This medley, then, is a poetic and imaginative wedding of various and seemingly conflicting elements of the Victorian age, an age of such great diversity that perhaps its nostalgia and brisk pragmatism, its conservative fears and radical dreams, could most appropriately be represented in such a form. The elements in the medley include the fairy-tale tone, the scientific interests at the beginning and end, and the question whether marriage is a contract between a master and his natural inferior or a relationship of equals. The most significant scientific influence on the poem, Killham suggests, is that of Robert Chambers' *Vestiges of the Natural History of Creation* (1844), with its conception of nature as evolving process and its implication—for Tennyson and for others as well—of an intellectual and, above all, moral evolution leading toward a higher, better human race of the future. The "woman question" in which Tennyson is interested includes the matter of education; only four years before *The Princess* was published, Mrs. Hugo Reid's *Plea for Women* (1843) formally proposed university training for women, and one year after the poem's publication, Queen's College, Harley Street, was founded.[10] As for the problem of marriage, the Saint-Simonians, in general,

10. This was the period when, in America as in Britain, the first women's colleges were being founded; from the late forties to the late fifties an extraordinary number of such institutions sprang up. It was the period, too, of women's first distinguished leadership in education, in and out of the academy.

preached the perfect equality of husband and wife, while
Robert Owen's lectures attacking Christian marriage (and
indeed most actual marriages) as a form of prostitution
were widely, if somewhat mistakenly, taken to condemn
any kind of marriage whatever. The question of marriage
is the final one considered in the central story of *The Princess*, and Tennyson distinctly relates the other elements to
it. Again, the true marriage signifies the furthering of
moral evolution and does not deny the aspirations—in fact,
the equal rights—of women, for Tennyson's vision of the
better future is one that sees men and women, though still
different, becoming more nearly alike.

The conception of the mutual influence of the sexes is
frequent in Tennyson.[11] *In Memoriam* cix praises "manhood fused with female grace" (p. 962). "Locksley Hall
Sixty Years After" both praises a woman with "all the
breadth of man" and refers to Christ as the ideal "man-
woman." And as late as 1859 the poet published lines on
the secondary characteristics of the sexes that echo parts of
The Princess, lines on a man "who affected an effeminate
manner":

> While man and woman still are incomplete,
> I prize the soul where man and woman meet,
> Which types all Nature's male and female plan
> But, friend, man-woman is not woman-man.   [p. 1424]

Presumably the somewhat cryptic final statement contrasts
effeminacy of voice and gesture with feminine sensitiveness. But feminine men and perhaps masculine women as

11. His 1832 "Dream of Fair Women" speculates on how "In
some far aftertime, the gentler mind / Might reassume its just and
full degree / Of rule among mankind" (p. 442).

well can represent for Tennyson a movement toward the reconciliation of opposites, of male aggressiveness and female responsiveness.

Sometimes the subject is very difficult to manage. The narrator may puzzle, if not embarrass, us when he begins his tale within a tale, the main story of the *Princess*,

> A Prince I was, blue-eyed, and fair in face,
> Of temper amorous as the first of May,
> With lengths of yellow ringlet, like a girl.   [p. 751]

There is a medieval tradition behind this poem, and one may be reminded of Chaucer's squire. The problem here is Tennyson's failure to recognize what a dramatic figure can say about himself. We hear something like smug narcissism in these lines—to say nothing of the effeminacy the poet deplores in later verse—just as we hear insufferable priggishness in Galahad's "My strength is as the strength of ten, / Because my heart is pure," and monstrous priggishness or something worse in Arthur's "I forgive thee, as Eternal God / Forgives." But *The Princess* is marked by more difficulties than this one of dramatization, this Tennysonian inability to grasp what a character must reveal instead of say. The prince's female garb is very odd, and his boyish plea to Princess Ida, finally, to "accomplish my own manhood," is at least problematic.

There can be no doubt as to the ultimate seriousness of Tennyson's purpose in this strange and fascinating work. *The Princess* provides, as Killham puts it, "reflections of an age"; it also gives us important reflections of a poet's mind, of his psychological depths.

Tennyson was fond of using a modern framework to show the immediate relevance of old tales. He sets this nar-

rative about feminism and the relations of the sexes in a
socially, politically, and ethically changing age, his own.
The Tory opinions of Sir Walter Vivian in the Prologue
are echoed by the bluff old king, the princely wooer's
father, in the tale. Finally, Sir Walter's elder son, concerned
with the ancient order and with British self-sufficiency and
not with the "social wrong" that his college friend the tale
teller recognizes, associates the doctrine of women's rights,
the modern version of the fantasies of "our wild princess"
Ida, with political upheaval and social instability, "revolts,
republics, revolutions." And Sir Walter's young daughter,
who is bold and almost a revolutionary in the Prologue, like
a feminine and more passionate Mill on the subjection of
women, is finally quiet—just as Ida in the main story, her
fictional counterpart, is wooed away from feminism to a
more conventional femininity and to marriage. But, clearly,
the conclusions of the poem are not really simple or conventional.

The tale of Princess Ida begins with the condition of the
prince, cursed so that he cannot distinguish "the shadow
from the substance" and subject to visions and seizures.[12]
Like Arthur in the *Idylls*, this would-be husband is associated with the shadowy and mysterious. There is no
doubt, however, that Ida, betrothed to him by proxy when
they were children, is substantial—and strong-minded. "She
had a will," "loved to live alone / Among her women, certain, would not wed" (p. 752). The fair prince's mission,
then, is to find and woo the wife he has not seen. With his

12. "In 1851 the 'weird seizures' of the prince were inserted. His
too emotional temperament was intended from an artistic point of
view to emphasize his comparative want of power" (*Alfred Lord
Tennyson: A Memoir*, p. 209).

friends Cyril and Florian ("my other heart, / And almost my half-self") (p. 752) he sets off on this mission. They discover from Ida's father, ineffectual old King Gama sitting blandly in his "mother-city thick with towers," that the princess has been fed upon the theories of two widows, "maintaining that with equal husbandry / The woman were the equal to the man," and "prophesying change / Beyond all reason" (p. 755). She has gone with her female entourage to the royal summer palace, to found there a sexually segregated college for women.

Ida's breaking of the marriage contract dramatizes once again the conflict of convention, of law, with individual freedom. Her emphasis on woman's equality with men introduces a revolutionary social theme. And the poem is concerned as well with the nature of sexuality, feminine and masculine. The strict feminism of Ida, exemplified in her college rules and lectures, forbids marriage and insists upon the separate equality, not the joining, of the sexes:

> "everywhere
> Two heads in council, two beside the hearth,
> Two in the tangled business of the world,
> Two in the liberal offices of life . . ." [p. 764]

Although it is not clear if Ida's ideal world would be as chaste and asexual as a Shaker community, the conventional view of proper marriage relations is certainly ignored if not denied.

What cannot, however, be ignored or denied is the existence here and now of a child. The widow Psyche, who discovers that the trio—the prince, Cyril, and Florian—are really men disguised as women, proves to be the most "feminine" of Ida's women; she keeps their secret. Her tenderness is associated, not only with the fact that Florian is her brother, but also with her motherhood. When Blanche, the enemy of Psyche and a hater of men—"she was wedded to a fool"—reports this treachery to the princess, Ida takes Psyche's child, a girl of course, away from her. And it is only when Ida herself is touched by feelings both sexual and maternal that she is willing to return the child to her mother. In fact, Ida's earlier opinions on "love, children, happiness," the traditional concerns of women, are distinctly not maternal:

> Yet we will say for children, would they grew
> Like field-flowers everywhere! we love them well:
> But children die. . . .
> . . . great deeds cannot die.   [p. 780]

But there *is* a child in *The Princess*, and this child's appeal to feminine feelings, along with the childlike prince's appeal, leads at last to the reconciliation of Princess Ida and the prince.

Of the well-known songs that punctuate the narrative, a number were added after the completion of the poem.[13] As Tennyson commented, these songs are meant to hold the work together: "The child is the link through the parts, as shown in the Songs . . . which are the best interpreters of the poem."[14] At least some of them—"As thro' the land at eve we went," perhaps "Sweet and Low," and certainly "Home they brought her warrior dead"—are concerned with the reconciliation of the sexes or the reconciliation to life of a lone, bereft woman through the existence of a child.

13. The six songs between sections of the poem were added in 1850; the blank verse lyrics, however, were in the original 1847 version of *The Princess*.

14. *Alfred Lord Tennyson : A Memoir*, p. 212.

At the end, the prince, who is often himself like a child, seems to regard Ida almost as a mother. In a curious outburst on the ideal woman, he apostrophizes his mother and sees Ida as following her pattern. The wife's function is defined here as virtually maternal in a way that anticipates her married state and her actually giving birth.

Being maternal means first of all being sexual, being a woman and, in the words of "The Two Voices," wearing the "rose of womanhood." Throughout *The Princess*, flower imagery is used to define women. The rose suggests literal sexuality, and the lily, here as in "The Lady of Shalott," is the flower both of chastity and of infertility, of death. Both flowers, both red rose and white lily, represent elements of each woman's character. First there is the modern girl who inspires this story, whose name is Lilia—although, when she speaks of women's rights and wrongs, she is "a rosebud set with little thorns." Princess Ida, in the tale, is a projection of this Lilia; and the disguised Cyril tells Ida that the prince worships her as his "one rose in all the world"—although she is white-robed and virginal. Melissa, the daughter of Blanche, is "lily-like," as one might expect a Blanche's daughter to be, but she is also described as a "rosy blonde." And when Cyril makes love to this rosy but cloistered beauty, he says, "Pale one, blush again; than wear / Those lilies, better blush our lives away" (p. 774). For much of what modern readers will find vaguely sexual in the poem—the phallic towers of Gama's "mother-city" (p. 754), the amazon-like women, each "like a rock . . . a spire," and the pipe organ "groaning for power" as "six hundred maidens in purest white" proceed (p. 772)—the poet almost certainly had no conscious sexual intention. It is hard, however, to believe that the symbolism of red and white flowers was not consciously intended. The narrator, the prince, explicitly denies his father's assertion that women are "game," "creatures of the chase" to be hunted down and tamed, and explicitly asserts that, instead, women are like flowers. One metaphor is brutal; the other is sentimental and perhaps asexual, if the emphasis is on the delicate pale flower. In fact, the problem with this imagery is to reconcile the sexual rose with the chaste lily, or fruitful flesh with unsullied spirit. That problem is lyrically addressed in the lyric, "Now sleeps the crimson petal, now the white."

Bringing together the red and the white, the flesh and the spirit, is as difficult as truly bringing together the two sexes. Yet marriage implies all of this. It implies not a loss of distinction between flesh and spirit or man and woman—

> Woman is not undevelopt man,
> But diverse; could we make her as the man,
> Sweet love were slain; his dearest bond is this,
> Not like to like but like to difference

—but, to a considerable extent, equality. And the social equality of the sexes, the raising of woman from a subordinate position, will depend, not only on an acceptance of the sexual body together with the chaste spirit, but also on the lessening of distinct secondary sexual characteristics that are merely social and arbitrary.[15]

15. Sir Charles Tennyson quotes a draft passage (*Nineteenth Century*, CIX [1931], 633):
> And if aught be comprising in itself
> The man, the woman, let it sit apart
> Godlike, alone, or only rapt on heaven—
> What need for such to wed? or if there be

Yet in the long years liker must they grow;
The man be more of woman, she of man;
He gain in sweetness and in moral height,
Nor lose the wrestling thews that throw the world;
She mental breadth, nor fail in childward care,
Nor lose the childlike in the larger mind;
Till at the last she set herself to man,
Like perfect music unto noble words;
And so these twain, upon the skirts of Time,
Sit side by side, full-summed in all their powers,
Dispensing harvest, sowing the To-be,
Self-reverent each and reverencing each,
Distinct in individualities,
But like each other even as those who love.
Then comes the statelier Eden back to men:
Then reign the world's great bridals, chaste and calm:
Then springs the crowning race of humankind.

[pp. 838–839]

This imperative amounts to the moral evolution of mankind toward a race of virtual supermen and superwomen. And the prince's hope is that he and Ida can be types in the present of what is to exist more generally in the future.

"Dear, but let us type them now
In our own lives, and this proud watchword rest
Of equal; seeing either sex alone
Is half itself, and in true marriage lies
Nor equal, nor unequal: each fulfils

Men-women, let them wed with women-men
And make a proper marriage.

Although this "proper marriage" might well be supposed to be ironical, Tennyson often emphasizes the importance of a man's having certain feminine qualities and a woman's having certain masculine qualities.

Defect in each, and always thought in thought,
Purpose in purpose, will in will, they grow,
The single pure and perfect animal,
The two-celled heart beating, with one full stroke,
Life." [p. 839]

The modifying of the sexes, or of two sides of the poet's imagination, seems necessary if the hidden warfare of sexual opposites, disguised as marriage, is to be transformed into fruitful and mutually satisfying relations. It implies a new definition of manhood—and of womanhood. The one is no longer to be fully defined as potency, the sexual, social, even crassly commercial power of the Carlylean hero, of whom the prince's brutal and stupid father in this poem is a parody. The other is no longer to be defined as passivity, the sexual, social, and cunningly hypocritical slavishness of the "Victorian" female, the type sweet young Psyche in this poem is in danger of becoming. Neither the bloody brute nor the bloodless lily is an appropriate image for a marriage partner, for a human being. At the same time, true marriage is not consistent with a simple reversal of contemporary stereotyped sexual roles, the man becoming wholly passive and the woman self-sufficiently aggressive. In spite of the element of parody, with men in women's clothes and a pretty hero who lives in visions like the Lady of Shalott, with the segregated blue-stockings and an Amazon-like heroine, the conclusion toward which this whole work moves is that the ideal marriage demands something other than conventional sexual types.

But there is still some caution, some uncertainty, in the dramatic expression of the ideal. The frame conclusion is again lighter in tone, and allows for conservative skepticism about all such dreams of perfect marriage. To be sure, the ideal contemplated sympathetically is far from pompously "Victorian," far from the attitude toward marriage and the wife that we might associate with the aging reactionary Tennyson. Yet this vision of the possibilities of a sexual union is given in the form of fantasy, set in the vaguely distant past, and the hero and heroine can be only types that anticipate, for the poet and his readers, a general realization of true marriage in the vaguely distant future.

In Memoriam: Marriage as Metaphor and Symbol

The ending of *In Memoriam* also deals with marriage, sexual relations, and the evolving of the race toward an ideal future. But until that ending the elegy—or series of elegies— is concerned with deeply felt friendship, not with explicitly sexual love, and so references to marriage, no matter what psychological significance modern readers may find in them, are almost entirely metaphorical.

The marriage metaphor occurs again and again in the lyrics, as the poet describes his spiritual relationship with the dead Arthur Henry Hallam.[16] Sometimes there is no

16. On this metaphor, and on Tennyson's relations with Edmund Lushington, see *Poems*, ed. Ricks, pp. 932, 936. Several critics have commented on the homosexual implications of *In Memoriam*, raising a question that generally occurs to modern students and other readers—and one about which Tennyson himself was apparently nervous. The poet's family background, with a sympathetic mother and a violent and unpredictable father, could create an extreme oedipal attachment and consequently strong latent homosexual feeling; Tennyson's frequent imaginative identification with women in his early poetry, his tendency to write of situations in which sexual union is frustrated, and his revulsion from feminine sexuality in the *Idylls* all support this psychological reading as much as the language and emotion of the elegy do. So does the emphasis here on sexual idealism and the movement from typing

more than a passing comparison. The speaker asks of the maiden whose beloved has suddenly died (a familiar kind of figure in the early Tennyson),

> O what to her shall be the end?
>   And what to me remains of good?
>   To her, perpetual maidenhood,
> And unto me no second friend.   [lyric vi, p. 870]

He compares himself, not to the maiden, but to the wooer whose love is "gone and far from home"(viii). And his tears are like those of a sorrowing widower (xiii).

Sometimes, too, the language of the poetry absorbs a comparison, which becomes a basic metaphor. The poet's life is a "widowed race" (xviii). And the phrase "widowed hour" refers to his bereavement (xl). But the most remarkable use of the marriage metaphor is in lyric xcvii.

Woman as Soul to typing Woman as degraded Sense. Rougemont repeatedly insists that the woman-worshiping troubadors, with their contempt for marriage, were actively homosexual. But even if one speculates on Tennyson's (for the most part, surely, unconscious) sexual feelings, there is a great difference for both psychology and literature between a writer who has deep homosexual stirrings, unacknowledged and hardly articulated to himself, and a writer whose homosexuality is avowed, because the conscious and evident intentions of each artist make up a large part of his life and work. Some modern psychoanalytical critics of literature appear to believe that the true and single "meaning" of a work equals the sum of deducible urges and frustrations (mostly sexual) of which the writer was unaware; yet surely the whole sense of, say, a complex poem also importantly involves what the poet was *aware of* and *intended*, since the words of his text have the logical and commonly accepted meanings of such verbal structures for its readers. Having properly scouted the "intentional fallacy" in criticism, we may now be in danger of an equally simple-minded "unintentional fallacy."

Two partners of a married life—
  I looked on these and thought of thee
  In vastness and in mystery,
And of my spirit as of a wife.

. . . . .

Her faith is fixt and cannot move.
  She darkly feels him great and wise,
  She dwells on him with faithful eyes,
"I cannot understand: I love." [pp. 949, 950]

The first quatrain at once suggests the turning point of "The Two Voices," but there is no child here. As the poet's vignette of a happy marriage is developed, the docile and admiring wife who can only love, not understand, her husband seems to be far removed from Princess Ida. This is because she continues to represent the poet's own spirit, admiring, loving, but not yet comprehending Hallam.

This metaphor of Tennyson's and Hallam's friendship as a spiritual marriage is carried very far indeed. The long and especially interesting lyric LXXXV, addressed to Edmund Lushington in its expanded final version, avows a determination to give up mourning and turn to a new friendship, and it refers to "love" and "friendship" as "equal powers / That marry with the virgin heart."[17] But the poet still thinks of himself as "the divided half of such / A friendship as had mastered Time." It is not surprising that the most often quoted lines of *In Memoriam*, in the first stanza of this lyric, are commonly supposed to be about a

---

17. As Princess Ida says, children die, but great deeds (and perhaps great poems) do not; this is only one of the points at which—so commentators have suggested ever since the publication of the elegy—*In Memoriam* resembles Shakespeare's sonnet sequence. The comparison, interestingly, embarrassed Tennyson.

man's love for a woman: " 'Tis better to have loved and
lost, / Than never to have loved at all." Yet the fact remains that the poet's spirit as a wife can have as children
only these poems.

His friendship, furthermore, may have "mastered Time"
to be "Eternal," but time still exists, and real men actually
live in time: the seasons—summer, spring, and autumn, cited
in these lines—continue to appear. And, living in this seasonal reality, the poet imagines Hallam's own voice telling
him to "seek / A friendship for the years to come." It
seems appropriate, and much more than coincidental, that
this friendship, which within time will replace one now
made eternal, is to be a bond with a brother-in-law. As Hallam was to have married the poet's sister Emily, Lushington
will marry his sister Cecilia.

The two voices of *In Memoriam* are not simply those of
grief and reconciliation to life. Rather, the division within
the poem is between two tendencies, two conceptions of
life and love. One tendency is to transcend time and transform all life into an eternal life, either in a Carlylean way,
so that personal identity is lost and only force is real, or in
an apparently Christian way, as when the poet hopes that
Christ will reach at last to him and his friend "and take us
as a single soul" (LXXIV). The other tendency is to find answers in the immanent, experienced reality of time rather
than in the transcendental reassurance. The first makes
marriage a spiritual union—in a sense, then, a metaphor. The
second makes marriage a substantial experience that may
result in the birth of a child. *In Memoriam* sometimes reads
like a groping toward the vision of eternity—like the poem
of Christian consolation that Queen Victoria, along with
most Victorian readers and the compilers of hymn books,

took it to be. It sometimes reads like a distinctly non-Christian, wholly time-involved argument for moral evolution toward a future superrace. In a somewhat ambiguous way the epilogue or ending—the wedding song—combines the two ideas: that of a spiritual, time-transcending love, and that of love physically expressed in connubial relations and conception. It seems that this ending practically transforms the metaphor of marriage into a sexual reality within human history—in effect, into a symbolic act. A symbol, unlike a metaphor or the extended metaphor called allegory, implies general meaning by being itself. And the persons and events in this poem are real.

So is the seasonal time that is often evoked in this work. If "The Two Voices" is really a poem about threes, *In Memoriam* is a poem of fours: it is written in quatrains, and in tetrameter; it is arbitrarily divided by three Christmases, each marking a stage in the poet's developing response to death, into four sections; and it is very often concerned with the temporal cycle of the four seasons. One way of putting the central anxious question in these lyrics is, does the cycle of season after season, year after year, century after century mean nothing but continuity and recurrence —a recurrence in which "nothing will die," and yet "all things will die"? Can the seasons be redeemed? Do single lives form part of one significant progress? It may not be too fanciful to say that Tennyson's development in poetic numerology is from an inspiring vision of a three-in-one of marriage to a hoped-for dynamic in which the seasonal four is transformed into the Hegelian three-into-four: thesis, antithesis, synthesis, which then becomes a new thesis, as the child grows into the man. *In Memoriam* finally defines the single life as a link in the evolution of the race. The pattern may be divine and spiritual; its historic embodiment is human.

So the work, which begins in grief as an elegy on the beloved dead man, ends in subdued joy as an epithalamion. Tennyson again turns from death and isolation to life, to marriage, to conception and new birth. This is the last sentence of the marriage song, which is the last sentence in the whole sequence:

> Again the feast, the speech, the glee,
>   The shade of passing thought, the wealth
>   Of words and wit, the double health,
> The crowning cup, the three-times-three,
>
> And last the dance;—till I retire:
>   Dumb is that tower which spake so loud,
>   And high in heaven the streaming cloud,
> And on the downs a rising fire:
>
> And rise, O moon, from yonder down,
>   Till over down and over dale
>   All night the shining vapor sail
> And pass the silent-lighted town,
>
> The white-faced halls, the glancing rills,
>   And catch at every mountain head,
>   And o'er the friths that branch and spread
> Their sleeping silver through the hills;
>
> And touch with shade the bridal doors,
>   With tender gloom the roof, the wall;
>   And breaking let the splendour fall
> To spangle all the happy shores
>
> By which they rest, and ocean sounds,
>   And, star and system rolling past,
>   A soul shall draw from out the vast
> And strike his being into bounds,

And, moved through life of lower phase,
   Result in man, be born and think,
   And act and love, a closer link
Betwixt us and the crowning race

Of those that, eye to eye, shall look
   On knowledge; under whose command
   Is Earth and Earth's, and in their hand
Is Nature like an open book;

No longer half-akin to brute,
   For all we thought and loved and did,
   And hoped, and suffered, is but seed
Of what in them is flower and fruit;

Whereof the man, that with me trod
   This planet, was a noble type
   Appearing ere the times were ripe,
That friend of mine who lives in God,

That God, which ever lives and loves,
   One God, one law, one element,
   And one far-off divine event,
To which the whole creation moves.   [pp. 985–988]

The most remarkable fact about this conclusion is that these forty-four lines make one sentence, a long, smoothly continuous yet extraordinarily complex single statement of the major ideas of *In Memoriam*. The unbroken rhetorical line seems almost to evolve, as the idea of moral evolution is developed, into a triumphant climax. But the climax, the final word, is *moves*, and the sense of movement is not quite broken even at the end.

The imagery here is no longer that of darkness but of kindly moonlight. The idea of the wedding bond, cele-

brated by the formalities of feast, toast, and dance, is part
of the whole idea of an order, of orderliness within bounds
or limits: so the conception of the child is described as a
soul's striking "his being into bounds"—just as, in "Crossing
the Bar," the soul is "that which drew from out the boundless deep."[18] The sense of an ordering of sexual impulse,
relating the experience of the wedding night to a cosmic
plan, makes possible another remarkable fact: Tennyson's
deeply serious and philosophic work ends with a passage
on sexual intercourse and conception.

As in *The Princess*, the child conceived of this marriage
is to be a link, not only of the parents to each other but also
of present to future and to past. Implicit in all this is the
link between the poet himself and Hallam—and, indeed,
between the spiritual, metaphorical "marriage" of these
friends and the physical as well as psychological marriage
of man and woman. The phrase "crowning race" echoes
the words of the passage on marriage and the future in *The
Princess*. Hallam has been a "type" of the future man, just
as the prince and princess were to be types of the future
man and wife.

The last stanza combines, now in religious language, the
idea of spiritual pattern or type and that of historical movement. God is both law and goal; He "lives and loves" yet
is a "far-off divine event," not wholly realized here and
now. One can read these lines in the light of Mill's melior-
ism, expressed by the essay "Nature" ("the Principle of
Good *cannot* at once and altogether subdue the powers of
evil"), so that "God" is a principle to be worked out in
time, or in the light of Christian eschatology, within which

18. Christopher Ricks compares the phrases (*Poems*, p. 986).

created time is to be redeemed and to be ended. In any case, the emphasis at last is on progress; and the way of progressing toward the divine future, the reconciliation of divine love with human life, is marriage, conception, birth.

In Memoriam is more than an autobiographical and elegiac work. It might be called, among other things, the poet's mortality ode. And the answer to its burden of mortality is not clear Christian reassurance of a personal resurrection or a joyous identification of life with Life but another vision of man, woman, and child. Again, as in *The Princess*, the concluding marriage is a type foreshadowing an Eden yet to be, while it is the means of humankind's evolving toward that fuller life of the future. The work is designed to move from death and grief to marriage—an actual, sexually consummated marriage—and the birth of hope.

Maud: Marriage as Falsehood

"The Two Voices," *The Princess*, and *In Memoriam* express Tennyson's most hopeful conception of marriage—marriage as an alternative to isolation, to despair and death. *Maud* and *The Idylls of the King* present his increasingly dark idea of marriage: in these works, it is imagined as impossible or disastrous within the real world of time, space, and human society. *Maud* moves from love through madness to war. The *Idylls* series moves from marriage through adultery to death.

Yet the germ of *Maud*, a section in Part II of the completed work, is a lyric of grief that is closely related to those of *In Memoriam*: it was written soon after Hallam's death, it almost certainly was inspired by his death, and it

expresses the poet's own mourning.[19] In so far as *Maud* is
a psychological, even novelistic, poem about history, it can
be contrasted with the earlier *Princess* and the later *Idylls*,
set in ancient times, and compared with *In Memoriam*.
Why and how does it arrive at a dramatized attitude so different from that in the epithalamion that concludes the
elegiac series? The poem can be read as the exploration of
a morbid mind, so that the speaker's responses to sex and
war need hardly be ascribed to the poet. But both Tennyson's general practice—he is rarely, like Browning, interested only or mainly in the odd psychology of a dramatic
figure—and some quality intense and immediate in *Maud*
have made readers from his time to ours think of the poem
as more than a monodrama, as a working-out of emotions
implicit in its germ and perhaps as a dark counterpart to *In
Memoriam*. The extraordinary difference in the endings of
In Memoriam and *Maud* may even result from the dramatic
poem's being essentially and consistently more personal and
direct, more an expression of the poet's feelings—not his
hopes but his deeper feelings—than the elegiac work is.

What might be called the basic situation of *Maud*—its
speaker is a thwarted young man whose beloved marries
another man because of his money and position—reminds
one of other poems by Tennyson, especially of "Locksley
Hall." And it seems clear that a number of personal experiences have been drawn upon in this poetic monodrama of
frustrated love, false marriage, madness, and violence.[20]

19. See George O. Marshall, "Tennyson's 'Oh! That 'Twere
Possible': A Link between *In Memoriam* and *Maud*," *PMLA*,
LXXVIII (1963), 225–229. "By expressing his own despair in 'Oh!
that 'twere possible' in terms of the grief of a lover over a dead
woman, and not of a man for a man as in *In Memoriam*, Tennyson
sought emotional release by objectifying his emotions" (p. 228).
20. Ralph W. Rader shows that one source of *Maud* is the poet's

Most important for the moment, however, is the clear relation between the loss of love dramatized and given lyric expression in *Maud* and the loss of earthly friendship—called a spiritual marriage—in *In Memoriam*. This relation makes especially striking the different ways in which the two works end. The conclusion of *In Memoriam*, with its vision of marriage here and now and of an Eden in the future here on earth, might be said to give a sort of typical or foreshadowing validity to the metaphorical marriage, the spiritual unity of friend and friend. But the unity of men arrived at by the end of *Maud*, as an alternative to frustrated desire for love and marriage, is not the unity of friendship temporal or eternal, but the unity of men at war: "I am one with my kind, / I embrace the purpose of God" (p. 1093). Both social oneness and individual nobility can be found now only by means of a destructive common action.

Ever since the poem was first published, its glorification of war has raised difficulties for readers. Whatever one thinks of the statement near the end of Part II that "lawful and lawless war / Are scarcely even akin" (p. 1090), one has to recognize in *Maud* a thematic and psychological consistency on this subject. The speaker insists from the very beginning that peace in his world is a delusion, a lie, and that open warfare is an honest and therefore better expression of what men are like—at least in modern society. This insistence helps to explain how the two main concerns in the poem are related: on the one hand a passionate love, on the other a commitment to the idea of warfare. Because the first fails, the second is advanced as an alternative to iso-

---

unhappy love for Rosa Baring; see *Tennyson's "Maud": The Biographical Genesis* (Berkeley, 1963), especially chapter iv, "*Maud* as Autobiography," pp. 88–121.

lation and madness. The distraught single voice implies that
the type or pattern of human life is not marriage but battle.
The speaker does not vow to go to war because it is "lawful," a just and inspiring cause. He needs a war, just or not,
to be the psychological equivalent of his frustrate passion
for the dead Maud. As in the later *Idylls*, love and marriage give way to warfare, and the sexual impulse is transformed.

The red flower that is feminine sexuality—the wife's red
"rose of womanhood" in "The Two Voices" and the whispering rose in Maud's dark garden—becomes a sublimated
object of desire, of lust, becomes the "blood-red blossom
of war with a heart of fire" (p. 1092).[21] This final metaphor of *Maud* questions, if it does not entirely deny, the
validity of friendship, love, and marriage. Now Tennyson's
voice, like Arnold's in "Dover Beach," speaks of the world
of human society as a battlefield; but Tennyson's speaker
embraces this vision as an alternative to loneliness, insanity,
suicide, instead of turning away from it to Arnold's alternative of love. Now we are well on our way from the
views of marriage expressed in "The Two Voices," *The
Princess*, and the concluding epithalamion of *In Memoriam*
—on our way to the views suggested by the last scenes in
The Idylls of the King.

The Idylls of the King: Marriage as Warfare

Maud was published in 1855, the year when, according
to his son Hallam, Tennyson "determined upon the final
shape" of the *Idylls* (*Memoir*, p. 522).[22] The first install-

---

21. E. D. H. Johnson's short article "The Lily and the Rose"
traces this change in poetic symbolism.
22. An account of the genesis and the gradual alterations in

ment, consisting of "Enid," "Vivien," "Elaine," and "Guinevere," appeared in 1859. The last published part of the series was "Balin and Balan," written between 1872 and 1874 but not printed until 1885. Tennyson devoted over forty years to his grand Arthurian project: his serious interest dates from at least the 1830's, and his "Morte d'Arthur" of 1842 is incorporated into the final "Passing of Arthur." During that time his ideas about its scope and possibilities grew, shifted, became in some ways richer and more complex, in some ways vaguer and more ambiguous.

His choice of an appropriate poetic form changed from pure allegory to masque to the eventual partly epic, partly allegorical verse narrative. One may well ask what the completed *Idylls* really is—or are; a question about the number of that verb is a serious question about the nature of the work. A group of romances? A modern epic? A consistent allegory? All or none of these? The very title *Idylls* suggests a series of beguiling tales. The division into twelve books and the introduction and farewell to Arthur suggest the epic. The increasingly moral and religious language of the later idylls suggests, not only symbolic meanings, but specific allegorical intention. As for its coherence, the work is difficult to comprehend as a whole, no matter how its poetic form is defined. Even though Tennyson de-

---

Tennyson's plan for his Arthurian work is given by Ricks (*Poems*, pp. 1460–1466), with the relevant passages from Hallam Tennyson's *Memoir*. J. Phillip Eggers points out that the first idylls were composed while the poet was still involved with *The Princess* and argues for a "link between the two": the *Idylls* concern "woman's role in private and public life"; the Round Table poems "relate events that reflect modern relations between men and women" (*King Arthur's Laureate* [New York, 1971], p. 144).

clared, "These idylls group themselves round one central
figure" (*Memoir*, p. 529), Arthur is truly the central figure only at the beginning and the end. The point usually
made, one supported by the poet himself, is that the *Idylls*
are all about soul battling evil in the world, but betrayed
as an ideal order here on earth is betrayed and destroyed
by the treachery of the senses—specifically, by adultery.[23]
This reading seems to make the *Idylls*, from a social point
of view, more than Byzantine in otherworldiness, and,
from a Christian point of view, one-sided if not heretical.
It also fails to explain, according to criteria for any literary
form save that of a loose collection of tales like Malory's,
how a number of idylls in the "Round Table" group fit in.
Although the emphasis on the allegorical theme of Arthur
as a pure soul fighting a losing battle in and against a sensual world is appropriate to the last idylls—last in the final
order, not in order of composition and publication—there is
a larger and more adequate theme that draws "The Round
Table" together: the theme of sexual love, of marriage and
its failure.

The titles of these ten tales suggest that theme. The second is "The Marriage of Geraint." And half of the titles
consist of pairs: "Gareth and Lynette," "Geraint and
Enid," "Balin and Balan" (about twin brothers, not man
and woman, but this pair, too, takes on sexual meaning),
"Merlin and Vivien," "Lancelot and Elaine," "Pelleas and

23. Although Tennyson did not like to give neat and absolute
allegorical interpretations of Arthur and the *Idylls*, he apparently
approved of such comments as Dean Alford's on the "conflict" in
the work "between spirit and the flesh"; and his son asserts that its
unifying principle is "the world-wide war of Sense and Soul"
(Hallam Tennyson's *Memoir*, pp. 524, 526).

Ettare." The final idyll of "The Round Table" is "Guinevere," and it is about a fallen wife. Although the first two
pairs, Gareth and Lynette and Geraint and Enid, figure in
stories with apparently happy endings, the man and woman
in each pair are in discord caused by pride and jealousy
virtually throughout each tale—*and* the men and women in
the other pairs are pointedly unmarried, adulterous, or incompatible. Actually, "The Round Table" is about the failure of all marriage and the resulting social chaos. Tennyson himself encouraged the idea, still widely accepted, that
the failures and the corruption of Arthur's world stem directly from the infidelity of Guinevere. But a serious question is whether this interpretation can be sustained by a
close reading of the work. Does Guinevere really cause the
destruction of the Round Table?

The *Idylls* begin with love, desire, and marriage. They
end with death—or, in Tennyson's own terms, not perhaps
the death but certainly the "passing" of Arthur. Perhaps
the King cannot die; perhaps, in the earthly, fleshly, sense,
he never lived.[24] In any case, the movement of *In Memoriam* from death to marriage and hope for new life is almost precisely, if not consciously, reversed. The ideas of
both marriage and warfare are involved here, as in *The
Princess* and *Maud:* the hope for a true marriage of man
and woman becomes a disillusioned belief in the inevitable
conflict of opposites, translated into the warfare of Soul
and Sense. But the basic and repeatedly varied yet repeat-

24. If Arthur is taken seriously as a Christ figure, the whole work
must be read as a Manichean document; the King is either a
heretical version of Christ, an emanation of God that is not incarnate, or an antichrist, an illusion of the Manichean, anti-incarnational mind.

edly stressed subject of the stories is the dramatic or stated
denial of harmonious marriage; the realities are egoism, or
willed isolation; conflict, or the warring of dualities; and
sterility, death, destruction.[25]

After all, Tennyson can hardly alter his sources so as to
end Arthur's married life happily, deny his "passing," or
avoid entirely the adulterous intrigues that Malory's prede-
cessors, on the whole, accepted easily. But he has chosen
the Arthurian material, and he has chosen to emphasize
certain aspects of it in his narrative and by his imagery.
His emphasis on the need for, and failure of, love and marriage begins in "The Coming of Arthur."

In fact, the first sentence of "The Coming of Arthur" is
about Guinevere. Arthur feels her attraction at once and
declares,

> "What happiness to reign a lonely king,
> Vext—O ye stars that shudder over me,
> O earth that soundest hollow under me,
> Vext with waste dreams? for saving I be joined
> To her that is the fairest under heaven,

25. Gerhard Joseph comments on "the contradictions implicit in
the dialectic of Western love" that are revealed in the attempted
union of Arthur and Guinevere. "The simultaneous principles of
attraction and repulsion that inform [this union] capture the interplay of sense and soul in archetypal Western love" (*Tennysonian
Love: The Strange Diagonal* [Minneapolis, 1969], pp. 164–165).
On Guinevere's warmth and Arthur's cold, unsympathetic qualities, see pp. 169–173. Joseph's study is full of insights, and his
ascription of two kinds of love to the *Idylls*—*eros* and *agape*, or
Dantean and Platonic—is very interesting. But one must ask if
there is really an interplay of sense and soul here, if there is not
instead in the "allegorical drift" a warfare between the two, an
apparent marriage that is actually a conflict between sexual and
spiritual opposites.

> I seem as nothing in the mighty world,
> And cannot will my will, nor work my work
> Wholly, nor make myself in mine own realm
> Victor and lord. But were I joined with her,
> Then might we live together as one life,
> And reigning with one will in everything
> Have power on this dark land to lighten it,
> And power on this dead world to make it live."
>
> [p. 1472]

There are both echoes and ironic implications in this passage. The stars and hollow earth and the vexing "waste dreams" suggest lines in *In Memoriam*, as does the idea that only a continuing communion of two persons can give value to mortal life. The words about marriage—"live together as one life"—almost repeat Tennyson's language in *The Princess*. But we know that this marriage will fail, that the King and Queen will not live together as one, that Arthur will first succeed in part and then entirely fail in his mission to lighten the dark land and make the dead world live. This suggests that when true marriage fails, civilization fails. In this story, or these stories, both are doomed. And increasingly, by an increasingly allegorical stress, the doom is made to seem inevitable, even universal.

The question of Arthur's birth, central in this idyll, bears on the matter. Some think him "less than man," some "more than man" and "dropt from heaven"; the most credible story for loyal Bedivere is that Arthur is the son of fierce King Uther and his unhappy wife Ygerne, forced into marriage immediately after Uther killed her first husband. To Bedivere, then, the King is the child of a cruel and unhappy marriage, itself the result of war, destruction, death. But Arthur's supposed half-sister Bellicent, daughter

of Ygerne, casts doubt on this genealogy and tells the story
of Arthur's coming from a ghostly winged ship, from the
sea in flame to Merlin's feet: "from the great deep to the
great deep," as Merlin riddles (p. 1480).[26] And if one anticipates the allegorical development of Arthur as pure
Soul, more than mortal man, this story offers no more hope
than the other for his marriage to mortal Guinevere. Holy
Dubric marries them and says,

> "Reign ye, and live and love, and make the world
> Other, and may thy Queen be one with thee,
> And all this Order of thy Table Round
> Fulfil the boundless purpose of their King!"

And the knights sing, "Let the King reign" (p. 1482). But
in all this the irony is clear when Arthur declares, "The
old order changeth, yielding place to new" (p. 1752).[27]
Arthur himself will reign "for a space." The world will
not be changed. The Queen will not be one with the King.

The first of the "Round Table" idylls, in the final arrangement, is "Gareth and Lynette." It was published in
1872, later than any other part of the sequence except
"Balin and Balan." This fact makes more interesting the
relatively light tone and apparently happy ending, for it
indicates that the growing darkness of tone and theme in
the whole series is artful and not only a reflection of
changes in Tennyson's mood over the years of composition.

---

26. Clyde Ryals emphasizes the importance of this riddle in his
study *From the Great Deep* (Athens, Ohio, 1967).

27. Allan Danzig finds in this statement a central idea for the
Idylls and for Tennyson ("The Contraries: A Central Concept in
Tennyson's Poetry" *PMLA*, LXXVII [1962], 577–585).

Yet even here, in tone and ending, there is something odd. The delicate Lynette is so offended by Arthur's assigning a kitchen knave to champion her that when Gareth defeats her enemies she disdains him: "thou smellest of the kitchen still," she complains, and seems almost to hope for his ultimate defeat (p. 1508). Although there is no source in Malory for the earlier part of this story, the disdainful maiden and her apparently low-born champion are traditional. Tennyson, however, underlines the persistent hostility of the fair Lynette, and it is only at the end that she relents. Even then there is ambiguity:

> he that told the tale in older times
> Says that Sir Gareth wed Lyonors,
> But he, that told it later, says Lynette.[28]

In "The Marriage of Geraint," Geraint's possibilities as a husband seem no greater than Lynette's as a wife. This doting knight becomes almost a version of harsh Walter in the Clerk's tale of Griselda in *The Canterbury Tales*. The story told in Tennyson's two idylls about Geraint and Enid—first published as one—comes from Lady Charlotte Guest's *Mabinogion* (1838–1849) instead of from Malory. Tennyson has chosen from a wealth of Arthurian material, and this story of a marriage sweet and sour fits well into his sequence

Hallam Tennyson glosses the second Geraint idyll, "Geraint and Enid," "The sin of Lancelot and Guinevere begins to breed . . . despair and want of trust in God and man."[29] And the poet has deliberately introduced an ele-

---

28. According to Hallam Tennyson's note in the Eversley Edition, the earlier narrator is Malory, the later "my father" (V, 467).
29. In the Eversley *Idylls* volume (VI, 473).

ment not in the *Mabinogion* tale to give a pretext for Geraint's leaving Camelot with his wife Enid:

> But when a rumour rose about the Queen,
> Touching her guilty love for Lancelot,
>
>   .   .   .   .   .
>
> Geraint believed it; and there fell
> A horror on him, lest his gentle wife,
> Through that great tenderness for Guinevere,
> Had suffered, or should suffer any taint
> In nature.   [pp. 1526–1527]

This horror may be thought directly relevant to what happens in the rest of these idylls, and Tennyson intended it
to seem so. Yet Geraint's turning against his wife cannot be
and is not explained by his anxiety about Guinevere. When
he overhears Enid thinking aloud of her fear that she is the
reason for her uxorious husband's neglect of his knightly
duties, Geraint misinterprets her words. But the point is
specifically made that he does not suspect his wife of adultery. His jealousy and his later monstrous egotism, even in
Tennyson's version, can no more be traced to Guinivere's
and Lancelot's affair than can Lynette's disdainful pride.

Most of "The Marriage of Geraint" consists of Enid's
memories about how Geraint championed, wooed, and married her. But Geraint's suspicion and his dour command to
her—"put on thy worst and meanest dress / And ride with
me" (p. 1530)—cast a shadow over these memories.

"Geraint and Enid" continues the story of this husband's
demanding behavior. As in "Gareth and Lynette," again it
is significant that the man and woman do not ride together.
She must go into the woods ahead of him, and he com-

mands her, on her "duty as a wife," not to speak a word
except in reply to him. Another element not in Tennyson's
source is Geraint's throwing away his purse, in effect an
angry gesture of denial that he is "effeminate": he intends
that both he and his wife shall live dangerously. But his attempt to prove his manliness is as surly as brave, and at last
it becomes a childish insistence on being reassured of love
at any expense—specifically, at Enid's expense.

Enid twice warns her lord of men about to assault him,
and both times, although he evades danger and wins a battle
because of her warning, he is rude and resentful at her
breaking silence. The two are taken into the hall of Enid's
old suitor the Earl Limours, who woos her again as Geraint
sits sullenly apart; and when she tells her husband, he only
taunts her the more. After he fights and defeats the impetu-
ous earl, he continues to sneer about her being "right honest." Finally, wounded by the men of Limours and bleeding
under his armor, Geraint collapses, and both he and Enid
are captured by the bandit Earl of Doorm. In the evil earl's
hall, he pretends to be dead, "That he might prove her to
the uttermost, / And say to his own heart, 'She weeps for
me' " (p. 1566). This situation is introduced by Tennyson
into the *Mabinogion* story, as if to emphasize the fact that
Geraint can play the role of Lynette's male equivalent. Her
pride and coldness give way only to motherly pity; his
pride and brutality give way only to childlike and emotionally parasitic self-indulgence. What is false and dangerous
if not destructive in the marriage of Geraint and Enid—
and he confesses plainly that he has done her great wrong—
is, in Tennyson's telling of the tale, a result of the hus-

band's personality, not of Guinevere's and Lancelot's sin breeding want of trust. Geraint's least forgivable behavior, his feigning of death, occurs when he has no doubt about Enid's complete love. One can argue that the first three idylls of "The Round Table," the only stories in the whole sequence that seem to conclude with love and the bright promise of true marriage, contain more reasons for misgivings about the open, nonmanipulative relations of the men and women in them than do Tennyson's earlier narrative poems.

In "Balin and Balan" there is no question of happy endings, of love, or of marriage. The story is a precise negation of these things, and it distinctly introduces a grim sense of sexuality as a fearfully destructive rather than a creative force. Again, the relation of Tennyson's story to his source is illuminating. In Malory there are two brothers, Balin and Balan, who unwittingly kill each other. Everything else in this idyll is original, including the symbolic and narrative underlining of the sexual theme. Again, too, Tennyson has deliberately linked events—the two wild brothers' battle and deaths—to the sin of Guinevere and Lancelot. He has also, effectively if almost certainly without conscious intention, introduced with the two figures of the brothers the ideas of sexual violence, inversion, and passion leading, not only to destruction, but to self-destruction as well.

The disillusionment of the brothers who have taken the Queen as their ideal of civilizing womanhood begins when Balin sees and overhears a meeting between Guinevere, pacing in the roses, and Lancelot, in a walk of lilies. Once more the two kinds of flowers and the colors, red and white, represent the sexual urge and the appeal of chaste isolation.

Lancelot, in the lilies, tells his paramour of his dream about a

> "maiden saint who stands with lily in hand
> In yonder shrine. . . .
>   all the light upon her silver face
> Flowed from the spiritual lily that she held. . . .
>   As light a flush
> As hardly tints the blossom of the quince
> Would mar [the] charm of stainless maidenhood."
>
> "Sweeter to me" she said "this garden rose
> Deep-hued and many-folded!"   [p. 1583]

Guinevere may well agree with Cyril of *The Princess:* "Than wear / Those lilies, better blush our lives away." In contrast, Lancelot, who is not, after all, a maiden knight, seems to pluck his roses with his eyes upturned—seems, that is, to live according to a double standard.

Shaken by this scene, suspicious now of Guinevere, Balin is further shaken by Sir Garlon's open accusation of the Queen and then by wily Vivien's stories of her and Lancelot, stories false in fact but not far from the truth in essence. Suspecting his feminine ideal of the very worst, he goes into a frenzy, shrieking and defiling his shield:

>   that weird yell,
> Unearthlier than all shriek of bird or beast,
> Thrilled through the woods; and Balan lurking there
> (His quest was unaccomplished) heard and thought
> "The scream of that Wood-devil I came to quell!"
> Then nearing "Lo! he hath slain some brother-knight,
> And tramples on the goodly shield to show
> His loathing of our Order and the Queen.
> My quest, meseems, is here. Or devil or man

Guard thou thine head." Sir Balan spoke not word,
But snatched a sudden buckler from the Squire,
And vaulted on his horse, and so they crashed
In onset, and King Pellam's holy spear,
Reputed to be red with sinless blood,
Reddened at once with sinful, for the point
Across the maiden shield of Balan pricked
The hauberk to the flesh; and Balin's horse
Was wearied to the death, and when they clashed,
Rolling back upon Balin, crushed the man
Inward, and either fell, and swooned away.
                                        [pp. 1590–1591]

As in *Maud*, the roses turn to blood. The bloody mood of
Balin is more like a child's horror at the facts of male and
female life than like the disillusionment with life in general
that an idol's guilt inspires. And it is far from accidental
that the knight Balin encounters is his brother, his other
self: discovering that his rose is no lily, he turns from
woman worship to self-destructive violence. The two
brothers die locked in each others' arms. Pellam's spear,
reputedly one that pierced Christ's side, gives a strange religious overtone, but the most striking quality about this
scene, with the bloody piercing of the maiden shield, is
violently and morbidly sexual. This is the one vivid, if symbolic, representation of close personal contact in the *Idylls*,
and it is both narcissistic and suicidal.

In this idyll the rumor of adultery does affect the action.
Yet even here, the compulsive personality represented by
Balin-Balan, the necessity either to idolize woman as the
sacred lily or reject her as the wicked rose, a fallen creature, can account for the result at least as well as Guinevere's radical imperfection. From now on in the *Idylls*,

sexuality almost always means beastlike sensuality, while the feminine sexual nature—the "rose of womanhood"—becomes an object of horror. And this attitude does not always focus upon Guinevere.

Another example of the sensual woman is the enchantress Vivien, in the next idyll, "Merlin and Vivien." She was originally called Nimuë, in the 1857 trial edition, *Enid and Nimuë: The True and the False*, and in the later story she still represents feminine falsehood in human relations, specifically in sexual love. Once more, Tennyson departs from his sources. In Malory, Nimuë is wooed by Merlin, who bores her, and she is hardly a wily vamp or practiced deceiver (Arnold is closer to Malory's spirit at the end of his "Tristram and Iseult"). In the Vulgate *Merlin*, translated by Southey, Viviane is genuinely attracted to the magician, enchants him only in order to hold him as her lover, and finally repents her action. In Tennyson, Vivien is the daughter of a knight killed by Arthur; she was born of her dying mother on the battlefield. Her motivation is hatred for the King and his court, and she enters that court, pretending to be a pure maiden in distress, intending to corrupt or harm it in any way she can—and actually attempting to seduce the obtuse King.

From the beginning, this idyll is concerned with sexuality in and out of marriage. A minstrel in the court of Mark, the Cornish king and Camelot's great enemy, tells how the knights of Arthur follow Lancelot by fighting in the Queen's name, vowing the chaste vows of the angels, who "love most, but neither marry nor are given / In marriage."

> It more beseems the perfect virgin knight
> To worship woman as true wife beyond
> All hopes of gaining, than as maiden girl.

> They place their pride in Lancelot and the Queen.
> So passionate for an utter purity
> Beyond the limit of their bond, are these,
> For Arthur bound them not to singleness.   [p. 1596]

"Balin and Balan" reveals one conclusion to that woman-worship: disillusionment and death. Even though here, as in "The Holy Grail," the King himself does not set the super-normal goal, he does not discourage, and in some sense may even inspire, it. (Early in the *Idylls*, Gareth is told by the old seer that the King sets "such vows, as is a shame / A man should not be bound by, yet the which / No man can keep") (p. 1491). When Merlin upbraids Vivien for her slander of the knights Valence, Sagramore, and Percivale, and then extenuates the love of Lancelot and Guinivere, she attacks even Arthur: "Man! is he man at all, who knows and winks?" He is "King, coward, and fool." Merlin knows that this is both false and unfair, that Arthur would have "all men true and leal, all women pure." But Vivien's question haunts the *Idylls* in a more serious sense than she has quite intended: "is he man at all . . . ?" (p. 1616). She has insisted to Mark that all flesh is foul:

> "This Arthur pure!
> Great Nature through the flesh herself hath made
> Gives him the lie! There is no being pure,
> My cherub; saith not Holy Writ the same?"   [p. 1597]

The answer to her question is, of course, No. But the irony of cynical Vivien's speech lies not simply in Arthur's seeming a Christ figure; as Soul personified at war with flesh, instead of as the incarnate or fleshly divine, Arthur becomes a Manichean version of Christ, a heretical version and therefore an anti-Christ. In fact, Vivien's cynicism about the flesh is not at all out of keeping with Merlin's melancholy as he sees

> An ever-moaning battle in the mist,
> World-war of dying flesh against the life,
> Death in all life and lying in all love.   [p. 1601]

Revulsion against the flesh becomes more and more apparent in the *Idylls* now, and it is focused upon woman as a fleshly creature. Here, once more, is something like the madonna-harlot syndrome, like the tendency of a Rossetti to see women as pure and spiritual or fallen and fleshly. Speaking as a male, Merlin responds to Vivien's playful boast that man's wit cannot mount as high as woman's:

> "Not mount as high"; we scarce can sink as low:
> For men at most differ as Heaven and earth,
> But women, worst and best, as Heaven and Hell.
>
> [p. 1616]

The double standard operates again and in just one direction, as Vivien, called "harlot," traps Merlin in the enchantment he has at last revealed to her and mockingly bids farewell to him as a "fool."

Vivien is an ascetic idealist turned sour. She does not, finally, disagree with Arthur's Manichean attitude toward the flesh; she simply sees that living beings cannot escape the flesh. Her destructive hatred of Arthur results from his killing of her father, and her corrosive cynicism comes from her acceptance of Camelot's impossible idealism; neither derives from the sin of Guinevere and Lancelot, even though she cites that sin with glee.

Wanton and fool—Guinevere the penitent and Dagonet the King's jester—all the people in the later *Idylls* seem to agree about the corruption of the flesh. The only ideal

feminine figure is the virginal girl, pining away in her lilies:
the Lady of Shalott, now called Elaine the lily maid of
Astolat.

As Enid stands in contrast to Vivien, the true to the supposedly false, so Elaine is a foil for Guinevere: the chaste
set against the spoiled, the isolated lily maid against the
Queen with all her jewels and her roses. And Lancelot,
neither wooer of the one nor husband of the other, stands
between the two. Guinevere's relationship with him has a
direct bearing on what happens to Elaine—or what does not
happen. But, again, it is doubtful that the adultery is genuinely causal; Elaine is part of a dark world in which chastity
denies sexual passion, the lily denies the rose.

"Lancelot and Elaine" includes echoes and reminders of
earlier idylls and other poems, and it foreshadows the yet
darker idylls to come. Gareth, the brave young man of the
first idyll in "The Round Table," has deteriorated with the
rest of Camelot, and he is now

> a good knight, but therewithal
> Sir Modred's brother, and the child of Lot,
> Nor often loyal to his word.   [p. 1637]

He is one of the knights of the Round Table, along with
Gawain and Tristram and Lancelot himself, who all once
seemed noble if not pure and who will increasingly seem
ignoble if not hopelessly corrupt. The diamonds in this
story, given as prizes in Arthur's tournaments, come from
the crown of a king, one of two brothers who fought together and killed each other "at a blow"; one is reminded of
the fratricide in "Balin and Balan." These gems, won by
Lancelot and given to Guinevere, who throws them into
the river, also suggest the jewels that are to be offered as

a prize in "The Last Tournament"—jewels again from the dead and jewels that will lead to death; yet those gems will not be pure diamonds but red rubies, stones associated with dark passion and with spilled blood. The Queen's speech sounds like another echo of Vivien's cynical comment when Guinevere laughs scornfully at Arthur for "swearing men to vows impossible":

> the faultless King,
> That passionate perfection, my good lord—
> But who can gaze upon the Sun in heaven?
>
> . . . . .
>
> He is all fault who hath no fault at all:
> For he who loves me must have a touch of earth;
> The low sun makes the colour.   [pp. 1624–1625]

The Queen's legal *bond*—the term is repeatedly used in Guinevere's and Lancelot's speeches—is with Arthur, but her free love is Lancelot's, for he has warmth and color. Color signifies earthly passion, and this passion is represented by the bright colors that contrast with the white purity, not only of Arthur, that "passionate perfection," but also of the pale Elaine.

Elaine, too, seems to be an echo. As a later, more real, more complex version of the Lady of Shalott, she reminds one still of all the Tennysonian maidens who are lily-like but long for love, and who choose death when they cannot have love. The difference, and once more this may be an anticipation of what is yet to come, is that even though she blushes once in the tale, when kissed by her brother, Elaine remains essentially the pure white foil to a colorful, passionate, and ultimately destructive force. There is no Guinevere in "The Lady of Shalott." But Elaine of Astolat is part of the larger fictive world. And we have seen that, while there are some virtuous maidens in this world of the *Idylls*, there is hardly another woman who is both virtuous and happy; the reader has misgivings about every sexual liaison. (The single exception, the one Tennyson clearly meant to function positively, as "the true," is Enid, in whose halls "arose / The cry of children, Enids and Geraints / Of times to be" (p. 1576), and her sketchy portrait as the mature wife and mother represents troth in marriage; but it comes in an early idyll almost as a "happily ever after" formula given in only a half-dozen bald lines.) A question hardly implicit in the early poem takes on force here in Arthur's kingdom: could an Elaine live on, marry, be realized as a flesh-and-blood woman, and not be corrupted? She would then have to become a sexual object, associated not with lilies but with roses, and a part of the world of the flesh. And could Lancelot marry Elaine? The wounded knight loves his fair nurse, the lily maid,

> with all love except the love
> Of man and woman when they love their best,
> Closest and sweetest.   [p. 1645]

There is virtually no close and sweet marriage in the *Idylls;* and of course the bond between the Queen and Lancelot—"not the bond of man and wife," as both say—is marred by her jealousy and his sense of guilt. The issues of legal marriage and free love are involved here.[30] But even

30. Lancelot says that "free love will not be bound," and Arthur replies that "free love, so bound [by "what is worthy love"] were freëst." Yet Lancelot cannot, like John Stuart Mill, advocate divorce (for the King and the Queen). And Arthur does not, like Coventry Patmore, specifically argue that a strict marriage law is

more significant is the question whether any sexual relation can be imagined in Arthur's realm as consummated and not guilty. If the soul is at war with the flesh, Guinevere may illustrate the problem, but she does not create it.

The next idyll, "The Holy Grail," bears in an oblique way on this matter. Tennyson fairly often relates religious to sexual feeling, although it seems unlikely that he means to do so except when he follows tradition by suggesting that the life of the religious may atone for guilty sexual acts: Lancelot will "die a holy man"—these are the last words of "Lancelot and Elaine"—and Guinevere will die an abbess. "The Holy Grail" is the idyll in which a purportedly religious form of sublimation is most striking. In a sense, the poet's ambivalence about marriage has a counterpart in his mixed feelings about the otherworldly quest for the Grail, bathed in pure light and yet rosy red.

In Percivale's search for the Grail, the first illusion of earthly happiness to crumble before his mind's eye, according to Tennyson's own comment, is the illusion of "wifely love and love of the family":

> And then behold a woman at a door
> Spinning; and fair the house whereby she sat,
> And kind the woman's eyes and innocent,
> And all her bearing gracious; and she rose
> Opening her arms to meet me, as who should say,
> "Rest here"; but when I touched her, lo! she, too,
> Fell into dust and nothing, and the house

---

still a better guide than, and should bind, true love. The only resolution, if it can be called that, will come in a cynicism less explicit yet far more sweeping than Meredith's in *Modern Love*, in a revulsion against physical passion and against the physical basis of marriage.

> Became no better than a broken shed,
> And in it a dead babe; and also this
> Fell into dust, and I was left alone.   [p. 1673]

Leaving behind the dream of marriage and the child—a dream turned into a nightmare—Percivale meets Galahad in a holy hermit's chapel and hears him describe the Holy Grail, which moves with him,

> Fainter by day, but always in the night
> Blood-red, and sliding down the blackened marsh
> Blood-red, and on the naked mountain top
> Blood-red, and in the sleeping mere below
> Blood-red.   [p. 1675]

Then Galahad disappears, following the "rose-red" Grail into a "spiritual city." Percivale proceeds to a fair town and soon is welcomed by a woman, now a widow, who in his early youth was his first love:

> The Princess of that castle was the one,
> Brother, and that one only, who had ever
> Made my heart leap.   [p. 1678]

She wishes to give herself to him, and her people beg Percivale, "Wed thou our lady, and rule over us" (p. 1678). So the temptation of "wifely love" is repeated and intensified. But he goes on, rejoins Galahad, and forgets at last that temptation to break his "burning vow."

Of all the knights other than Galahad, only humble Percivale and modest Bors have clear glimpses of the Grail. Gawain tells the King he soon gave up the quest and instead dallied with his "merry maidens." Lancelot, though half-maddened by his guilty love as he approaches the holy object, comes close to the vision—but the Grail is veiled to him. Arthur concludes the idyll ambiguously with a comment on the need to do one's duty and not to wander on visionary quests while land and city go to ruin; yet he sees Galahad as the highest of his order, and he himself appears to be a visionary, in this world but not quite of it. Speaking of himself, he says,

> Let visions of the night or of the day
> Come, as they will; and many a time they come,
> Until this earth he walks on seems not earth,
> This light that strikes his eyeball is not light,
> This air that smites his forehead is not air
> But vision—yea, his very hand and foot—
> In moments when he feels he cannot die,
> And knows himself no vision to himself,
> Nor the high God a vision, nor that One
> Who rose again.   [p. 1687]

The curious quality of this idyll derives largely from its double attitude toward the otherworldly quest, an attitude in part articulated by the King. The doubleness is in fact expressed by Tennyson in his direct comment on the idyll —Tennyson, with his visions and his love of holy places and relics but his distaste for these things when used by such literally believing Christians as King Pellam, who in "Balin and Balan" is the caricature of a Catholic. He writes of "The Holy Grail," "Faith declines, religion in many turns from practical goodness to the quest after the supernatural and marvellous and selfish religious excitement," but also, "I have expressed there my strong feeling as to the Reality of the Unseen."[31] Of course the two comments could be reconciled by pointing out that the purely visionary life is

31. See Hallam Tennyson's notes in the Eversley Edition, VI, 487–488.

not for most men, as the poet and his Arthur do clearly say.
Yet both Percivale and Bors have the vision, even Lancelot
comes close to it, and all are deeply affected, largely for
good, by the Grail quest; only the corrupt and obtuse cannot thus see and be uplifted. Or one could adopt the Hindu
version of mysticism contained in the Bhagavad-Gita and
insist that a world-transcending vision raises one above one's
earthly duties, which one nevertheless pursues. But Arthur's
actual tendency (and at least one of Tennyson's) is alter-
nately to insist on temporal duties and to deny that time
and space have any value—perhaps, even, any reality. In
this, temperamentally, Arthur is close to the views of the
prophetic Carlyle, who praises dictatorial heroes and rants
about contemporary politics but also declares, first and most
strikingly in *Sartor Resartus*, that the only reality is the
visionary's, the mystic's, and that temporal things are sheer
illusion.[32] It seems clear that Carlyle's combination of the
here-and-now religion of work with a basically anti-Christian, anti-incarnational transcendentalism influenced Tennyson greatly, most of all in the *Idylls*. The internal contradiction is closely related to an internal contradiction of
attitudes toward marriage and sexuality in this idyll that is
essentially about both religious experience and sexual experience—about a religious vision and sexual temptation and
guilt.

The story seems, in spite of Arthur's practical misgivings, to glorify a pursuit of the unearthly vision, in which
a temporal and sexual object, the rose, which is also an

32. Hallam Tennyson comments, "Arthur suspects that all the
material universe may be but vision," and he quotes his father on
"the two dreams of Space and Time," in the Eversley Edition VI,
498.

image that can merge frighteningly into the bloody rose of lust and violence, is now safely sublimated as the rosy Grail. One need not strain to find the Grail a conventional (or Freudian) symbol of feminine sexuality, but a quite unconscious one, when the poet repeats insistently its color—"rose-red," "blood-red"—in phrases that echo the language of sexual and ultimately destructive passion in *Maud.* This idyll insists upon the crumbling away of wife and babe, the denial of marriage—in Percivale's vision. And it does so against the background of a civilization that is crumbling for lack of day-to-day and down-to-earth attention. The whole situation is a mirror image and commentary on the treatment of marriage throughout the *Idylls:* the joining of man and woman is seen at the beginning as a necessary first step toward the revival of the dead dark world, and yet Arthur's own quest is increasingly described in language that transcends, denies, is divorced from, the sexual, even the physical. The divorce is not apparently caused by Guinevere.

The tendency to divorce red and white or sense and soul is more evident than ever in the next two idylls, "Pelleas and Ettarre" and "The Last Tournament." "Pelleas and Ettarre," which is adapted from Malory's story, includes elements and motifs from most of the earlier "Round Table" idylls: the proud disdainful woman and her modest knight, in "Gareth and Lynette"; the disillusionment of wild and natural innocence, in "Balin and Balan"; the false voluptuous female of "Merlin and Vivien"; the tournament for a precious prize that is to be disdained, from "Lancelot and Elaine." More important, it uses again, not only the story of the innocent man and the false sensual woman, but also the sexual imagery of the corrupt red rose to reinforce a sense that true marriage cannot be realized in a world where there is only lust, not love.

When the naïve Pelleas first sees haughty Ettarre, she seems almost a Princess Ida, almost masculine in her feminism: playfully, but significantly too, she says to him, "We are damsels-errant, and we ride, / Armed as ye see, to tilt against the knights" (p. 1689). Once more the strong woman, set off in striking contrast to the rare pure maiden, has a perversely strong will and despises the man who is meek and mild. Ettarre soon assumes the manner of a guileful Vivien, wheedling Pelleas into winning for her the golden circlet in Arthur's Tournament of Youth. She despises him as Lynette despises Gareth, Vivien despises Merlin, and even Guinevere despises Arthur. She avoids him and at last betrays him. Poor Pelleas has an inkling of her nature when he is vexed by a remembered song:

> "A rose, but one, none other rose had I,
> A rose, one rose, and this was wondrous fair,
> One rose, a rose that gladdened earth and sky,
> One rose, my rose, that sweetened all mine air—
> I cared not for the thorns; the thorns were there.
>
> "One rose, a rose to gather by and by,
> One rose, a rose, to gather and to wear,
> No rose but one—what other rose had I?
> One rose, my rose; a rose that will not die,—
> He dies who loves it,—if the worm be there." [p. 1698]

In the context, this song seems simply to reflect on Ettarre as a sexual object and a false creature; the sexuality and corruption are inextricable. But the image is no more simple than, say, Blake's "sick rose." Tennyson's roses are essentially ambiguous here, in *Maud*, and, for another important instance, in the echoing last line of "The Vision of Sin": "God made Himself an awful rose of Dawn." The rose of the remembered song, then, is more than the image of one woman: it is an elusive and awful object, perhaps sacred as well as sexual, desired as the rose-red Grail is, mortal, supremely fair, and ultimately mysterious.

The emphasis is on corruption: the worm is in the rose of fleshly womanhood; and the words "if the worm be there" combine a sexual association with the idea of death. (In this respect, the song even anticipates the knight's finding his rosy lady in bed with Gawain, the dying of his love and innocence, his temptation to kill them, and his transformation into a bitterly vengeful and deadly figure.)

And there is falsehood now, not only in the love of man and woman, but also in the "troth" of man and man, for here, as in *In Memoriam*, sexual love and friendship are associated. Only now both are corrupt. Gawain, the "light of love," promises Pelleas to win his lady for him, and he promptly betrays that promise by seducing Ettarre. The strategy of Gawain's telling her that he has slain Pelleas as a means of making her love the supposedly dead knight is not very clear in either Malory or Tennyson, but it may dimly suggest the motive of Geraint, who wants to be assured of Enid's love by her grief when she thinks him dead.

In any case, Gawain's scheme is hardly a success. When Pelleas discovers false Gawain and Ettarre asleep in each other's arms, he cries,

> "O towers so strong,
> Huge, solid, would that even while I gaze
> The crack of earthquake shivering to your base
> Split you, and Hell burst up your harlot roofs
> Bellowing, and charred you through and through within,

> Black as the harlot's heart—hollow as a skull!
> Let the fierce east scream through your eyelet-holes,
> And whirl the dust of harlots round and round
> In dung and nettles! . . .
>   . . . disgraced,
> Dishonored all for trial of true love—
> Love?—we be all alike: only the King
> Hath made us fools and liars. O noble vows!
> O great and sane and simple race of brutes
> That own no lust because they have no law!
>   .   .   .   .   .
> I never loved her, I but lusted for her—
> Away."   [p. 1701]

The association of towers and harlots is to occur again in
the bitter imagery of the next idyll, along with this denial of
love and disgust at its pretense.

Pelleas leaves his sword between the false pair and dashes
away, to meet and to be bested by Lancelot, of whose
adultery he learns. When Pelleas discovers from Percivale's
inadvertent remark that the Queen herself is false, he asks,

> "Is the King true?" "The King!" said Percivale.
> "Why then let men couple at once with wolves.
> What! art thou mad?"   [p. 1703]

In fact, Pelleas is maddened and is all but mad. He calls out,

> "I am wrath and shame and hate and evil fame,
> And like a poisonous wind I pass to blast
> And blaze the crime of Lancelot and the Queen."
>   [p. 1704]

Finally, defeated by Lancelot, faced by the suffering
Guinevere, he springs into the dark—to reappear in the next
and yet darker idyll.

In this idyll, "The Last Tournament," the main and the bitterest spokesman for the disillusioned point of view is Dagonet, Tennyson's version of the tragic fool and seer—almost a version of Lear's fool. His foil is Tristram, the amorous knight who wins the ruby carcanet that is the prize in Arthur's tournament. The antagonist is not yet the final enemy of Arthur, Modred, but the symbolic anti-Arthur, Pelleas—now known as the Red Knight.

Along with intensified sexual imagery and language, that of towers and harlots, the idyll uses an intensified color scheme, so that the dim white of Arthur's purity is opposed both to the natural green of Tristram and to the passionate and bloody red of Pelleas, with his earthy, fleshly court. Arthur and Dagonet are concerned with black and white, with earthly foulness and spiritual shadow; Tristram of the Woods dresses all in green and is associated with fresh fruitfulness as the essential lover, while Pelleas the Red Knight transforms the bright color of the rose and ruby into that of violent bloodshed, of wrath destroying and destroyed. The color red comes to dominate the scene: a ruby is the prize; in Arthur's Tournament of the Dead Innocence, it is given by Tristram not to his wife, Isolt the White, but to Mark's wife Isolt, and it seems to turn her hands a bloody red; finally, at the very end of the idyll, Mark strikes, and Tristram dies a bloody death. Apparently all Camelot, except Arthur and Dagonet, now prefers red to white. The women at the tournament soon tire of being "white-robed in honour of the stainless child," dead Innocence, and throw off the guise of the "snowdrop" that "would make the world as blank as Winter-tide," and wear gay colors (p. 1709). And when Arthur's knights attack the Red Knight's castle, the result is a ghastly "red dream" of massacre, of men and women murdered, of red wine, red blood, red fire in the ravaged and "red-pulsing" tower. Once more the images suggest that sexual lust is transformed into a lust to kill and to destroy.

The polar opposites here are represented by the child Innocence, found in an eagle's nest, and the harlots in the Red Knight's tower. The child inevitably dies, as innocence dies in this world but also as the promise of marriage, for not only harmony but also a living future has to die in a world where true marriage is impossible—in a poetic world whose great theme is not marriage but divorce, the divorce of man and woman, white and red, spirit and flesh. Yet the very ruby that becomes a symbol of destructive lust is found at first upon the child Innocence, as if to suggest that there has been some promise in this maiden of a reconciliation between innocence and the senses.

On the other hand, words of Pelleas and Tristram, meant dramatically to show their bitterness and moral decay, actually function imaginatively to criticize the divorce as something impossible in human life. Pelleas, scorning Arthur, says,

> My tower is full of harlots, like his court,
> But mine are worthier, seeing they profess
> To be none other than themselves. . . .
> My knights are all adulterers like his own,
> But mine are truer, seeing they profess
> To be none other.   [p. 1707]

This attack on hypocrisy echoes the cynicism of the sour man in "The Vision of Sin"—of Pelleas, too, it can be said that "conscience made him sour"—but it comes disturbingly close to a truth.

At last the red tower triumphs by being destroyed; for Arthur's knights, in their lust to destroy it, enter into its spirit and become red knights. So they act out a harsh criticism of Arthur's order which Tristram voices when he scorns the King's attempt

> To bind [his men] with inviolable vows,
> Which flesh and blood perforce would violate:
> For feel this arm of mine—the tide within
> Red with free chase and heather-scented air,
> Pulsing full man; can Arthur make me pure
> As any maiden child?
>
>   . . . . .
>
> The ptarmigan that whitens ere his hour
> Woos his own end; we are not angels here
> Nor shall be. [pp. 1722–1723]

Dagonet comments, in effect, that if men are not angels they are swine (and presumably women, to "woman-worshipper" Arthur, are worse):

> I have wallowed, I have washed—the world
> Is flesh and shadow—I have had my day.
> The dirty nurse, Experience, in her kind
> Hath fouled me. [p. 1713]

There can be no reconciling of "free love," about which Tristram sings, with spiritual order if all flesh is foul. Dagonet may not be simply Arthur's spokesman—although his diction and the parallel with *Lear* make him seem a "wise fool"— but if his view here is extreme, it is an extreme toward which the *Idylls* progress. The grimness of "Pelleas and Ettare" and "The Last Tournament" is related to the view that Dagonet articulates, the apparently "right" view in Camelot. And there is no indication that Ettare, Pelleas,

and the fool respond as they do to sex and the senses because of Guinevere and Lancelot.

Guinevere comes to share this attitude and to speak like
the fallen wife in a popular play. In the idyll "Guinevere"
—the most difficult of the narratives for the modern reader
to like—she seems drearily conventional, yet at moments
touching. Arthur, too, invites an ambivalent response: he is
partly a shadow, an unincarnate Christ figure, and, because he talks as if he so regards himself, a monumental and
perhaps blasphemous prig; yet he is partly, if reluctantly,
a man. The question Vivien asks and Tristram echoes—"Is
he man at all?"—seems to be raised again when the simple
novice speaks to Guinevere of Arthur's miraculous coming
and recalls of the young king that,

> could he find
> A woman in her womanhood as great
> As he was in his manhood, then, he sang,
> The twain together well might change the world.
>
> [p. 1732]

When Arthur appears to Guinevere at the convent, he
sounds like a ghost and talks like the Almighty: "I, whose
vast pity almost makes me die / . . . Lo! I forgive thee, as
Eternal God / Forgives" (p. 1738). Yet, for all his revulsion at Guinevere's fleshliness, he appears to acknowledge
his own flesh:

> I cannot take thy hand; that too is flesh,
> And in the flesh thou hast sinned; and mine own flesh,
> Here looking down on thine polluted, cries
> "I loathe thee": yet not less, O Guinevere,
> For I was ever virgin save for thee,

> My love through flesh hath wrought into my life
> So far, that my doom is, I love thee still.
>
> . . . . .
>
> Hereafter in that world where all are pure
> We two may meet before high God, and thou
> Wilt spring to me, and claim me mine, and know
> I am thine husband. [pp. 1738–1739]

Still, Arthur's love, bred in the flesh, apparently can be realized in marriage only "where all are pure," outside the flesh. Arthur's unbearable priggishness and arrogance in part of this speech—in another part he is almost poignantly the real, wronged human being—is a result, not only of Tennyson's inadequate dramatization, but also of the persistent tendency to picture him as a mystical king, a being of shadows, a time- and earth-transcending ideal. Arthur reflects on his own generative force in the world when he says to Guinevere,

> Well is it that no child is born of thee.
> The children born of thee are sword and fire,
> Red ruin, and the breaking up of laws. [p. 1735]

In the *Idylls*, where no children are born and live (unless Enid's, alluded to once in a line and a half, are supposed to thrive), where the baby in "The Holy Grail" must crumble into dust and the infant Innocence in "The Last Tournament" symbolically dies young, no marriage seems altogether true and fruitful. At least Gareth's and Lynette's, Geraint's and Enid's, are in some doubt. There can be no marriage at all between Merlin and Vivien, Lancelot and Elaine, Pelleas and Ettarre, or Tristram and his dark Isolt.

The marriages of the last idylls, those of Mark, of Tristram, and at last of Arthur, are disastrous.

The convenient explanation, then, offered again in "Guinevere," that the Queen's infidelity inspires all other falsehoods and leads to the destruction of the court simply is no explanation for the personalities of Vivien, Ettarre, and Isolt. It is altogether too neat, and in suggesting it, Tennyson is unfair to his own complex imagination. One may be tempted to argue that the poet has unconsciously shown how Arthur's high-minded, "Victorian" distaste for the flesh brings about disaster; there is a good deal of truth to the argument, but this, again, is too simple. The failure of Guinevere to respond to Arthur and her preference for Lancelot make up the major focus in the *Idylls* for the central themes of sexuality and marriage, or animal impulse and social order. But the other situations are versions of these themes rather than direct results of Guinevere's passion. Finally, in yet another passage of color imagery, Guinevere declares,

> I thought I could not breathe in that fine air
> That pure severity of perfect light—
> I yearned for warmth and colour which I found
> In Lancelot—now I see thee what thou art,
> Thou art the highest and most human too.   [p. 1741]

These lines, spoken as the Queen, about to commit herself to the convent, looks forward to a marriage of reunion in heaven, echo but contradict her speech in "Lancelot and Elaine" on Arthur's lack of color. If color here again signifies earthly passion, as the color red so often does in Tennyson, the "highest and most human" being is one without earthly passion.

"The Passing of Arthur," Tennyson's somewhat extended version of the 1842 "Morte d'Arthur," is the frame idyll that ends the work. It stands apart from the other tales, however, retaining the flavor of romance but also the mysterious, magic quality of the first version. The poet is said to have intended the two frame idylls, as distinct from the ten of "The Round Table," to be strikingly archaic, and they are. One can argue that the central stories in the *Idylls* have social and moral themes, whereas the last idyll—and to some extent, the first—is essentially heroic and visionary. Here, as in other poems, Tennyson's frame seems distinct from the stories. The King is a commanding figure at the center of the narrative only in the two frame idylls, which are largely concerned with open warfare and not the conflicts of couples, or marriage warfare. It seems that only here do we see Arthur clearly; the shadowy king has hardly been involved in social strife or in marriage.

Tennyson's critics have, in various ways, suggested that the serious problem of the *Idylls* is the ideal Arthur's failure to be human within a fictive world of human actions.[33] We have seen, to give the problem focus, a contradiction between his first hopes for earthly marriage and his coming to represent a Soul at war with Sense, divorced from the flesh, and so denying earthly marriage. This denial is so striking partly because of the poet's early and repeated emphasis on marriage as a theme to be set off against that of isolation leading to death. The failure of men and women

---

33. "Despite his ideal manhood, or perhaps because of it, Arthur is conspicuously ineffective when brought into dramatic relation with the real men of the Round Table and the complex tumultuous woman who is his Queen. . . . As King, he is a shadowy background presence" (Buckley, *Tennyson*, p. 177).

within time and space—the long-ago time and bounded
space of Arthur's kingdom—to marry and give birth to children means more to Tennyson than the crumbling of Camelot. It means that he does not now conceive of moral evolution as an actual hope. There is change, as Arthur says:

> The old order changeth, yielding place to new,
> And God fulfils himself in many ways,
> Lest one good custom should corrupt the world.
>
> [p. 1752]

But the change in this cyclical, seasonal work—and the
Idylls stress the seasons of the year more insistently than do
the lyrics of *In Memoriam*—is not, it seems, progressive.

One is reminded of the allegorical sculpture in Camelot,
the city built to music and explained by art: first, that on
the great gate that dazzles young Gareth, on which the
Lady of the Lake is represented:

> And in the space to left of her, and right,
> Were Arthur's wars in weird devices done,
> New things and old co-twisted, as if Time
> Were nothing.   [p. 1490]

Then, the sculpture with its "mystic symbol[s]" in the
hall:

> in the lowest beasts are slaying men,
> And in the second men are slaying beasts,
> And on the third are warriors, perfect men,
> And on the fourth are men with growing wings,
> And over all one statue in the mould
> Of Arthur.   [p. 1669]

The hall sculpture might be thought to represent an evolu-
tionary pattern, like the one suggested by the conclusions
of "Locksley Hall," *The Princess,* and *In Memoriam.* Yet

this picture is hierarchical and static. Here are no "ringing grooves of change," no vivid, hopeful ringing-out of the old, ringing-in of the new. The matter is again ambiguous, and one may detect in Tennyson's ambiguity about man's moral development, about the promise of the future, an unresolved conflict between Carlyle's transcendental insistence that time *is* nothing and Mill's progressive belief that time is the only reality. In any event, this poet's one persistent means of asserting hope for progress, the theme of fruitful marriage and the saving child, is notably absent from the *Idylls*.

Later Poems: Isolation

True marriage is again thwarted in the other late poems on the subject: "Aylmer's Field," "Enoch Arden," and even "Northern Farmer New Style."[34] The last two are attacks, one heavy and one light, on what is termed in "Aylmer's Field" a "filthy marriage-hindering Mammon" that makes "the harlot of the cities." There is no "mammon marriage" at last in the story of poor Edith Aylmer and her Leolin, only because both die. Their narrative includes the proud blustering father and the radically changing social background—in this poem, the French Revolution—of *The Princess*, as well as the degrading imagery of woman as a creature to be hunted, the false imagery of the "mammon" world. It includes too a final emphasis on death as the al-

34. The most often quoted statement in "Aylmer's Field," "marriages are made in Heaven" (p. 1166), might be taken as an example of Tennyson's "Victorian" sentimentalism; it is, however, bitterly ironic in the context, for the poem shows that although true or ideal marriages may seem to be made in Heaven, the actual marriages of a commerical age are often made (on earth) by greedy and stupid people.

ternative to marriage and hope for the future. Proud Aylmer is broken at last by the words of Averill's sermon with its apt biblical echo, "My house is left unto me desolate." Aylmer's line dies with his child Edith's death.

"Enoch Arden," while not a consistently successful poem, is the most interesting of these verse stories. Like Arthur, Enoch knows that "all things human change." His death may even dimly suggest Arthur's: "So past the strong heroic soul away." Enoch, however, is a flesh-and-blood man, not a shadowy king: he has been a husband and a father. Yet, when he returns a changed being from his long ordeal at sea to find that he is thought dead and that his Annie has remarried, he becomes another version of Tennyson's almost archetypal figure, the bereft and isolated lover. The poem combines Tennyson's theme of marriage and children with that of individual isolation and death; so its over-all tone is both light and dark, or again bittersweet. With all its flaws, the dullness of parts, and the ludicrous flatness of the final line, "Enoch Arden" is a serious work on what remains for Tennyson a serious subject, and it has more dignity than many of the poet's critics have allowed. Its pathos represents one way, at least, to join the hopeful and the melancholy voices.

Marriage is often frustrated in Tennyson's early lyrical verse. Marriage is defined as a link to the distant future in *The Princess* and *In Memoriam*. The hope expressed in these works, however, seems to be destroyed by the greed of the modern world in *Maud* and in the later poems on mammon-marriage. *Maud* expresses also the poet's awareness of sexuality as a destructive force. And the very existence of fleshly sexuality, in conflict with otherworldly spirituality, leads to an apparent rejection of earthly marriage in the *Idylls*. These shifts in mood and emphasis reflect the poet's various attitudes toward Victorian society and the future; toward the hypocrisies, repressions, and distortions imposed on generous impulse by greedy mammonism; but also toward the apparently dangerous freeing of sexual desire that can overthrow the order of marriage and the order of the state. The appeal of marriage as an idea is deep and consistent in his poetry, but one asks why Tennyson so often observes or imagines its poignant failure here and now.

The tendency toward what we have called sexual idealism in Tennyson's work can lead to a rejection of the real, of the real woman and of real wedlock. When the poet tries to locate his spiritual ideal, not in the distant future toward which mankind can evolve, but in an imagined world of actual persons, the degree of actuality he achieves depends on the degree to which the ideal fails of realization. The idea of marriage means for Tennyson an escape from shadows and solipsism to the longed-for reconciliation of impulse and social order through a union of spirit and flesh, of the creative self and the responsive milieu, of woman and man.

But all these, including *woman* and *man*, are abstractions. When Tennyson writes of himself as woman or man, as the soul in "The Palace of Art" or the aged speaker in "Tithonus," the abstracted images, representing aspects of a whole personality, succeed. The poet's experience and imagination both, however, teach him that real women are not abstract soul or spirit; the resulting disillusion implies that he has a version of the "madonna-harlot" syndrome, the insistence on making *woman* either exalted or degraded. So this poet who begins by associating woman with spirit

and who can even insist that women and men should become more alike, at last, in the mood of the *Idylls,* seems to
fear the world, the flesh—and the woman. The feminine
figure that was Soul in early Tennyson becomes corrupting
Sense in the later Tennyson.

The frustrated and failed marriages in his poetry suggest
that he finds in life not a union but a divorce, a conflict, of
contrasting, complementary, and partial values—values, not
people. But Tennyson is not always true in his abstracting
and his allegorizing to his own profound imagination. In the
Idylls of the King he accepts the painful actuality of divorce, the negation of his own temporal and redeeming idea,
and he tries to make the divorce itself an ideal truth with a
Carlylean denial of the flesh, the real world, and history.
This paradoxical and doomed attempt helps to explain some
flaws both small and large in the poetically impressive, often
beautiful *Idylls:* the dimness of Arthur in "The Round
Table," his priggishness here and there as he detaches himself from the flesh, and especially the contrast—indeed, a
kind of divorce—between the central group of tales, about
women and men, and the heroic frame tales that fail to explain or relate to the "Round Table" world of difficult
social bonds. Yet Tennyson's imagination triumphs over his
avowed intentions: the *Idylls* demonstrate how a divorce
of the very ideas of Soul and Sense can mean in human
time only destruction and death. They demonstrate, finally,
how sterile the total polarization of the sexes is, the Victorian and later tendency to define women and men essentially, not as persons in the traditional religious way, but in
abstract sexual or antisexual ways: man as virile power *or*
as Soul, as sheer "spiritual" subject; and woman as chastity
personified *or* as Sense, as mere sexual object.

4 | Marriage and Divorce in Browning

The marriage poetry of Tennyson both reflects and raises questions about the conflict between convention or law and individual desire; the place of woman in society; the nature, creative or destructive, of sexual impulse; the possibility of a person's communion with another, the possibility for a marriage of true minds. Robert Browning's poems on love and marriage are often evidently concerned with the first matter, the conflict between law and free love, and the last, the question of enduring sexual passion; the other matters are at least implicit in his poetry. His emphasis is on vivid individuality, and now and then he represents a strong woman who asserts her freedom. And even though Browning associates love with creativity, even though his dramatic forms imply some communication between, if not communion of, persons, he shows again and again how people may use sexuality to manipulate or degrade others, as well as how they can be trapped by their own egos, how they are both ironically defined and isolated by the way they deceive others *and* themselves. Yet these subjects—law and freedom, the powers and rights of woman, the moral or vicious nature of sexual desire, the possibility of honest communion or true marriage within a society—are suggested rather than directly pursued in most of his works, in his dramatic poetry about love, binding or free, about marriage as a high ideal and as a cruel form of repression.

Paradoxically, with the usually dramatic poet Browning even more than with the often lyric poet Tennyson we may be tempted to see the poems on love and marriage as a direct result of the poet's own love and marriage; at the end of *Men and Women*, Browning almost invites us to do so. After all, even though Tennyson's delayed marriage in 1850 was a crucial event in a year of crucial events, his courtship and that marriage do not enter into his verse as obviously as does his love for Hallam or even as powerfully as does his blighted affection for Rosa Baring. Browning writes about daring love, elopements and escapes, and the sad loss of the beloved, in lines that inevitably make us think of the daring affair of the Brownings' elopement and the sequels. In any event, without turning from thematic criticism to speculative biography, we can divide the works of Robert Browning into those published before his marriage, those published after his marriage, and those published after his wife's death: first, *Pippa Passes* (1841), *Dramatic Lyrics* (1842), and *Dramatic Romances and Lyrics* (1845); then *Men and Women* (1855); finally, *Dramatis Personae* (1864), *The Ring and the Book* (1868–1869), and the long late poems.

In much of his early verse, in *Pippa*, *Dramatic Lyrics*, and *Romances*, Browning is concerned with the idea of sexual love as a creative force and, at the same time, with the experience—almost always the woman's experience—of marriage as bondage. In this early period, he seems not to realize that the two are related: that the notion of the creative man's dominating, supporting, even molding his mate into a beautiful form can be an idealized version of the selfish husband's treating his wife as an object, a possession that reflects his own taste and power. Browning contrasts the artist and lover with the possessive collector and husband; he fails in these early poems to indicate that they may be compared as well as contrasted. In the verse of *Men and Women,* he tends to move from the relatively distant, highly dramatized, and in a sense theoretical subjects of idealized lovers and criminally villainous husbands with victimized wives (all in the long ago and far away) to the psychological and immediate matter of marriage as an actual experience that often begins with ecstasy and ends with boredom and alienation. In *Dramatis Personae* and the poems that follow, Browning stresses the alienation so much that he appears to echo the bleak sentiments of Meredith in *Modern Love* and to anticipate the bleaker sentiments in much of Hardy's verse. The great work of this period, *The Ring and the Book,* reflects several earlier interests and emphases, with its villainous husband and innocent wife, its exciting escape, and finally the heroine's rejection of earthly marriage as a snare or a delusion.

Involved in all these poems about sex, love, and marriage is the problem, already implied, of what is wholly dramatic and imagined, and what may reasonably be thought of as personal. Browning's two earliest published poems have dramatic forms—one is a monologue of sorts, the other a closet drama—but they express very personal ideas and feelings. The burden of *Pauline,* the "clear idea of consciousness / Of self,"[1] led Mill to comment on its morbid and

1. *The Works of Robert Browning,* ed. F. G. Kenyon, Centenary

excessive self-consciousness.[2] The somewhat fragmentary
nature and murkiness of this work and of *Paracelsus* may
result largely from the poet's attempt both to reveal and
to mask himself.[3] It is only in *Pippa Passes,* the first of the
Bells and Pomegranates series, that Browning succeeds in
giving his ideas and attitudes dramatic expression, so that
each speaker in the poem represents an individual point of
view that is in contrast to others. Yet there is a controlling,
implicit point of view, the poet's own. This dramatic poem
—or poetic drama—has thematic coherence: it is about kinds
of love.

Pippa Passes: Marriage as Creation

The work begins with dawn, a new day, and a new
year; it is to dramatize turning points and new resolutions
for a number of people. There is dramatic irony, and finally
double irony, in the mill girl Pippa's imagining today the
lives of "Asolo's Four Happiest Ones." These are the

Edition (10 vols.; London, 1912), II, 130–131; all quotations of
Browning's poetry are from this edition, to which volume and page
numbers refer.

2. See the *Literary Essays of John Stuart Mill,* ed. Edward
Alexander (Indianapolis, 1967), pp. 47–48; and William C. DeVane,
A Browning Handbook (2d. ed.; New York, 1955), p. 47. Mill's
handwritten criticism (it was not published as a review) at the end
of his copy of *Pauline,* now in the Victoria and Albert Museum, is
reproduced in Norton B. Crowell, *The Convex Glass* (Albuquerque,
N. M., 1968), pp. xiv–xv.

3. On *Pauline* and *Paracelsus* as revelations of the poet's developing soul, see Roma A. King, *The Focusing Artifice* (Athens, Ohio,
1968), pp. 3–19. For a discussion of these works only not as self-
portraits but also as poetic experiments, see Park Honan, *Browning's Characters* (New Haven, 1961). For comments on love as a
saving passion in both poems, see Walter Houghton, *The Victorian
Frame of Mind* (New Haven, 1957), pp. 385–388.

town's four supposedly happiest couples: beautiful Ottima and her lover Sebald, who represent erotic—and illicit—love; newly wed Phene and Jules, who exemplify married love; Luigi and his mother, who express filial and maternal love; and finally the Monsignor, who, in his closeness to God, reflects and embodies divine love. The most obvious ironies are that "happy" Ottima and Sebald are adulterers and murderers whose love is turning to gall; Jules and Phene seem to be a mismatched pair whose marriage is the result of trickery; Luigi, in conflict with his mother, is torn between his love for her and his patriotic zeal; and the Monsignor, who comes from a thoroughly corrupt family, can at least be tempted by greed and villainy. Pippa does not realize that all these people who, she thinks, are quite happy and quite unrelated to her not only are caught in conflicts but are able to resolve them by hearing her own singing. The double irony, then, is that her songs, with their apparently naïve liveliness and optimism, actually are effective and that, because of Pippa, God does seem to be in his heaven and some of the world's ills seem to be righted.

Of the four episodes, three—"Morning," "Noon," and "Night"—have to do with love and marriage. In the first, Ottima's lover Sebald has just helped her kill her husband. As they face each other in the bleak dawn—they prefer the darkness to Pippa's vital sunlight—they are horrified by their crime, which does not unite but divides them. Hearing Pippa sing, "God's in his heaven— / All's right with the world" (II, 114), Sebald cries out to his mistress, "I hate, hate—curse you! God's in his heaven!" But Ottima, at this moment, can contemplate her own suicide and his and say, "Not to me—to him, O God, be merciful." These last words in their scene are especially interesting. The woman who seems, from Pippa's distance, to be simply rich, loved, and happy appears, on closer view, to be guilty of adultery and murder; yet our final impression must be that her guilty passion for Sebald is genuine. She is not "magnificent in sin" (II, 114), as she has wanted to be, but she is totally in love, so she stands in sharp contrast to Tennyson's vamps, to false Vivien and Ettarre. With her old rich husband and her need for love, Ottima seems more like Maud and other weak victims of mammon-marriage; but it is characteristic of Browning, as it certainly is not of Tennyson, that the unhappy wife who interests him, who is presented directly and dramatically, is the victim who acts, who rebels and breaks out of her marriage. Whether or not Ottima is quite redeemed by the passion of her last one-line prayer, her poignant words make more terrible the results of this conflict between worldly marriage and free love.

The second episode deals even more directly with marriage. The young sculptor Jules has been tricked by jealous fellow art students into believing that simple Phene, ward or daughter of the unsavory hag Natalia, is a cultured and sensitive young lady. By means of forged letters they bring about his proposal and marriage to the girl, with whom he has never spoken. When Phene does speak, after their wedding, to recite the malicious Lutwyche's taunting verses, Jules realizes that he has been tricked—but also that Phene is an innocent who has been used by others, an innocent who looks up to him with awe. At this crucial moment he hears Pippa singing, outside his house, the song of the page who loved Queen Kate, "Give her but a least excuse to love me!" And he reflects,

> If whoever loves
> Must be, in some sort, god or worshipper,
> The blessing or the blest one, queen or page,
> Why should we always choose the page's part?
> Here is a woman with utter need of me,—
> I find myself queen here, it seems!   [II, 130–131]

Finally, the sculptor Jules determines to create his own ideal, as the sculptor Pygmalion did, to shape blank, innocent Phene into the woman he thought she already was.

This resolution introduces several interesting ideas. First, although it is expressed dramatically and not as the poet's conviction, the idea that "whoever loves /[is] God or worshipper" may suggest an assumption that is different from Tennyson's about an ideal equality of devotion, in *The Princess* (published six years later). As Ottima, the mistress, is virtually worshiped by her lover, so Jules, the husband, is worshiped by his bride. There may well be inequalities—though not the conventional inequality of the two sexes—implicit in the poet's fascination with the man or woman of strong and vivid personality.[4] (It seems significant that Browning's most memorable characters, except perhaps the people in *Pippa* and Andrea del Sarto, dominate their situations and their auditors by being the sole speakers, in dramatic monologues; they do not take part in

---

4. DeVane comments on the "Queen-Worship" poems (grouped under the title in the *Dramatic Lyrics* of 1842), "Rudel and the Lady of Tripoli," and "Christina" in *A Browning Handbook*, pp. 120–123. His reading is essentially the one assumed here. But his reading of one poem is challenged by several critics: John W. Tilton and R. Dale Tuttle, in "A New Reading of 'Count Gismond,'" *Studies in Philology*, LIX (1962), 83–95; and Sister Marcella Holloway, in "A Further Reading of 'Count Gismond,'" *Studies in Philology*, LX (1963), 549–553.

marriage dialogues.) Second, the lover and husband in this episode is an artist, and the two functions of loving and creating beauty are closely related if not inseparable. This yoking of love and art, the virtual identifying of bold lover and successful artist, occurs again and again in Browning's poetry.

The third episode is less relevant to the subject of love and marriage. Luigi's mother tries to persuade him that life with the charming Chiara is preferable to dying in a perhaps vain attempt to assassinate the Austrian tyrant. And the evil Intendant's plan to remove Pippa herself, the unknowing heiress to the fortune of the Monsignor's family, is to turn on her being seduced by the blond, blue-eyed Englishman Bluphocks. But Luigi is not to be distracted from his patriotic duty, and Pippa regards the blond foreigner's supposed interest in her as a joke perpetrated by the poor town girls, a joke that is interrupted by the Monsignor himself, as he calls for the Intendant's arrest. There are wheels within wheels. Pippa's singing has inspired, not only Luigi's courage, but also the Monsignor's resolution that saves her from being seriously tempted.

Finally, the emphasis of the poem is on facing up to reality and making moral decisions: the decision of Ottima to accept the results of her passion, her guilt, and her responsibility; the decision of Jules to accept the love offered him and to create his own ideal; the decision of Luigi to act according to his conscience; and the decision of the Monsignor to recognize and resist temptation. Ottima's decision involves the realization that although marriage can be a burden and frustration, freeing oneself from the burden may entail violence, sacrifice, and guilt—in effect, that "free love" in an imperfect world may impose a fearful cost.

Jules's decision is to accept marriage as a possibility, as a means of creating new order and beauty.

Dramatic Lyrics and *Dramatic Romances:* Marriage as Bondage

Marriage, then, in Browning's mature poetry, can be both a social limitation or constricting bond, perhaps to be broken—although the breaking is dangerous—and a challenging opportunity, perhaps to be accepted. The extreme and disastrous effects of breaking the bond—Ottima, for instance, is guilty of murder—are often understated, while the challenge of free and creative love is emphasized. Sometimes, to be sure, a free, true love seems poignantly impossible: Browning's imaginative sympathy for the trapped wife is evident in "My Last Duchess," the best known and the best of the 1842 *Dramatic Lyrics*. Here again the poet establishes a relationship between love and art: if the true lover is an artist, the tyrannical husband is a collector of art, one who regards statues, pictures, and also people as possessions, as objects instead of beings or living expressions of the human spirit. The Duke as collector anticipates other tyrant-husbands. The dead Duchess anticipates a number of later figures, including Pompilia. The women who speak in the later poems generally escape from the imprisonment of marriage, as the Duchess has not. A frequently prominent feminine character in Browning is the determined, the active, and, at last, the liberated woman. She may be an abused wife or a misaffianced girl or a falsely accused maiden like the speaker in "Count Gismond." Browning apparently meant in the two poems "Italy" and "France" ("My Last Duchess" and "Count Gismond") to show, as DeVane puts it, "the nature of the marriage bond—in Italy

the wife a chattel, in France an adored mistress."[5] It seems
significant that the wife in "My Last Duchess" is dead and
that the main effect in this brilliant work is that of the
speaker's, the Duke's, character: he is cold, selfish, evil, yet
polished and strong and somehow, curiously, impressive.
In "Count Gismond," however, the speaker is a living wife
whose marriage represents not bondage but freedom.

A third poem in the volume of 1842, "In a Gondola,"
shows again that Browning's lovers do not always escape
whole from their social bondage. This dialogue ends melodramatically with the stabbing of the lover by one of "the
Three," his beloved's guardians. But this man and woman
have not been defeated. Browning's favorite theme of apparent failure that is real success—and apparent success that
is moral failure or death-in-life—is evident here.

> The Three, I do not scorn
> To death, because they never lived: but I
> Have lived indeed, and so—(yet one more kiss)—can die.
>   [III, 317]

There are echoes of these themes in a lighter poem, the
monologue called "The Flight of the Duchess," in the 1845
volume *Dramatic Romances and Lyrics* (Part VII of *Bells
and Pomegranates*). These echoes seem almost playful, for
the monologue is witty and almost grotesque in its rapid
rhythm and its freely varied, sometimes comic, rhymes.
Yet the subject is quite serious, and the Duchess in this
poem is clearly a successful counterpart to "My Last Duchess." Her husband, a cold and conceited antiquarian, is another collector of things:

> the Duke's plan admitted a wife, at most,
> To meet his eye, with the other trophies,

5. DeVane, p. 107.

> Now outside the Hall, now in it,
> To sit thus, stand thus, see and be seen,
> At the proper place in the proper minute,
> And die away the life between.   [III, 352]

But the Duchess is not to be collected and put away. Described as a caged bird, she flies off at last to the gipsies,
choosing a life of freedom.

Perhaps the most striking part of the poem, which shifts
from virtual doggerel to something like high seriousness, is
the disquisition on love by the old gipsy woman who leads
the Duchess to her freedom, away from the castle, old customs, and her marriage.

> Art thou the tree that props the plant,
> Or the climbing plant that seeks the tree—
> Canst thou help us, must we help thee?
> If any two creatures grew into one,
> They would do more than the world has done;
> Though each apart were never so weak,
> Yet vainly through the world should ye seek
> For the knowledge and the might
> Which in such union grew their right:
> So, to approach, at least, that end,
> And blend,—as much as may be, blend
> Thee with us or us with thee,—
> As climbing-plant or propping-tree,
> Shall some one deck thee, over and down,
>   Up and about, with blossoms and leaves?
> Fix his heart's fruit for thy garland-crown,
>   Cling with his soul as the gourd-vine cleaves,
> Die on thy boughs and disappear
> While not a leaf of thine is sere?
> Or is the other fate in store,

And art thou fitted to adore,
To give thy wondrous self away,
And take a stronger nature's sway?   [III, 365–366]

This series of questions is first of all about the relationship of the Duchess to the gipsies; but it shifts to ask about her relationship to a lover. The partial blending here of weakness and strength—in the words of Jules, of page and queen —is once more unlike the union of female and male that Tennyson, in the *Princess*, imagines as the ideal marriage. One might even read Tennyson's lines, published in 1847, "In true marriage lies / Nor equal, nor unequal," as a reply to the 1845 passage in Browning, as an assertion that a man and a woman can do more than partially blend, can grow "into one," can "purpose in purpose, will in will . . . grow, / The single pure and perfect animal." Anyway, Browning projects no Tennysonian ideal for the future; indeed, in his view there is value in inequity, in both the giving and the taking of love. Once more, however, he suggests that the roles of strong and weak, supportive and dependent, are not necessarily identical with the sexual roles of male and female. Each poet in his own way, different though the ways are, is at pains to contradict the fairly conventional attitude of, say, a Coventry Patmore regarding the mastery of male over female (an attitude, one has to add, that Tennyson seems to accept in the later *Idylls*).

In fact, Browning makes a point in "The Glove," another monologue in the volume of 1845 (the speaker is Ronsard), of defending the beloved woman's right to make extreme demands on her wooer. Schiller and Leigh Hunt, in telling the story of a proud woman who throws her glove into the arena before a lion for her lover to retrieve, distinguish between selfish pride and true love. Browning deliberately disagrees: this imperious woman, who doubts the words of devotion she hears and requires proof by action instead, is apparently another "queen." In the end she has her "page," too, but he is not De Lorge, who retrieves her glove, then scorns her selfish vanity in setting such a task. A youth who has watched the scene follows her from the court—she is in disgrace—and at last marries her. Theirs, apparently, is a happier marriage than that of De Lorge, whose seemingly undemanding wife becomes briefly the king's mistress. Browning's moral, "What you'd get, first earn," does not quite fit, since De Lorge might be said to have earned the devotion of his first lady, although he resents her means of testing him. And the passage suggesting that his task was, after all, not very difficult is unconvincing, possibly because the verse is by no means Browning's most vigorous or most subtle. Indeed, it is difficult for the reader to follow, let alone sympathize with, the poet's reversal of Leigh Hunt's moral. In this version, the idea that beloved and lover are properly like a demanding queen and a servile page reminds one of the pattern of Tennyson's "Gareth and Lynette"—which is only an inversion of the more usual pattern in the *Idylls* of the dominant man and servile woman.

Men and Women: Marriage as Affinity and as Alienation

In September, 1846, Browning married. Less than four years later, influenced perhaps by both his pious mother's death and his wife's Protestant zeal, he published his first straightforward poem on religion, *Christmas-Eve and Easter-Day*. Then, in 1855, Browning published a work in two volumes that has always claimed the attention and admiration of readers, *Men and Women*. The title of the collection is significant. It suggests, not only that Browning is concerned with the great Victorian subject of people in society, but also that these poems deal mainly with the bonds between the sexes, with men *and* women. All of the poet's favorite subjects appear in these volumes: the arts of painting, music, and poetry in "Fra Lippo Lippi," "A Toccata of Galuppi's," "Master Hugues of Saxe-Gotha," and "How It Strikes a Contemporary"; religious faith in "An Epistle of Karshish," "Bishop Blougram's Apology," and "Cleon"; various forms of high aspiration in "Childe Roland to the Dark Tower Came" and "A Grammarian's Funeral." These matters are interrelated—they all figure, for instance, in "Saul"—and each is related as well to Browning's central subject of love, human and sexual, divine and cosmic. But the specific subject of love between men and women is the major one of this collection. Of the fifty-one pieces in the two volumes of *Men and Women*, more than half are about love and marriage.

"Love among the Ruins," the first poem in the collection, strikes a clear and apparently simple note with its last line, "Love is best!" But the spirited rejection by an imagined young lover of all ephemeral pride and worldly folly is not, in fact, simple. The poem's alternating three-syllable lines are like echoes, and the whole piece is an ironic echoing among the ruins of "centuries of folly, noise and sin." If the world's glory dies in time, so do lovers—and so can love itself, with its "blood that freezes, blood that burns." A number of Browning's other poems also reflect on both love and temporal mutability, only to emphasize this melancholy fact.

In his most nearly personal verse, the poet never suggests

the cooling or death of love. The central image in "My Star," which is usually considered a tribute to his wife, is sparkling but not inconstant. The evidently autobiographical "Guardian Angel" refers to Elizabeth Barrett Browning as "my angel" and suggests—so Betty Miller argues— the man's emotional dependence on his wife.[6] (Angel and poet, here, almost fit into the pattern of queen and page.)

Yet another personal poem in *Men and Women,* "By the Fire-Side," although it provides from imagination as well as memory an Italian setting for the married lovers' moment of perfect union, is essentially—that is, psychologically—autobiographical. In this poem about loving and growing old, which in a way resembles "Rabbi Ben Ezra," the two elements of love and time are in harmony. The relationship between the sexes is introduced early, in the sixth stanza, by a curious metaphor that refers to Italy as a

> woman-country, wooed not wed,
> Loved all the more by earth's male-lands,
> Laid to their hearts instead!   [III, 202]

But the speaker's beloved, "my perfect wife, my Leonor," has been both wooed and wed. The major theme of the poem, then, becomes not so much aging as marriage—the feeling at a crucial moment that two persons have indeed been wed, have been made one.

> At first, 't was something our two souls
> Should mix as mists do; each is sucked
> Into each now: on, the new stream rolls,
> Whatever rocks obstruct.   [III, 206]

This is unlike the gipsy's speech in "The Flight of the

6. *Robert Browning: A Portrait* (London, 1952), pp. 145–147.

Duchess" and the other passages in Browning about the relationship, in love, between dependency and dominance.

The sense of perfect unity seems to be qualified a few stanzas later: it does not, at least, come easily.

> Oh I must feel your brain prompt mine,
>   Your heart anticipate my heart,
> You must be just before, in fine,
>   See and make me see, for your part,
> New depths of the Divine!   [III, 206]

Still, the speaker is grateful that his beloved has not set up a bar to his love, has not, like De Lorge's skeptical lady in "The Glove," made him "strive and agonize / . . . For the hope of such a prize!" She has not had to test him, although she now can guide him. The belief, too, that there can indeed be inequality in love, as well as imperfection in marriage, is hinted at in these cryptic lines:

> If two lives join, there is oft a scar,
>   They are one and one, with a shadowy third;
> One near one is too far.   [III, 210]

Yet the final emphasis is on the momentary feeling of perfect union.

> A bar was broken between
> Life and life: we were mixed at last
> In spite of the mortal screen.   [III, 210]

The speaker says, "The forests . . . had mingled us so, for once and for good." He apparently means that this union will last until the end of the lovers' lives; he says, in effect, that their love triumphs, not over, but *in* time. There are certain curious elements, including the man's asking his Leonor—she is like the strong and faithful wife in Beethoven's *Fidelio*—to prompt and lead him. But one can argue that—like Tennyson's young prince wooing his Ida—the man who defers to his beloved so that the socially "feminine" characteristic of dependence is his and the supposedly "masculine" characteristic of leadership is hers counteracts the conventional inequality between the sexes to approximate that union of equals he has intuited, in a moment of insight, as the reality of marriage. In this poem, rather like the Tennyson who wants men to be in some ways more like women and women in some ways more like men, Browning implies as the ideal of marriage not necessarily an inversion of social roles—so that "Baron and Femme" becomes "queen and page"—but something like a natural unity of two persons.

In his most optimistic mood Browning even suggests that such love overcomes death, as the speaker in "Evelyn Hope" believes and as the poet himself virtually says in "Prospice," referring to his dead wife. These poems may both be seen as examples of Browning's interest in the Goethean doctrine of "elective affinities."

But Browning shows another aspect of love and life and evinces a less simply optimistic mood. In such sharp verses as "A Pretty Woman," about a coquette, and "A Light Woman," the monologue of a man who has taken his best friend's mistress in order to save the friend from her meretricious appeal, the lovers are badly mistaken about their affinities. In "A Lover's Quarrel" they may not be, but it is clear that disagreements over such matters as the virtues of Napoleon III and the validity of spiritualism (subjects on which, in fact, the Brownings disagreed) can lead to a rift—although the lover and speaker hopes at the end, as he thinks of his beloved, to "have her for evermore!"

One who has loved and lost, who has been rejected, or who has been mistaken about his affinity with the beloved, may still hope—or may nobly accept his or her loss. In "The Last Ride Together" the speaker begins by accepting his fate, his failure to win his lady's love, and only begs her once more to go riding with him; he ends by imagining that they may ride on forever, in "the instant made eternity." Whether he is inspired or mad—and at moments he sounds like Porphyria's lover, who wants to stop time in order to preserve his love—this speaker expresses the poet's own vitality and makes the rhythm of riding become the very rhythm of life, repetitive and constant, temporal and endless. The rhythm of riding may also suggest, at least to modern readers, a strong sexual quality in the poem.[7] But the monologue expresses a need to escape from the yoking of day-to-day time with love, because the lover's condition does not allow for such a harmonious relationship of the two as was intuited in "By the Fire-Side," a poem about one moment made eternal, outside time, yet also about a marriage within time, about growing old.

Many poems in *Men and Women* are concerned with the loss of affinity, the loss of love. In the little lyric "Misconceptions" a queen has misled, and presumably rejected, a would-be lover. "In a Balcony," as much a dramatic poem as a poetic drama, reverses this situation: the misconception is the Queen's, as she believes she is loved by Norbert, who

7. See, for example, Russell M. Goldfarb, "Sexual Meaning in 'The Last Ride Together,'" *Victorian Poetry*, III (1965), 255–261.

in fact is devoted to the Queen's cousin Constance. "In a Balcony" includes a number of familiar motifs and ideas. It begins with Norbert's "Now" and Constance's rejoinder, "Not now"; there is a contrast between the bold man's and the cautious woman's attitudes toward love and action, and a suggestion that the right point of view is the man's: love must be declared without delay or subterfuge, in order to redeem time, even if the result—as it is for the lovers of "In a Gondola"—is disaster and death. Norbert insists that love is best, better not only than glory but also than all the arts, and must avow itself. In fact, Constance's plan, which Norbert follows—he tells the Queen he loves her loyally and asks for her cousin in marriage because the cousin is so near the Queen that she "seem[s] a piece of her"—does lead to pain if not to disaster. The Queen misunderstands, takes Norbert's declaration as a mode of wooing *her,* and declares her love for him together with her intention to dissolve her own marriage and wed him. Constance, realizing the misunderstanding, gives herself completely at this moment—"now"—to her lover; yet she tries until nearly the end to keep the truth from the Queen, presumably to protect Norbert. At the ambiguous conclusion of this dramatic poem, the Queen has discovered the truth; guards approach the two embracing lovers in the balcony—perhaps, as the lovers and as critics have supposed, to arrest them (Norbert anticipates "some death"). Yet apparently Browning himself said casually that the guards come for the body of the Queen, who has died of grief.[8] If the ending is taken that way, the poet's final emphasis is as much on poignant

8. According to Katherine deKay Bronson, "Browning in Venice," *Century Magazine*, LXIII (1902), 578; cited by DeVane, p. 253.

misconception and the loss of love as it is on boldness and the intensity of love.

One-sided love is sometimes poignant in Browning, but he sometimes treats it almost humorously, as in "A Serenade at the Villa." But perhaps as painful, and even more relevant to the theme of marriage, is the cooling of love between two persons, married or not, who have been close. "Two in the Campagna," for example, contrasts with "By the Fire-Side" in that it longs for perfect unity but realizes that the wedding, the union, of its two lovers is imperfect.

> I would that you were all to me,
>   You that are just so much, no more.
> Nor yours nor mine nor slave nor free!
>   Where does the fault lie? what the core
> Of the wound, since wound must be?
>
> I would I could adopt your will,
>   See with your eyes, and set my heart
> Beating by yours, and drink my fill
>   At your soul's springs,—your part, my part
> In life, for good or ill.
>
> No. I yearn upward, touch you close,
>   Then stand away. I kiss your cheek,
> Catch your soul's warmth,—I pluck the rose
>   And love it more than tongue can speak—
> Then the good minute goes.
>
> Already how am I so far
>   Out of that minute?   [III, 219–220]

Often, in Browning's poems of this period, the perfect minute, the time when love and unity seemed complete, has passed.

In other poems from *Men and Women* it is clear that

Browning's specific subject is married love—its problems and, sometimes, its failure. Three sets of two poems explore this matter, first from the man's and then from the woman's point of view: "Love in a Life" and "Life in a Love"; "One Way of Love" and "Another Way of Love"; "In Three Days" and "In a Year."

"Love in a Life," with its speaker's imagery of hunting through "room after room" for his wife, suggests something of the isolation felt by the married couple in Meredith's *Modern Love*. But even if the husband seeks and fails to find, to understand and, in that sense, to hold his wife, she is nevertheless determined to hold him. "Life in a Love" begins,

> Escape me?
> Never—
> Beloved!
> While I am I, and you are you,
>   So long as the world contains us both,
>   Me the loving and you the loth,
> While the one eludes, must the other pursue.   [III, 234]

Who, then, really is the pursuer? The man thinks he is, but the word order in these lines cited may mean, if "the loving" is the one who eludes and "the loth" is, paradoxically, the one who pursues, by being elusive the woman holds onto her man. In any case, both have a sense of incompleteness in their relation, of a marriage that is still imperfect.

The next set of poems that deliberately contrast a man's with a woman's point of view toward love is "One Way of Love" and "Another Way of Love." DeVane comments that the speakers are man and wife, and they almost certainly are, although we can guess it only from her phrasing ("Well, Dear, in-doors with you!").[9] He sounds more like a frustrated wooer than a happy husband; she apparently thinks that he finds in her calm only the "serene deadness" of marriage. If so, and if he is dissatisfied, he can leave—so she seems to say.

The third set of poems is about, first, a physical separation, and then, a psychological one. The husband's speech anticipates a reunion with his wife in three days, and the happy anticipation is marred only slightly by a hint, a faint fear, that in these days of being apart and, more significant, in the years to come, love and good fortune may drastically change. Betty Miller suggests that this is a personal poem written by Browning while he was in Paris and separated from his wife.[10] At any rate, the companion piece, "In a Year," spoken by the woman, is about an imaginary development. A serious change has indeed occurred:

> Never any more,
>   While I live,
> Need I hope to see his face
>   As before.
> Once his love grown chill,
>   Mine may strive:
> Bitterly we re-embrace,
>   Single still.   [III, 237]

Her theme now is "love's decay"; again, time and love are at odds, and she can anticipate only death.

More astringent in its implications about modern marriage—marriage within which, once more as in Meredith,

9. P. 273.
10. P. 181.

the wife is intelligent and sensitive—is the dramatic monologue "Any Wife to Any Husband." The repetition of
"any" in the title is especially surprising, because this is a
wife's complaint, about not only her husband's coolness,
but also his infidelity. In a sense, it anticipates the subject
of *Fifine at the Fair*, although the point of view here is that
of the woman who is the victim of a double standard. The
bitterness in some of these lines is remarkable. The wife
(any wife!) reflects in almost acid language on her husband, her "strong" man; finally, and with biting irony, she
cites the tradition that man is the nobler and woman the
inferior creature, a tradition that was under attack in 1855
but that was being in some quarters reaffirmed:

> And yet thou art the nobler of us two:
> What dare I dream of, that thou canst not do,
>   Outstripping my ten small steps with one stride?
> I'll say then, here's a trial and a task—
> Is it to bear?—if easy, I'll not ask:
>   Though love fail, I can trust on in thy pride.
>
> Pride?—when those eyes forestal the life behind
> The death I have to go through!—when I find,
>   Now that I want thy help most, all of thee!
> What did I fear? Thy love shall hold me fast
> Until the little minute's sleep is past
>   And I wake saved.—And yet it will not be!   [III, 217]

The second stanza imagines a husband faithful after the
wife's death, and then, in the harsh last words, realizes that
this cannot be. (DeVane suggests that Browning is both reacting to his own father's new romantic attachment shortly
after his mother's death and anticipating his feelings about
his affair with Lady Ashburton after his own wife's death.)
The woman's knowledge that if her husband were to die

first she would be faithful to his memory adds special point to the ironic phrase in which she calls him the "nobler of us two."

In one way or another, each of these poems on love and alienation within marriage implies serious criticism of the institution. Passion dies; men are frustrated or unfaithful; women are trapped or are left alone and, like Tennyson's heroines, can only weep and wilt. From a strictly legalistic and moralistic (rather than moral) point of view, however —the point of view of a Coventry Patmore—Browning is more shocking in other poems; he seems to approve the ignoring or breaking of merely legal marriage bonds. In the verses ironically entitled "Respectability," the speaker contrasts his true and free love for his mistress, which would be condemned by society, with the false and hypocritical public display of feelings (specifically, in the French Academy), of which society approves.

More shocking—and the poem did shock some of Browning's contemporaries—was "The Statue and the Bust." This poem is one of the few in English—along of course with Shelley's "Ode to the West Wind"—to make successful use of terza rima. It seems a particularly appropriate form here, because Browning's story is about three persons; he pictures, not the Tennysonian triad of man, woman, and child, but the love triangle or, more accurately, the intertwined lives of husband, wife, and lover. There could hardly be a more striking contrast in moral attitudes than the one between this poem and the *Idylls of the King* (the first of the idylls was published four years after *Men and Women*), in which Tennyson condemns Guinevere for breaking her marriage vows as strongly as Browning condemns his lady for not breaking hers. Like Guinevere, Browning's lady, who has just been married, sees her true love for the first time, riding by. Like Lancelot, Duke Ferdinand also falls in love with the lady. Unlike Arthur, her husband perceives their love, and he sequesters his bride in order to keep her. He acts, that is, like several other tyrant-husbands in Browning, including the husband in "My Last Duchess" and Guido in *The Ring and the Book*. But the two lovers do not act, and this is a fault, for their inertia amounts to a moral flaw. The lady determines to escape to her would-be lover at once: "I save my soul—but not to-morrow." Then she procrastinates: she will wait one day. The Duke, too, vows to act at once but then reflects, "Yet my passion must wait a night." Failing to obey Norbert's imperative at the beginning of "In a Balcony"—"Now"—they go on waiting until the end of their lives and at last virtually become dead images of themselves; her bust in the window looks outward, and his statue in the square looks upward. (The window here suggests another comparison with Tennyson: like the Lady of Shalott, this lady looks out the window, but she fails to complete her action by leaving her prison— her chamber and her marriage.) Her youth and vitality die, until she seems finally as unearthly as Rossetti's blessed damozel.[11] The Duke's youth, too, dies and his "dream escapes."

11. One parenthetical passage virtually echoes Rossetti's "The Blessed Damozel," which was first published in 1850, about five years before this poem. These are Browning's lines:

(And, leaning out of a bright blue space,
As a ghost might lean from a chink of sky,
The passionate pale lady's face—

Eyeing ever with earnest eye
And quick-turned neck at its breathless stretch,
Some one who is ever passing by—) [III, 400]

They are at last condemned by the narrator in a passage of unorthodox moralizing: "They see not God, I know," because they failed to act on their own deepest and truest impulses. Browning is aware of how unorthodox his moral will seem, and he anticipates objections.

> I hear you reproach, "But delay was best,
> For their end was a crime."—Oh, a crime will do
> As well, I reply, to serve for a test,
>
> As a virtue golden through and through,
> Sufficient to vindicate itself
> And prove its worth at a moment's view!   [III, 401]

It is hard to take these lines as anything but ironic, although a good many of Browning's readers have managed to do so. Would the poet say that a man who deeply desired to murder someone and postponed the act until his chance was gone had lost his soul and forfeited heaven because he failed to carry out that act? A crime may serve for a test in this instance only if the poet means what respectable society calls a crime, not if he means a genuinely evil act. The shift to a generalized moral at the end—"Let a man contend to the uttermost / For his life's set prize, be what it will!"—only thinly camouflages the fairly clear fact that the ethical point of view expressed in this poem not only condones but actually insists on the goodness of free love and the necessity of breaking false or mistaken marriage vows. (If this were not so—to look ahead to a later and major work—Guido in *The Ring and the Book* should be praised for acting on his impulse and having his wife killed.)

Rossetti's poem, which begins, "The blessed damozel leaned out / From the gold bar of Heaven," has a number of such extended passages enclosed in parentheses.

Browning appears to hedge his moral position in the last stanzas of "The Statue and the Bust," appealing to "you of the virtue" to strive, to act, as those moved by a lawless love in this tale did not act. In the very hedging there is irony.

> The counter our lovers staked was lost
> As surely as if it were lawful coin:
> And the sin I impute to each frustrate ghost
>
> Is—the unlit lamp and the ungirt loin,
> Though the end in sight was a vice, I say.
> You of the virtue (we issue join)
> How strive you? *De te, fabula!*   [III, 402]

Everything else in the poem has made it clear that the frustration of love—not of just any desire—is deadly and evil and that the unlawful pursuit of love is not truly a vice, as the shocked and self-righteous "virtuous" ones in the reading public will suppose.

Critics have commented on the tension in Browning's poetry between an urgent concern for untrammeled expression of love and aspiration on the one hand and, on the other, an awareness of demands for conformity made by religion and by society. E. D. H. Johnson, for one, finds in the tension another instance of the Victorian poet's "alien vision."[12] But, very much a man of his age, Browning tends

12. "Browning's conviction that the passionate intensity of romantic love is incompatible with conventionalized social morality leads him to glorify one at the expense of the other. . . . The decision to give all for love more often than not involves some course of action at variance with established codes of conduct" (*The Alien Vision of Victorian Poetry* [Princeton, 1952], p. 103). For a suggestive discussion of Browning's anti-"Victorian" views on the relations of the sexes (men are more intellectual, women more emo-

ironically to modify (as in "The Statue and the Bust"),
dramatize (as in "Fra Lippo Lippi"), and give distance and
objectivity (as in *The Ring and the Book*) to attitudes toward such matters as marriage and the relations of the sexes
when they might be offensive.

The modern reader is likely to suspect another sort of
refraction and modification in "Women and Roses," a poem
that DeVane says is "not at all in Browning's usual manner . . . [but] stands by itself in his verse."[13] In fact, the
imagery and phrasing of the poem strongly suggest Tennyson's dreamlike lyrics about fruits and flowers, especially
those about roses. As in Tennyson, the rose represents feminine beauty.

> I dream of a red-rose tree.
> And which of its roses three
> Is the dearest rose to me?

The three roses are the ideal woman of the past, the real
woman of the present, and the yet unborn woman of the
future. The first exists in memory.

> Dear rose, thy term is reached,
> Thy leaf hangs loose and bleached:
> Bees pass it unimpeached.

The second is alive. She is described in language that seems
especially sexual.

---

tional, but emotional impulse may come closest to final truth), see
pp. 100-109, which touch on some of the poems discussed here and
also on others, such as "Mesmerism" and "A Woman's Last Word."

13. P. 259. It may remind the reader of Blake's "My Pretty Rose-
Tree," with its distinct and intended sexual meaning.

> Dear rose, thy joy's undimmed;
> Thy cup is ruby-rimmed,
> Thy cup's heart nectar-brimmed.

The third, a rosebud, may be the baby before birth.

> Dear rose without a thorn,
> Thy bud's the babe unborn:
> First streak of a new morn.   [III, 240–241]

The feminine image of the rose is not so characteristic of Browning as it is of Tennyson, although it occurs and has some erotic implications in other poems by Browning, including "One Way of Love" and "Another Way of Love." The traditional use of the imagery to suggest feminine sexuality, however, at least as old as the *Roman de la Rose,* tends to reinforce the sexual meaning that the reader may well associate with the flower—and the tree. These lines, then, link symbolic eroticism with generation, the future, the continuity of life—and finally, once more, with artistic creation: "I will make an Eve, be the artist that began her, / Shaped her to his mind!" (III, 241).

The idea of the artist-lover who reshapes his beloved seems almost to be inverted in "Andrea del Sarto." Yet in this poem, too, we can imagine that Andrea has partly created his wife's personality and situation. In doing so, he has revealed a degree of uncertainty (though not perhaps quite the male passivity of a Swinburne character), a sense of limitation, together with the expressive power and the soaring aspiration that we generally expect in Browning's artists. Andrea will do his work "to-morrow," not now; he denies his own freedom to act ("we are in God's hand . . . fettered fast") (IV, 118); and he looks to heaven for fulfillment instead of seeking it here on earth.

The well-known passage at the end of the poem sums up his ideas and specifically expresses both his strength of intention as an artist and his sense of frustration as an artist-husband.

> In heaven, perhaps, new chances, one more chance—
> Four great walls in the New Jerusalem
> Meted on each side by the angel's reed,
> For Leonard, Rafael, Agnolo and me
> To cover—the three first without a wife,
> While I have mine! So-still they overcome
> Because there's still Lucrezia,—as I choose.
>
> [IV, 260–266]

Earlier Andrea asked Lucrezia to stay with him, her hand in his hand, "both of one mind, as married people use" (IV, 117). But they are hardly of one mind, any more than are the married couples in the other poems of this volume that dramatize alienation. (The hint here, not only of alienation but of the wife's—not the husband's—infidelity, may have seemed to some of Browning's readers the most shocking thing yet.)

One need not go as far as Betty Miller in finding "Andrea del Sarto" a reflection of the poet's domination by his own wife (to the detriment of his art) in order to recognize again a theme that is central to *Men and Women* and an important subject now for Browning: how actual marriage, in contrast to the ideal of a perfect union in love, can be a source of discontent.[14] The poem does not, however, quite suggest the same social criticism that is explicitly in Mill's arguments for divorce and perhaps implied in Tennyson's

---

14. Betty Miller, pp. 175–176. She clearly implies but does not spell out the point.

verse about mammon-marriage. It it not the legal bond alone that brings about frustration in *Men and Women;* rather, as in Meredith's *Modern Love,* the fault is in the men and women themselves. Even though he feels fettered, fated, Andrea says at last that he chooses to have Lucrezia as his wife. And if it seems clear that some of Andrea's attitudes are less than admirable, that they are in effect rationalizations, still the last rationalization is given a dramatic basis. There may be, between the artist and his wife, an affinity that is inevitable. His personality has led him to choose and partly to create a dominating wife, and the result appears to have been a further weakening of his personality, of himself as man and artist. In any event, though she may be an unworthy wife, one can see in this marriage once more the pattern of page and queen.

Andrea contrasts with Browning's aspiring and successful artists: with Jules in *Pippa Passes,* who is a Pygmalion to his wife, and with Fra Lippo Lippi, who of course has no wife. But he also contrasts with other husbands—those in "My Last Duchess," "The Statue and the Bust," and perhaps even *The Ring and the Book.* Obviously, Andrea seems morally preferable to the Duke who has dominated and at last destroyed his "last Duchess." Yet the Duke displays the force and mastery that Andrea, in relation to his wife, largely lacks. One is too coldly self-sufficient, the other too much aware of limitations; both are unsuccessful husbands. In "Andrea del Sarto," however, the main concern is not with a woman cruelly trapped and broken by the marriage bond but with a man who has freely chosen marriage and, in spite of everything, confirms the choice.

We have observed that Browning's early poems on love and marriage, from *Pippa* through the 1845 *Dramatic Ro-*

mances and Lyrics, tend to emphasize the idea of a freely
accepted and mutually rewarding relationship between the
dominant and the dominated in a marriage (with the person
of either sex playing either role), as well as the perversion
of that ideal into a heartless relationship between owner and
object in a false and merely legal marriage. The poems of
Men and Women, however, tend to emphasize the ideal of
unity, not only the balance of roles but also the ecstatic if
momentary sense of oneness in marriage, along with the actual and melancholy experience of alienation, not one-sided
coldness and cruelty, in a marriage. To some extent, there
is a shift from social or legal situations to psychological
ones. Even in "The Statue and the Bust," the jealousy and
repressiveness of a husband is much less important than the
timidity, the inaction, of a wife and an, after all, extremely
powerful lover who is hardly the victim of his society. This
is not by any means a complete or simple shift in subject
matter and emphasis; but Browning's conception of marriage as an idea and as a social and psychological reality appears to have become—after his own marriage—a good deal
more complex.

Again, one serious difficulty arises because most of
Browning's poetry (including that of *Men and Women*)
takes dramatic form. We certainly cannot say that the innocent Pippa or even the wise gipsy in "The Flight of the
Duchess" speaks the full truth as conceived by Robert
Browning. The attitude expressed in "The Glove" is supposedly that of the poet Ronsard. And the three pairs of
monologues on marriage, by wives and husbands, are evidently fictive. It could be argued, indeed, that such psychological portraits as "My Last Duchess" and "Andrea del
Sarto" are "objective" in that they express without judging

the personalities of two men. The tendency to judge the Duke at Ferrara as a heartless collector of art and people instead of a true artist and lover, and Andrea as a too passive and procrastinating artist and husband, may result in part from a knowledge of other poems, of the whole tendency in Browning's work to glorify creativity, love, and action. And the judgments are partly suggested but also partly qualified by the texture of the poetry itself, as we must constantly remind ourselves in considering themes in imaginative literature. The speaker in "My Last Duchess," for example, is hardly to be admired on strictly moral grounds, but the polished ease of his language (during most of the monologue) and, above all, the rhythmic vitality of his speech communicate the vividness of character that marks some of Browning's worst rogues and villains, from the monk in the "Soliloquy of the Spanish Cloister" to Ned Bratts. In this respect, Browning is the most fascinating of poets. He has been called a moral guide, a prophet, a teacher; the verb *preach* has been used in this chapter. He has also been called the poet of dramatic objectivity and considered something of a precursor for modern and supposedly relativist writers who define, not truth or fact, but point of view. Each of these extreme opinions can be supported: in the dramatic poetry there are elements of both moral commitment and detached observation of the psychology of individuals.[15] Sometimes, however, Robert

15. In his chapter "*The Ring and the Book:* A Relativist Poem," Robert Langbaum emphasizes the psychological and artistic "relativism" of Browning's poetry, and specifically of his masterpiece. "Yet the judgments . . . are by no means 'relative'—if we mean by the word that no one is either good or bad but a bit of both." Rather, the poem "is relativist in that social and religious absolutes are not the means for understanding the right and wrong.

Browning emerges from the role of ventriloquist—and psychologist—and speaks in as nearly a direct and personal way as any lyric or didactic poet can. This occurs in the final poem of *Men and Women*, "One Word More."

In this epilogue to the fifty poems about men and women, and largely about husbands and wives, the poet addresses his wife. In doing so, he brings together several subjects that the other poems have dealt with: explicitly, the relation of art, painting as well as poetry, to love; implicitly, the nature of love within marriage. Again as in the other personal poems, his tone is completely unironic; his wife is the poet's Beatrice and, in the imagery at the end, his moon. So this collection, which includes many dramatic examples of gradual frustration and failure in marriages, ends as it began, in "Love among the Ruins," on the clear and simple note of ideal love. When the poet says, "Let me speak this once in my true person, / Not as Lippo, Roland or Andrea," the critic may assert that in fact he speaks his complex mind and feelings more fully in the dramatic than in the direct form. But both aspects are there. Deeply concerned about the bond between the sexes, Browning both celebrates the ideal of marriage and imagines the frequently imperfect, even painful, reality.

Dramatis Personae: Marriage as Failure

In 1861, Elizabeth Browning died. The first volume of poetry Robert Browning published afterward was *Dramatis Personae*, which appeared in 1864. The first poem in the

---

. . . They are for the most part barriers to understanding." The point is that "we must judge what is being said by who is saying it" (*The Poetry of Experience* [New York, 1957], pp. 110, 113, 115).

volume is "James Lee's Wife" (the original title was simply "James Lee," but it was changed in the 1868 collected works), a series of soliloquies spoken by an English wife living with her husband on the coast of Brittany. The opening section was originally entitled "At the Window"; the title was changed in the second edition (also 1864) to "James Lee's Wife Speaks at the Window." The poem begins,

> Ah, Love, but a day,
> > And the world has changed!
> The sun's away,
> > And the bird's estranged;
> The wind has dropped,
> > And the sky's deranged:
> Summer has stopped.   [IV, 215]

The rhymes in this first part of the first section predict the movement of the poem: *changed* and *estranged*, then *deranged*. The wife asks her husband, "Wilt thou change too?" She and he do gradually become estranged. And the final derangement, so to speak—not madness but a deep emotional disturbance—is suffered by the woman who speaks in these soliloquies. (The first four sections may possibly be monologues, that is, speeches addressed to a listener, to James Lee; but DeVane, comparing the whole poem to *Maud*, calls it a monodrama and thus suggests that it is soliloquy. In any case, the sixth through ninth sections are almost certainly examples of thinking aloud rather than of speaking to someone, so that the movement from marriage dialogue to isolation would be emphasized if one were to argue that the first parts *are* dramatic monologues.)

In the second section, "By the Fireside," the imagery is

that of "shipwreck wood": the James Lees are not quite
shipwrecked, but the fabric of their ship of marriage—on
"Love's voyage"—is now rotting. "In the Doorway," the
third section, repeats the rhyme words *change* and *estrange;*
a sense of a wintry coldness in the couple's love deepens
the uneasy drift toward alienation and spiritual divorce
which constitutes the movement of this whole poem.

The suggestion that this movement results from the
"lightness" of the husband, which makes the faithful wife
its victim, becomes explicit in the next part, "Along the
Beach":

> How the light, light love, he has wings to fly
>   At suspicion of a bond:
> My wisdom has bidden your pleasure good-bye,
> Which will turn up next in a laughing eye,
>   And why should you look beyond?   [IV, 220]

The settings in these vignettes—the changing weather,
the firewood, the swallow, the beach, the cliff and rocks
and sea—correspond to the wife's feeling of increasing loss,
alienation, and melancholy. Even the poem she reads in
"Under the Cliff" (later retitled "Reading a Book under the
Cliff"), which begins, "Still ailing, Wind?" becomes a subject for reflections that are really reflections on a dying
marriage; this part is especially interesting because in it the
woman is reacting to the young poet's, the young Browning's, own attitude:[16]

> Rejoice that man is hurled
> From change to change unceasingly.
> His soul's wings never furled!
>   . . . . .

16. The poem quoted is by Robert Browning himself and was
published twenty-eight years earlier.

> Nothing endures: the wind moans, saying so;
> We moan in acquiescence: there's life's pact,
>   Perhaps probation—
>
>   . . . . .
>
> Only, for man, how bitter not to grave
>   On his soul's hands' palms, one fair, good, wise thing
> Just as he grasped it! For himself, death's wave;
>   While time first washes—ah, the sting!—
> O'er all he'd sink to save.   [IV, 224]

The first half-dozen lines quoted here give what we think of as Browning's "philosophy"; the final lines are a woman's answer to it, to the idea that a man's reach should exceed his grasp. They also bring into question the belief expressed in "By the Fire-Side" that a momentary sense of communion, of grasping love fully, can establish a bond that lasts a lifetime. For James Lee's wife, as for the sad women who speak in the series of poems on marriage in *Men and Women*, time and love are not at all in harmony.

"James Lee's Wife" includes some passages that are clearly characteristic of Browning's thought and interests: the conclusion of "Among the Rocks"—"If you loved only what were worth your love, / Love were clear gain . . . / Make the low nature better by your throes!" (IV, 225)— and the comments in "Beside the Drawing-Board" about the artist who could not succeed in capturing with his pencil the beauty of his beloved's hand:

> And on the finger which outvied
>   His art he placed the ring that's there,
> Still by fancy's eye descried,
>   In token of a marriage rare:
>   For him on earth, his art's despair,
> For him in heaven, his soul's fit bride.   [IV, 226]

But even these passages are ironically undercut by the context. The speaker cannot, finally, live with the husband who may not be worth her love, and she can hardly anticipate being a bride in heaven when she says in the last section ("On Deck"), "I leave you, set you free" (IV, 228). Her "love that was life, life that was love" (IV, 229) has ended in separation, as, perhaps, "modern love" must, from the sensitive woman's point of view. DeVane suggests that Meredith's sequence of poems on marriage, which Browning admired, is about precisely "the same kind of tragic event" as this.

Since there are, however, in Browning's earlier work—especially in *Men and Women*—a number of poems concerned with just this subject, the slow breaking-up of a marriage and the woman's suffering, it is in relation to them, and to the poet's other passages and verses on married love, that "James Lee's Wife" seems most interesting. For here it appears that two aspects of Browning's art, and two aspects of his mind as well, are being revealed: his tendency toward ventriloquism, toward expressing through his characters his own ideas about art and life (both should reach beyond what can be grasped or what succeeds in the world) and his contrasting and complementary tendency to enter into the minds and emotions of various personalities, to be, as it were, objective. The poem shows his idea of the necessity for continual striving and his imaginative understanding of how a striving, changing, always inconstant life destroys in time such values as married love.

The specific causes for the failure of James Lee's marriage are not given in the poem, except the cooling of the husband's ardor.[17] But if he is supposed to be at all like the

17. Browning said simply that the man was "tired" (*Robert*

young poet, the young Browning himself, to whom the wife mentally replies (in "Under the Cliff"), with his "pride / Of power to see" (IV, 222), James Lee's growing weary of the married state may be only one aspect of his restless nature. And it is clear that the married woman cannot be happily striving, changing, and free, as Browning's often stronger men can be.

"Dîs Aliter Visum" ("To the Gods It Seemed Otherwise") is another poem about the failure of love, and its scene is, again, the coast of France. Again, too, the speaker is a woman. But she reflects on not one but two failed marriages—her own and her would-be lover's—and on the failure of a love (and a marriage) that might have been. Like a feminine version of Arnold's speaker in the last of the poems to Marguerite, she addresses the one who might have wooed and have won her, and she speaks with scorn of his failure to act ten years earlier. In this poem, however, the man who has failed to act on his deepest impulse is a poet—and a successful one—while the spokesman for Browning's "philosophy" is the woman he did not wed. She realizes that everything human, including the love and marriage of human beings, is imperfect; the man she speaks to is older than she, and when they met she was an inexperienced girl. But, she asks,

> Was there nought better than to enjoy?
>
> . . . .
>
> No wise beginning, here and now,
>   What cannot grow complete (earth's feat)
> And Heaven must finish, there and then?

Browning and Julia Wedgwood, ed. Richard Curle [New York, 1937], p. 109).

> No tasting earth's true food for men,
> Its sweet in sad, its sad in sweet?
>
> No grasping at love, gaining a share
>   O' the sole spark from God's life at strife
> With death, so, sure of range above
>   The limits here? For us and love,
> Failure; but, when God fails, despair.   [IV, 246–247]

The failure of men and women to love means the failure of God to be effective in the world. No man or woman is a perfect whole, in body and spirit, "but what's whole, can increase no more, / Is dwarfed and dies, since here's its sphere" (IV, 247).

All this is familiar Browning doctrine, and it perhaps accords with the doctrine of elective affinities. It does not provide an answer to the suffering here and now of James Lee's wife. Nor do the other poems in *Dramatis Personae* that have to do with broken or failed marriages and love not seized in time: "The Worst of It," "Too Late," "Youth and Art," and (perhaps) "Confessions." "The Worst of It" is either a soliloquy or a monologue spoken by a husband to his unfaithful wife. If it is taken to be a monologue, an actual speech addressed to the wife, it becomes reminiscent, not only of *Modern Love*, but also of Arthur's last words to Guinevere in the *Idylls of the King*. In either case, this poem is concerned with the ubiquitous Victorian subject of the fallen woman, familiar not only in such works as Augustus Egg's narrative triptych *Past and Present*, a triad of paintings that show the disgrace of a faithless wife, but in more or less serious work as well, from D. G. Rossetti's unfinished picture *Found* to Wilde's play *Lady Winder-*

mere's Fan. The traditional "Fall of Man" appears to have been transformed, for many Victorians, into the "fall of woman." Her story is made more poignant by the madonna-harlot syndrome that conceives of woman as essentially an angelic creature. The story is based in large part on grim social and economic reality—the reality of the factory girl virtually forced into prostitution but also of the woman forced into a loveless mammon-marriage. It is difficult to know just how the speaker in Browning's poem is to be judged, as a suffering lover, a self-righteous prig, or a decent deceived husband—a sort of George Meredith—or as none or all of these. But one detects irony on Browning's part when the man says he could forgive the erring wife, "but what will God say?" and when he concludes, "In Paradise, / If we meet, I will pass nor turn my face"—especially if one keeps in mind the moral of "The Statue and the Bust."

"Too Late" and the rather lighter "Youth and Art" and "Confessions" again dramatize the sad failure of would-be lovers to act, to elope and marry. Once more, it seems striking that the treatment of love and marriage in this volume, as in *Men and Women,* is consistently pessimistic. Lovers fail to marry, and marriages fail to last.

The Ring and the Book: Marriage as Crime

Browning's masterpiece was first published in 1868–1869. *The Ring and the Book* combines, in one poem of twelve books totaling over twenty-one thousand lines, all of the main preoccupations of the mature poet. It is about the truth of art, the various and relative points of view from which people see reality, and the necessity in life for courageous, even impulsive, action. It is also very much about love and marriage.

Although he had found the "Old Yellow Book" in a bookstall in Florence some time before his wife's final illness and death in 1861, Browning did not begin to write his poem on the subject of that document—the late-seventeenth-century trial of a nobleman who killed his wife—until 1864. Still, the memory of Mrs. Browning may be said almost to haunt this novel in verse, as Henry James called it, this story of a pure woman trapped in an unhappy home, of her escape to temporary freedom, and of her dying. Book I, called simply "The Ring and the Book," includes the celebrated and sometimes criticized image of the ring, the work of art, or poem, which is an alloy of the poet's imaginings and the pure gold of factual truth.

> Such labour had such issue, so I wrought
> This arc, by furtherance of such alloy,
> And so, by one spirit, take away its trace
> Till, justifiably golden, rounds my ring.
>
> A ring without a posy, and that ring mine?   [V, 44–45]

The "posy" is the final evocation of the poet's dead wife, "lyric Love, half-angel and half-bird / And all a wonder and a wild desire."[18]

18. The dedication underlines what commentators have often observed about a parallel between the story Browning tells here and his own elopement. "While there is little overt resemblance between Pompilia and Elizabeth Barrett . . . it is likely that Pompilia is in some ways a much idealized version of Browning's dead wife, or, perhaps more accurately, a substitute figure. The terms of the invocation . . . forge a strong implicit link between the women whom Caponsacchi and Robert Browning had rescued respectively from the marital prison at Arezzo and the invalid's

Book I apparently presents the poet speaking in his own person, as do the epilogue to *Men and Women* and the prologues and epilogues in a number of later long poems. This section not only outlines the story of a young wife's escape from her harsh husband to her foster parents, with the aid of a chivalrous canon; it also makes clear the poet's ultimate judgments, in the imagery that describes Pompilia as a pure white soul, Guido Franceschini as an evil star, his kin and followers as a fox, a cat, a monkey, and werewolves, and Caponsacchi as a St. George. Although Browning enters imaginatively into the personalities of his various speakers in the ten central monologues of the work, there is no real doubt, from almost the beginning, about the moral truth: Pompilia is essentially an innocent girl and finally a saint, Guido a rapacious monster, and Caponsacchi a soldier of God.

Therefore, in Book II, "Half-Rome," we judge the moral insight—or lack of it—revealed by the speaker in relation to the impression of the characters that has been established. The first dramatic speaker is sympathetic to Guido, and his imagery is strikingly different from the poet's in Book I. Now Pompilia is a minnow, a piece of bait that has been set by her foster mother, Violante, to catch an aristocratic husband, and Violante and Pietro are called cat and dog; women in general are a "beast-fellowship"; later Pompilia is

---

couch in Wimpole Street" (Richard D. Altick and James F. Loucks II, *Browning's Roman Murder Story* [Chicago, 1968], pp. 19–20). Altick and Loucks also comment interestingly on "marriage and the church" in *The Ring and the Book*, emphasizing the parallel between a marriage contract and religious vows but showing as well how Guido and his defenders can distort this parallel as they jumble and misuse biblical passages for precedents to argue that wives should be totally submissive to husbands (pp. 208–212).

a snake and her canon, Caponsacchi, a fox. From the first speaker's point of view, Guido's only fault as a husband is his not having been stricter earlier; his having Pompilia and the aged couple murdered is justified as serving a social purpose.

> The better for you and me and all the world,
> Husbands of wives, especially in Rome.
> The thing is put right, in the old place,—ay,
> The rod hangs on its nail behind the door,
> Fresh from the brine: a matter I commend
> To the notice, during Carnival that's near,
> Of a certain what's-his-name and jackanapes
> Somewhat too civil of eves with lute and song
> About a house here, where I keep a wife.
> (You, being his cousin, may go tell him so.)   [V, 91–92]

It is evident that the attitude of "Half-Rome" results directly from his being a jealous husband.

The speaker in Book III, "The Other Half-Rome," is unmarried; his view of matters is very different from that of the speaker in "Half-Rome" and is consistent with the attitude implicit in Book I and finally to be made explicit. But the emphasis of this tender-hearted bachelor is on Pompilia's youth and beauty as much as on her innocence and Guido's malice. And he is inclined toward sentimentalism, as even his use of varied and lively images suggests: he frequently refers to Pompilia as a flower, a rose or lily, a lamb, or a fruitful tree, in the most interesting imagery of all—while Guido is a rat, a fox, a wolf. This speaker is as idealistic about marriage as the one preceding him is cynical. But he sees in Guido and Pompilia's marriage a perversion and parody of true wedlock.

Imagining the marriage of Pietro and Violante (on the basis of very little evidence, as we come to see), he says of the idealized couple, not too young or old, too poor or rich, that they were, seventeen years earlier,

> All at the mean where joy's components mix.
> So, again, in the couple's very souls
> You saw the adequate half with half to match,
> Each having and each lacking somewhat, both
> Making a whole that had all and lacked nought.
> The round and sound, in whose composure just
> The acquiescent and recipient side
> Was Pietro's and the stirring striving one
> Violante's: both in union gave the due
> Quietude, enterprise, craving and content,
> Which go to bodily health and peace of mind. [V, 96–97]

The language, apparently echoing the metaphor of Aristophanes in the *Symposium*, also reminds one again of Tennyson's prescription for ideal marriage near the end of *The Princess*. But it is significant that this language is used by a man who is not himself married to describe a couple about whom he really knows very little, a couple in whose marriage there has, in fact, been deceit and trouble. Even he realizes that the unfallen Adam and Eve he has conjured up must be, if they are real, imperfect, and that what appears to be their Eden must prove to be less than a paradise.

When, he says, they decided to add to their lives the one element missing, a child, they let corruption in:

> Out of the very ripeness of life's core
> A worm was bred—"Our life shall leave no fruit."

. . . . .

> " 'Tis in a child, man and wife grow complete,
> "One flesh: God says so: let him do his work!"
>
>   [V, 145, 154]

Eve-Violante falls, and, through her, Adam-Pietro also falls,
by adopting a child and pretending that it is their own.

> Well, having gained Pompilia, the girl grew
> I' the midst of Pietro here, Violante there,
> Each, like a semicircle with stretched arms
> Joining the other round her preciousness—
> Two walls that go about a garden-plot
> Where a chance sliver, branchlet slipt from bole
> Of some tongue-leaved eye-figured Eden tree,
> Filched by two exiles and borne far away,
> Patiently glorifies their solitude.   [V, 99–100]

Into this Eden-in-exile, where Pompilia is both the precious
tree that is the occasion for a fall (perhaps hers is forbidden fruit) and the treasured tree to be guarded, as in the
story of the Hesperides, comes Lucifer-Guido. He per-
suades Violante to allow him secretly to marry Pompilia,
and she tells Pietro that, tempted, she fell. Now Eden is lost
indeed. And its polar opposite is a quagmire, the mire of
this new, this secret and doomed marriage. In the latter part
of this book, Pompilia is spoken of as a trapped bird, and
the Franceschini household is repeatedly alluded to in imagery of enclosure, darkness, the stifling prison that is like
a tomb. When she at last escapes that household with the
aid of Caponsacchi, she is a bird uncaged, a creature freed.
Finally, the innocent and lovely creature is destroyed by
the wolves and her diabolic husband.

"The Other Half-Rome" has moved from an early idealistic conception of the Eden-like marriage of Pietro and

Violante to an idea of the doomed and deadly marriage of the contrasting Guido, worldly and cruel, and Pompilia, naïve and innocent. The first part of the monologue is filled with the imagery and rhetoric of balance and unity, of half and half made whole, of roundness; the latter part is entirely about division, divorce, the opposites of wolf and lamb, white and black, devious husband and pure wife.

Book IV, "Tertium Quid," might seem to be a speech that mediates between the extremes of "Half-Rome" and "The Other Half-Rome." Its urbane speaker wants to weigh the evidence and reach a balanced judgment—or to give the impression of doing so. Yet the sense of this section is more that of a judicious compromise than that of a judicial conclusion. The imagery used here is drawn partly from "Half-Rome" and partly from "The Other Half-Rome." Pompilia may be a flower, but, if so, she is a "rose above the dungheap," and Violante and Pietro are "selfish beasts" who have used her, again, as bait upon their hook. As for Guido, he may or may not be such a villain as some say. "Tertium Quid" objects, in fact, to the moral and rhetorical extremes of partisans on both sides of this debate; Guido's may well go too far, and perhaps he should be punished—though probably not with death and certainty not with torture—while Pompilia's champions "must have her purity itself, / Quite angel—and her parents angels too," and must have Guido a "monster," when in fact "he's a mere man," "is noble, and he may be innocent." The key phrase finally is "on the other hand," and this speaker seems at last to be more interested in compromise than in clear-cut justice.

The first monologue of the husband, which has his full title as *its* title, "Count Guido Franceschini" (Book V), shows him as he presents himself, formally and cleverly, to the world. He represents himself as a docile creature, a fish who has been hooked—once more that image—and the victim of Pietro's and Violante's "dog-like" greed. But he also speaks of Pompilia as a mere piece of property, a bird he has bought and owns, in a way that recalls the noblemen in "My Last Duchess" and "The Flight of the Duchess." And his comment on marriage to the ecclesiastical court is especially revealing:

> Am I to teach my lords what marriage means,
> What God ordains thereby and man fulfils
> Who, docile to the dictate, treads the house?
> My lords have chosen the happier part with Paul
> And neither marry nor burn,—yet priestliness
> Can find a parallel to the marriage-bond
> In its own blessed special ordinance
> Whereof indeed was marriage made the type:
> The church may show her insubordinate,
> As marriage her refractory.   [V, 215]

The argument is that a husband is like a superior in the hierarchy of the church, whom a plain monk, like a mere woman, must obey. Guido's appeal to church officials is cleverly calculated, and very near the end of it he sketches an ideal state of things:

> Husbands once more God's representative,
> Wives like the typical Spouse once more, and Priests
> No longer men of Belial, with no aim
> At leading silly women captive, but
> Of rising to such duties as yours now.   [V, 255]

Guido's conception of marriage smacks a little of late Tennyson and a good deal of Coventry Patmore.

The speaker in the Book VI, "Giuseppe Caponsacchi," is just such a member of the clergy as Guido cites—and *he* is also appealing to the ecclesiastical court. His is the voice of the convert, of a man who has been converted from worldliness to faith and courage by a woman's purity—converted to a manhood that is identical with true priesthood. In Caponsacchi's monologue there is once more an extensive and varied, almost a jumbled, use of animal imagery. Pompilia is a pure white dove and a version of the Madonna, Pietro and Violante are mice in a cat's cage, and Guido is like a bear, a hawk, a scorpion.[19]

Perhaps the most interesting book of all is Book VII, Pompilia's own monologue. It begins with affecting simplicity: "I am just seventeen years and five months old" (VI, 3). Although this simple girl may now and then

19. W. David Shaw argues that the whole poem is a conversion of raw fact into myth and that "the hero of this myth is the Messianic deliverer, Caponsacchi, whose crusade to right the wrong choice made by the first Eve [Violante] issues in his rescue of the second Eve, Pompilia, his victory over the Edenic serpent, Guido, and his redemption of what is at once a society and a bride" (*The Dialectical Temper: The Rhetorical Art of Robert Browning* [Ithaca, 1968], p. 285). One has to add that the bride is not Caponsacchi's, however, and that Pompilia's own view of marriage is that it can be truly realized only in heaven, not in human society. Shaw also suggests, along with some earlier commentators, that "of all the speakers, Caponsacchi [instead of the Pope] comes closest to being Browning's surrogate"; and he sees a relationship between Browning's "adoration" of his wife and Caponsacchi's of Pompilia, fusing "renunciation and possession . . . into one attitude" (p. 285). In contrast, Altick and Loucks cannot accept a Messianic Caponsacchi; to be sure, he represents in part the "church militant," but he is still, in his burning anger, and in spite of the great change made in his life by his response to the saintly Pompilia, a proud man and a "fallible human" (*Browning's Roman Murder Story*, p. 56).

sound like Robert Browning speaking on his favorite
themes, the self-portrait is on the whole remarkably moving
and real. The result is that the girl's comments on love and
marriage seem to have some of that apparent naïveté and
actual wisdom that we attribute to Pippa. Unlike Pippa,
however, Pompilia has been deeply disillusioned on these
matters.

> Everyone says that husbands love their wives,
> Guard them and guide them, give them happiness;
> 'Tis duty, law, pleasure, religion, well,
> You see how much of this comes true in mine!   [VI, 7]

The imagery of flowers, of animals, and of traps occurs
here again, echoing and emphasizing concepts of earlier
passages in other sections.

But Pompilia's specific comments on marriage are startling. She declares that the archbishop who enjoined her, in
an interesting sexual metaphor, to "swallow the burning
coal [your husband] offers you" (VI, 24) gave her wrong
advice. She had longed to enter a convent and be chaste,
and now in retrospect her longing seems to have been for a
fate that would have been better. Speaking of sexual relations in marriage, the best Pompilia can say of Guido is that
at least he was not hypocritical.

> He never did by speech or act imply
> "Because of our souls' yearning that we meet
> And mix in soul through flesh, which yours and mine
> Wear and impress, and make their visible selves,
> —All which means, for the love of you and me,
> Let us become one flesh, being one soul!"
> He only stipulated for the wealth;
> Honest so far. But when he spoke as plain—

> Dreadfully honest also—"since our souls
> Stand each from each, a whole world's width between,
> Give me the fleshly vesture I can reach
> And rend and leave just fit for hell to burn!"—
> Why, in God's name, for Guido's soul's own sake
> Imperilled by polluting mine,—I say,
> I did resist; would I had overcome!   [VI, 26]

The conception of ideal marriage, the familiar idea of two souls' being "one flesh, . . . one soul," is expressed only negatively, only as something that has not been possible.

Pompilia is married and becomes a mother quite against her will. The other sympathetic persons in her account—Caponsacchi and the Pope—are celibate. Very near the end of her speech, Pompilia refers to her canon and champion.

>   He is a priest;
> He cannot marry therefore, which is right;
> I think he would not marry if he could.
> Marriage on earth seems such a counterfeit,
> Mere imitation of the inimitable:
> In heaven we have the real and true and sure.
> 'Tis there they neither marry nor are given
> In marriage but are as the angels: right,
> Oh how right that is, how like Jesus Christ
> To say that! Marriage-making for the earth,
> With gold so much—birth, power, repute so much,
> Or beauty, youth so much, in lack of these!
> Be as the angels rather, who, apart,
> Know themselves into one, are found at length
> Married, but marry never, no, nor give
> In marriage; they are man and wife at once
> When the true time is: here we have to wait
> Not so long neither!   [VI, 58]

This rejection of earthly sexuality—of connubial relations—
in a dramatic monologue is certainly not so thoroughgoing
as the apparent rejection of all sensuality and of the very
senses at the end of Tennyson's *Idylls*. It is an extreme instance of a woman's reaction to a marriage in which she is
a piece of property, a mere sexual object. Dramatically,
perhaps, the second speech of "Guido" is the high point of
this whole poem; philosophically, so to speak, the Pope's
monologue is the crucial one. But when *The Ring and the
Book* is regarded as a treatment of love and marriage, this
passage at the end of Pompilia's testimony can be considered
the central moment in the poem. It sums up from an innocent woman's point of view the radical contrast between
the ideal and the reality of marriage.

The opposing lawyers in Guido's trial are caricatured in
the next two sections, "Dominus Hyacinthus de Archangelis" (Book VIII) and "Doctor Johannes-Baptista Bottinius"
(Book IX). Significantly, the defender of Guido, the
"wronged husband," is a family man, devoted above all to
his young son, and the prosecutor is a single-minded bachelor pedant who cares less about Pompilia or justice than
about his own eloquence and his own career.[20] These are
set pieces of characterization, however, and it is interesting
that Guido's defender now, unlike "Half-Rome," is more

20. The defense of Guido rests on the sanctity of marriage and
the consequent duty of a wronged husband to avenge the wrong.
The defending attorney, Archangelis, does not seem, like "Half-
Rome," to be himself a jealous husband; he praises family life and
is glad not to be, like his rival the Fisc, "yet bachelor." It seems
interesting, however, that for Archangelis the happily married man
(can there be in his name an ironic echoing of Pompilia's insistence
that only angels marry spontaneously and happily?), family life

sympathetic than the speaker on the other side, the advocate who is very willing to admit some stain an Pompilia's
honor for the sake of his case.

The great soliloquy of "The Pope" (Book X) has usually
been taken to represent Browning's own point of view or
something close to it. The argument for Guido that the
Pope has to consider is

> That in this case the spirit of culture speaks,
> Civilization is imperative.
>
> . . . . .
>   Take
> Guido's life, sapped society shall crash,
> Whereof the main prop was, is, and shall be
> —Supremacy of husband over wife!
>
> . . . . .
> And there's but one short way to end the coil,—
> By giving right and reason steadily
> To the man and master: then the wife submits.
>
> [VI, 219–220]

To this argument Browning's Pope replies at once by condemning Guido and his followers to death.

In the husband's second speech, called simply "Guido"
(Book XI), the brilliant, cold, and finally desperate and
almost hysterical villain begins rather plausibly but then reveals himself for what he is, a wolf hiding behind sheep's
rhetoric. Even the beginning of his speech hints at this
truth.

> All honest Rome approved my part;
> Whoever owned wife, sister, daughter,—nay,
> Mistress,—had any shadow of any right

---

is mainly a matter of concern for, and delight in, not a wife but
a son.

> That looks like right, and, all the more resolved,
> Held it with tooth and nail,—these manly men
> Approved!   [VI, 224]

Guido still thinks of women as objects to be owned by
"manly men." Yet by the end of his long speech, during
which he gradually deteriorates and seems less and less
urbane and self-controlled, the condemned murderer can
cry out, "Pompilia, will you let them murder me?"

The story and its meaning are finally summed up in "The
Book and the Ring" (Book XII), which ends—thus ending
The Ring and the Book—with another address to Browning's "Lyric love." There may be irony, though hardly
deliberate, in the fact that this poem about a false and fatal
marriage concludes with a reference to the poet's dead
wife. In any event, the last explicit concern of "The Book
and the Ring" is with how art—the art of poetry—can obliquely show forth an essential truth.[21] One element of

21. The relationship of truth and art and Browning's conception of truth in *The Ring and the Book* have become subjects for
doubt, debate, and frequent disagreements. See, for example, Shaw's
recent study, and J. Hillis Miller's section on Browning in *The Dis-
appearance of God* (Cambridge, Mass., 1963), both of which tend
to question the poet's attainment of a clear, final, and single "truth."
For discussions of fact, art, and truth as represented in the ring
metaphor and Browning's several passages on those matters, see
Paul A. Cundiff, "The Clarity of Browning's Ring Metaphor,"
PMLA, LXIII (1948), 1276–1282, William O. Raymond, "Truth
in *The Ring and the Book*," *Victorian Newsletter*, Fall, 1956, pp.
12–13; Langbaum, *"The Ring and the Book,"* in *The Poetry of
Experience;* Cundiff, "Robert Browning: 'Our Human Speech,'"
Victorian Newsletter, Spring, 1959, pp. 1–9; Donald Smalley,
"Browning's View of Fact in *The Ring and the Book*," *Victorian
Newsletter*, Fall, 1959, pp. 1–9; Cundiff, "Robert Browning: 'Indis-
putably Fact,'" *Victorian Newsletter*, Spring, 1960, pp. 7–11;

Browning's truth, one interpretation of the poem, involves a realization of the conflict between the lovely idea of marriage made in heaven and the grim fact of marriage made on earth.

It is not at all surprising that the story in the "Old Yellow Book" appealed to Browning. The historical document contains or implies a number of situations and ideas that, it is evident from earlier poems, fascinate him: a young woman's unhappy marriage to a cruel but in some ways a fascinating husband, her escape to freedom, her poignant death; but also the question of evil, what its essence is; the fact of vastly differing and relative modes of understanding experience; the final problem, what is truth?

The Pope's reflections in the poem bring these events and themes into one focus. He confesses to himself that he may misjudge, that no man can be certain of attaining to full or ultimate truth. But he makes it clear, too, that a man can often detect, in himself and others, flagrant falsehood. Falsehood, conscious or in large part unconscious, distinguishes the goats from the sheep in Browning's cast of characters. All the speakers save three have ulterior motives and distort facts to deceive themselves, others, or both. "Half-Rome," "The Other Half-Rome," and even "Tertium Quid" project their own motives into the story and so distort it. Worse than this distortion is the professional and unquestioned hypocrisy of the lawyers, whose whole prac-

---

Langbaum, "The Importance of Fact in *The Ring and the Book*," *Victorian Newsletter,* Spring, 1960, pp. 11–17; George R. Wasserman, "The Meaning of Browning's Ring-Figure," *Modern Language Notes,* LXXVI (May, 1961), 420–426; and L. J. Swingle, "Truth and *The Ring and the Book:* A Negative View," *Victorian Poetry,* VI (Winter, 1968), 259–269.

tice of rhetoric is a deliberate attempt to turn plain truths into ambiguities. Worst of all is Guido's guile; his outer self, Count Guido Franceschini, belies his naked self, malevolent and pitiful Guido.

Facts are stated directly but, more important, emotions and attitudes are expressed and even analyzed scrupulously by Pompilia, Caponsacchi, and the Pope himself, who specifically condemns Guido not only for a murder but, first of all, for a lie. This lie, the man's essential sin, which resulted from greed and led to violence, was Guido's wedding of Pompilia.

> He purposes this marriage, I remark,
> On no one motive that should prompt thereto—
> Farthest, by consequence, from ends alleged
> Appropriate to the action. . . .
> The best, he knew and feigned, the worst he took.
>
> [VI, 175]

His was, then, "a marriage—undertaken in God's face / With all those lies so opposite God's truth" (VI, 176). This "wedded lie" is the corruption beneath and behind the husband's and murderer's guilt; and this corruption seems at last virtually to be the essence of evil in *The Ring and the Book*—not to perceive, communicate, and act openly, but to distort, lie, and manipulate. Browning suggests very early in the poem that he is aware of a paradox here, for his own poetic art is one of refraction, of fictiveness, of using and caricaturing people; but he finally defends this art as telling "truth / Obliquely."

The lie in life, not art, the use of false words and false poses—this basic sin in *The Ring and the Book* is a sin of which most people in the work are to some degree guilty, not only the speakers in the series of monologues but also, and notably, Pietro and Violante. And the implication may be that ordinary men, neither murderers nor patrons of murderers, who enter into mammon-marriages, false and loveless marriages, whether in ancient or modern times, are as sinful in kind as the treacherous Guido.

The Ring and the Book is a very complex poem about a relatively clear story on the meanings of which a relatively simple, unambiguous judgment seems finally to be made. Its complexity results from its being psychological as well as moral, dramatic as well as didactic; it results from the tension, if not the conflict, between the two aspects of Browning's art. The ideal of truth in human relations, and especially in marriage, the most intense of such relations, is only an illusion in so far as earthly experience is concerned, while the personal relations Browning dramatizes, except for the chaste relations of Pompilia and Caponsacchi, are more or less false.

The poem makes a further connection between the idea of love and the idea of art. Often in Browning's poetry the lover is also an artist, just as the possessive husband is a collector; often the artist's creative act and the gesture of love are identical. In *The Ring and the Book*, the lover, the honest man in a close protective relationship to a woman, is Caponsacchi, a man who does not woo and cannot wed; and the artist, who comments on art, is not a lover, not even a dramatic character, but the speaker at the beginning and end of the poem, the poet himself. The poet's vision now is largely one of falsehoods and earthly failure, and he suggests that he can express the truth of that vision only indirectly. The possibility of a true sexual love in Pompilia's world is uncertain, and the artist's very "truth" may seem ambiguous.[22] For Tennyson, the idea of sexual love, of marriage, may represent the relationship of the isolated soul to the world of society and of sense—or the failure of that relationship—but it may also specifically suggest the relationship of the solitary artist to his own society—or the failure of that relationship. It may be exaggerating to declare that, like Tennyson, Browning apparently comes to doubt the spiritual creativity of sex, even to fear sex. Pompilia, after all, is a dramatic character. Yet at the end of *The Ring and the Book* the possibility of honest sexual love and perhaps even "honest" art remains uncertain.

Later Poems: Marriage as a Problem

Browning's long poems of the seventies touch in various ways on domestic love, inequities in marriage, and infidelity. *Balaustion's Adventure*, published in 1871, is a version

22. Perhaps Browning has invited, with his passages on fact and imagination, on truth in art, the attacks sometimes made on his historical accuracy as well as the disagreements referred to in the preceding note. *The Ring and the Book* is presented as an attempt to achieve a perfect marrying of literal reality and poetic insight—not only the creation of a poetic, virtual reality that reflects on various experiences in life. But do the "Old Yellow Book" and the other historical documents necessarily yield the very truths at which Browning's oblique and dramatizing art arrives, for all its psychological "relativism"? As Langbaum puts it in *The Poetry of Experience* (p. 135), the poem raises the question "whether facts really can speak for themselves" in poetry. If not, *The Ring and the Book*, although for the most part a brilliant success as a novelistic poem, fails to do what the poet apparently wanted to do, to fuse or wed fact and the poet's intuitive knowledge to form a metaphorical gold ring. If the poem fails to persuade us that it is as much historically as imaginatively true, and that the two truths are literally one, Browning's ring is not a wedding ring.

of the *Alcestis* of Euripides. Browning's girl from Rhodes, Balaustion, comments on the story of Alcestis, a wife who is willing to die for her husband and is returned to life only by the power of Heracles; finally, Balaustion changes the story. She would have it that the husband, Admetus, is reluctant to accept the sacrifice of Alcestis and later feels remorse for having done so. As DeVane points out, Browning follows here the example of Morris; and, as Betty Miller suggests, he may also project into the character of Admetus his own remorse about having proposed to Lady Ashburton after his wife's death.[23] *Prince Hohenstiel-Schwangau, Saviour of Society*, published in 1871, tends to present the poet's side of what had been a long-standing disagreement with his late wife on the merits of Napoleon III. The most extraordinary reflection of Browning's mixed feelings about sexuality and marriage, the memory of his wife, and his own brief unfaithfulness to that memory is—several critics have observed—the complex poem *Fifine at the Fair.*

Fifine is a curious poem for several reasons. It is often associated with D. G. Rossetti's "Jenny," a young man's soliloquy about a prostitute that shocked many readers in 1870, and with the "Fleshly School" controversy begun by Robert Buchanan's attack on Rossetti and Swinburne. It is true that Rossetti himself responded to *Fifine* as a veiled or implicit attack on his work; and DeVane comments that Browning's poem has "a situation clearly similar to Rossetti's [with] his young and thoughtful man of the world in Don Juan, and his harlot in Fifine."[24]

Yet the differences between the two poems are signifi-

23. DeVane, p. 356; Betty Miller, pp. 268–269.
24. DeVane, p. 367.

cant. *Fifine* is a monologue; the husband addresses his wife
(or her memory), and the likelihood of his going to the
gipsy girl, Fifine, is only hinted at finally. "Jenny," which
Rossetti regarded as a comment on the evil of prostitution,
has much less moral ambiguity than Browning's poem,
which may shock readers because the Don Juan who deftly
justifies his infidelities also speaks, often persuasively, with
the voice of Robert Browning on art, religion, and the
world at large. To be sure, some of his imagery seems to
place him with the Duke at Ferrara and other husbands in
Browning, revealing him as an urbane and intelligent collector instead of a lover, a creator. He compares Elvire,
his wife, with a Raphael painting and his light-o'-love of
the moment—perhaps Fifine—with a book of pictures by
Doré, suggesting that although a man may tire for a brief
while of even the highest art and be amused by mere illus-
trations, it is the great art that has lasting importance. His
conclusion to the passage in which he develops this imagery
is interesting: if, while he were at his Doré, he asks, he
were told that the picture gallery containing the Raphael
was on fire,

> Would not I brave the best o' the burning, bear away
> Either my perfect piece in safety, or else stay
> And share its fate, be made its martyr, nor repine?
> Inextricably wed, such ashes mixed with mine!
>   . . . . .
> For which I get the eye, the hand, the heart, the whole
> O' the wondrous wife again!   [VII, 194]

In spite of the ending, the husband's willingness even to die
in order to keep his wife, and the *Liebestod* theme of a
wedding of ashes, Don Juan thinks of women as beautiful

things to be owned and enjoyed—even his precious wife Elvire. This attitude would seem, from the poet's point of view, to condemn him.

There are more fully developed images that create more complexity. The prologue to *Fifine*, titled "Amphibian," is about swimming in a bay, and this Swinburne-like subject is dealt with in a strange way: the air is the spiritual realm, and the butterfly that hovers over the swimming poet is the spirit of his dead wife; the dry land is the everyday world of "noise and dust"; and the sea is the sphere of "passion and thought" (VII, 165).[25] Swimming, then, is immersing oneself in passion and thought, and for the poet that means immersing himself in poetry.

But his character Don Juan uses the same imagery differently. He, too, is a man of passion and thought, but his equivalent for poetry is sexual adventure. His defense of such adventure to his wife uses this very imagery, and it is one of the most remarkable of all psychological explanations of the sex-obsessed personality of Don Juan. He speaks of an impulse to rise from the false to the true, and he seems to equate falsehood with illicit sexuality and truth with marital fidelity, just as Tennyson does in the *Idylls*. His extraordinary argument is that he can best aspire to the air when he is in the sea; he can most nearly understand, imitate, and momentarily approach free spirituality when he is immersed in free sexuality. There is some sense here that the sea of gross and temporary passions is the opposite of the blue sky, which represents pure spirit, but that in the briny alien sea, spontaneous sexual passion, a

25. One critic, Henry C. Duffin, suggests the importance of this curious passage by entitling his study of Browning *Amphibian* (Cambridge, 1956).

man best grasps pure spirit—because his sexuality is base and false to this spirit, but also because physical passion is a parody, and therefore a version, of spiritual passion.

Don Juan has other lines of fanciful argument. Women, he says, are more valuable than men as conquests (sexual relations are for the moment incidental) because they give themselves completely and inspire men to reveal their best selves, or at least—and this is more likely—to pretend to be better than they have been. Don Juan demonstrates that despite his high-sounding reasons he is still a manipulator, using falsehood, flattery, and attractive dissimulation; he wants to "mimic grace," not have it. Finally, his comment that "Elvire is land not sea— / The solid land, the safe," suggesting his willingness to abjure passionate sexuality *and* aspiration to the spiritual in favor of everyday marital fidelity, may be undercut when he leaves to find the gipsy girl Fifine—for just five minutes, he says.

Yet Browning's Don Juan is still in some respects an impressive man. Even the poem's epilogue, "The House-holder," in which the poet imagines his dead wife's appearing to him and anticipates joining her in death, does not quite resolve the questions in the poem or destroy the speaker's appeal. He is certainly unlike Byron's Don Juan (just as his lines on the delightful but briny and alien sea are perhaps deliberately unlike Byron's apostrophes to the ocean in *Childe Harold*): he is no innocent child of nature. Still, although he is as false in his way, and as false to his marriage obligations, as Guido in *The Ring and the Book*, he articulates a feeling about the attraction of a natural, oceanic existence, which has its claim on the man just as a solid, dry-land, safe existence, with sanctioned and conventional marriages, does. Like Arnold in "The Forsaken Merman," Browning here suggests a contrast between the two: spontaneity and passion in the deep, order and duty on the dry land. And the poem does not provide an explicit enough frame, an unambiguous moral point of view, to insist quite clearly on the necessity of choosing only one.

Red Cotton Night-Cap Country, published in 1873, deals with contemporary events, as Browning's poetry rarely does, for all its distinctly Victorian sensibility and the contemporary relevance of its themes. Here the poet is concerned with the conflict in the darkening mind of a man who is torn between his illicit but true attachment to his mistress, a married woman, and his religious feelings, or, in the language of *Fifine*, his attraction to the airy realm of spirit. At the end, crazed, he leaps from a church tower into the air and, when no hoped-for miracle occurs, is killed. A narrative rather than a dramatic poem, this work has usually been considered unsuccessful. It does, however, indicate again Browning's interest in the relationship between sexual passions and spiritual ideals—a relationship that, once more, cannot be easily resolved, as it is by the Tennysonian Arthur, who is all spirit in the war between Soul and Sense.

Browning's next work, *Aristophanes' Apology*, was published in 1875. It is another defense of Euripides, using again the character Balaustion. In the same year *The Inn Album* appeared, the retelling in verse of a forty-year-old scandal in which a vicious roué attempts to pay a gambling debt by blackmailing the woman he once seduced. Clearly, in this story which ends with violence and death, Browning shows once again his interest in the specifically sexual ways in which men and women—especially women—can be exploited.

The later poems are somewhat less concerned with love and marriage than those of Browning's middle period. The *Pacchiarotto* volume of 1876 is largely about art and the artist. *The Agamemnon of Aeschylus* (1877) is a translation of sorts. *La Saisiaz* and *The Two Poets of Croisic* (1878) have to do with personal immortality and with literary careers. The *Dramatic Idyls* of 1879 are for the most part studies of conscience, of guilt and remorse. The second series of *Idyls* (1880) is of relatively little interest.

There are poems on love in *Jocoseria* (1883), *Ferishtah's Fancies* (1884), *Parleyings with Certain People of Importance in Their Day* (1887), and *Asolando* (1889). Three poems in *Jocoseria* are noteworthy: "Cristina and Monaldeschi," a monologue by the Swedish queen, who commands that her unfaithful lover be killed (she is almost as cool as the speaker in "The Laboratory"); "Mary Wollstonecraft and Fuseli," in which a Mary Wollstonecraft who is very little like that real writer and propagandist for women's rights declares her love for the painter; and "Adam, Lilith, and Eve," an anecdote about the first love triangle. In the *Parleyings*, the one entitled "With Daniel Bartoli" includes yet another story of a strong-minded woman, who breaks off her engagement to marry a duke, for his sake, and becomes a younger man's wife.

More interesting are the rather personal late lyrics and passages on love. In *Ferishtah's Fancies*, the stanzas that start "Not with my Soul, Love!" at the end of "Plot-Culture" come as an almost startling conclusion to a remarkable poem that in some ways goes further than "The Statue and the Bust" (or *Fifine at the Fair*) in seeming to counsel free sexual love; this lyric, addressed to Mrs. Bloomfield-Moore, insists that pure "Soul-love" is not enough, that physical expression is needed to make love incarnate. Finally, in *Asolando* there is a series of love poems that are strikingly passionate: "Now," "Humility," "Poetics," and "Summum Bonum." It is evident from these and other late lyrics that Browning retained his interest in the subject of sexual love until the end of his poetic career.

The subject of marriage is not, perhaps, so thematically central to the art of Browning as it is to that of Tennyson, for whom the harmonious joining of the sexes represents both the transcending of deep-seated conflicts and a promise, for the future, of a moral as well as physical evolution of mankind, and for whom the warfare of the sexes, or the divorce of soul and sense, means both a denial that there is any cooperative human order and a belief that history is sterile. Yet for Browning, as for Tennyson, this subject has profound, recurrent importance; for Browning, too, it raises questions of social justice—the "woman question" and, more specifically, the question of divorce—as well as questions about men's urgent sexual drives in and out of marriage and about the psychological possibility of such a union of diverse persons as the poet sometimes imagines and sometimes, apparently, claims for his wife and himself.

Browning's tendency, as he moves from his early to his late poetry, is toward a fuller understanding of how complex the subject is. He tends, in fact, to dramatize or otherwise express all of the possible attitudes toward sexuality that we have considered. In *Pippa* and many other poems, the sexual love of man for woman is a form of creativity, akin to the artist's, and it can in a sense mold the pliant woman. This love is a version of the sacramental analogy, in which sexual passion represents God's creative love of the soul and, by implication, the woman, the wife, is a sort of creature of the man, the husband. Some other poems, however, picture the woman at best as a "Queen" and often as a noble lady imprisoned in marriage, and they suggest the romantic theme of woman worship with its frequent contempt for marriage. Finally, there is a strain of psychological realism in Browning that tends to qualify if not to counter these categorical and traditional attitudes toward love, tends to show the brief experience of apparently perfect affinity but also the frequent experience of alienation within marriage and even to realize that sexual bonds may be worse than meaningless, may be virtually criminal when entered into falsely, with wholly selfish intent. These three attitudes toward sexual relations can be clarified, perhaps, by stressing how each one conceives of the woman: she is, for Browning's version of the sacramental point of view, a creature with potentiality; for his romantic and idealizing point of view, a queen or noble captive; for his more psychologically realistic and thus secular point of view, a limited, perplexed being but an independent person.

In the earlier poems, then, the spiritual ideal of marriage may evidently be betrayed for social and selfish reasons, but it still seems possible for the bold man, the artist like Jules who represents the heavenly principle of creative striving, to approximate that ideal by perceiving and then molding the beauty of the woman. Later, it is clear that some women offer more or, in another sense, less than natural potentiality—although the husband of Elizabeth Barrett Browning never dramatizes a creative woman, not a singer, not an actress, not even an amateur writer or artist! (His Mary Wollstonecraft is only a woman in love, and James Lee's wife throws "the faulty pencil" away.) Finally, the ideal of a perfect union, whether the union of strong and weak or the almost mystical oneness of equals, does not correspond to various actual experiences. The same creative imagination that marks the artist makes him, makes the poet, realize how rare perfect troth—or truth—is in human relations: how men can be variable, faithless, how women can be trapped by the legal and religious institution of marriage.

There are personal implications for the poet in all this—as a husband, as a widower, but also as a man essentially much more given than, say, Arnold or Tennyson to cosmic optimism that appeals to values transcending politics and history. Sometimes there is a tension, if not an open conflict, between the visionary wish to idealize deep impulse and the dramatic compulsion to imagine human situations. Again and again, directly or dramatically, Browning suggests a parallel between the artist's creativity and the sexual drive. He also implies, in *The Ring and the Book* and elsewhere, that being fully true, even telling the truth, if it is possible somehow in art, may be only intermittently and rarely possible in the most intimate of human relationships, a relationship that is not in this world always heavenly or ideal.

5 | Victorian and Modern

Parts of this study suggest that the major Victorian poets regarded contemporary marriage as a largely false institution that encouraged lies. Although that proposition is more true than the familiar one that all Victorians, including all writers, held marriage and the home to be sacred, the matter is not at last so simple. Great anxiety is expressed in the literature of this period about the nature of sexuality and the need to channel its force, to idealize it in romance or spiritualize it in marriage, together with profound uneasiness about the effect of the marriage contract on people, especially on women. The Romantic upheaval of ideas and sensibility, in philosophy, politics, and the arts, had produced an assumption about the value of spontaneity—including, as Blake for one made clear, sexual spontaneity—and had challenged social bondage. If Victorians generally responded skeptically to the assumption, if they were fearful that greed and cruel lust are after all inherently human, they were nevertheless, and in spite of Carlyle, affected by the moral force of the challenge. The implications of Carlyle's parallel between wives and slaves, and of the yet more shocking parallel between women and domesticated animals, were not lost on many thoughtful and influential Victorians.

These mixed and complex reactions to sexual questions that are necessarily simplified in the prose of argument and even to some extent in the prose of fiction find a fuller and often more subtle expression in the poetry of the age.

Complications

Not only is the body of Victorian poetry on sexual matters more complicated than present-day readers may assume it to be; the widely received judgments about the work of individual poets often need to be modified if not disputed. Swinburne, for example, often thought of as the one Victorian poet who celebrated carnal passion, has so paradoxical a mind that for him sexual desire is at once transformed into the idea of pain and the idea of death; and it is the idea much more than the experience of either on which he concentrates, so that, far from being fleshly, his is the most abstract and even spiritual verse of the period (and is in this Shelleyan sense the most Romantic). Sexual yearning cannot be satisfied on earth, according to Swinburne's poetry, which serves to remind us not only of the destructive power of sex but also of the existential limitation, the frustration, inherent in the very fact of being sexual. On the other hand, Arnold, the most elegiac of Victorian poets, the one for whom all experience, including love, is tinged with sadness, with a sense of frustration and ultimately of loss, is also the poet who gives clearest voice—in "Dover Beach" especially—to men's and women's deep, often desperate, yearning for love as a value to replace faith in nature, in religion, in humankind's tragic significance. Tennyson's fastidious spirituality, with its tendency to withdraw from strife and from the earthly, and Browning's aggressive optimism, with its zeal for endless striving on earth—qualities that we may consider central and simple in the work of each—are themselves profoundly qualified by the imagination of each. Indeed, in much of their best work, the poets' apparently single-minded attitudes are subjected to an oblique but nevertheless powerful criticism—what might be called unconscious self-criticism.

Tennyson's melancholy and his recurrent dream of a womblike place of escape from the pain of active life are well known. But in his verse he consistently opposes an ideal of sexual union and fruitfulness to this mood, this dream. And if the ideal fails of realization because it becomes too spiritual, becomes less real than the physical, animal facts of life the poet seems to fear, that very failure is a trenchant criticism by the poet's imagination of his intellectual contradictions, his excessive, even Manichean, idealizing. Radically different in attitude as they seem to be and in a sense really are, *The Princess, In Memoriam, Maud,* and the *Idylls* are consistent in revealing the human need for intercourse, for the proximate marriage of true minds if not of bodies, and in revealing that the alternative to this intercourse is an isolation which leads to madness or death for the individual, or a political abuse of sexuality, a state of warfare—military aggression, commercial exploitation, the warfare of ego against ego implied by total individualism—which leads to chaos for the society.

Browning's supposedly bland optimism, too, is very much qualified in his poetry of experience. One obvious instance is "James Lee's Wife," in which the woman bereft of love reads and responds to Browning's own most optimistic verse of striving, his praise of change and challenge. In *The Ring and the Book,* as well, there is a criticism, represented by the figure of the pure young woman who is both an unloved wife and a spiritually noble lady: Pompilia has striven bravely, as a Browning heroine should, to escape imprisonment and a wedded lie, yet she must at last be passively resigned to death and the hope for heaven; striving, art, and love are hardly meaningful for her in this world where people marry and are given in marriage.

The value, the truth, of marriage as experienced by men and women is repeatedly doubted by these poets. But their doubts are of several kinds. They are hardly in agreement about sexual relations and sexual spontaneity. Swinburne may idealize spontaneous sexuality, but he does not do so in the interest of sexual freedom, at least not in the sense we now might give that phrase; for him, erotic passion expresses an existential bondage. Arnold may emphasize human beings' lack of freedom, especially to express their passions, but for him the limitations through which love longs to break are personal or natural, not sacramental or merely legal. Tennyson may be disillusioned with the bonds of marriage, but he is unable to praise or finally to accept free love. And Browning, who seems again and again to celebrate the free and spontaneous acting-out of sexual desire, is haunted by the fear that passionate spontaneity itself may be ephemeral, just as the laws that arbitrarily govern it are constricting.

Sexuality as a Theme: Victorian and Modern

In Swinburne, Arnold, Tennyson, and Browning, furthermore, the very ideas of sexual order—the religious or legal bonds of marriage—and of sexual freedom or spontaneity—the freedom to express oneself sexually that can be denied to men as well as to women—may be intermixed, often ironically. Not one of them presents directly or dra-

matically a truly sacramental view of marriage that would
define it as strictly as Patmore does. Not one—not even
Arnold—is strictly and totally secular in attitude, as Meredith seems to be, with his concern for the liberating of sexual impulse and for the liberating of women from being
sexual objects. But in each there are sacramental overtones,
and in all except Swinburne the tendency to idealize sex,
even to worship Woman, is sharply qualified by a secular
awareness of sexual and psychological realities.

Questions about sexual freedom, women's rights, the perhaps essentially biological (and in itself morally neutral)
nature of sexual response, sexual order, the sexual differentiation of social roles, and the perhaps essentially demonic
or sacred nature of erotic passion—these were virtually introduced to poetry by the Victorians. And the Victorians
were probably more concerned with the basic social and
moral issues than writers since have generally been. On the
other hand, they were more attracted to romantic woman
worship than serious modern poets are, so a certain tension,
even a kind of schizophrenia—at best a creative schizophrenia—characterizes the verse of the Victorian age.

The most striking difference between Victorian and
later poets in dealing with sexual matters is that important
modern poets may take either a sacramental or a secular
attitude, but almost none of them are drawn to a woman-
idealizing, romantic view of sexuality. Hardy might be said
to represent the transition from Victorian to modern, and
his stress is almost entirely on the theme, so familiar in Arnold, of short-lived passion, of dying and dead love; he regards men and women alike as limited, fated, usually pitiful
beings. Yeats, the first clearly modern major poet, does not,
for all his myth-making, transform human sexuality into

anything like the mythic and earth-transcending idea celebrated by Swinburne; his "Crazy Jane" poems insist, rather, on the earthy, the physical, the lowly basis of spiritual love.

Perhaps the two least secular of major modern poets in regard to the subject are T. S. Eliot and Dylan Thomas, one a Christian and the other a Romantic of sorts, but a Romantic who uses Christian language and ideas. Each, in his way, echoes Victorian poets. Eliot's "Love Song of J. Alfred Prufrock" is ironic, not only because it is not a conventional love song, but also because it seems at first to be a dramatic monologue in the manner of Browning or Tennyson but in fact cannot succeed in being one—for Prufrock cannot succeed in talking to anyone but himself. *The Waste Land*, a poem whose subject is the loss of sexual and spiritual vitality in modern life, uses the familiar Victorian method of linking sexuality with religion. It suggests, with its references not only to Antony and Cleopatra but also to the Wagner's *Tristan und Isolde*, the frequent Victorian fascination with love that is irrationally passionate, law-defying, love that leads to death. But if Eliot has in common with Swinburne a conviction that such love involves more life, more truth, than the casual seductions and boring marriages of our familiar world, he is, nevertheless, quite different in turning ultimately to a religious formulation that implies at least the sacramental value of sexuality, not a romantic and antisocial, antimarriage, antifleshly attitude.

Dylan Thomas, not a conventionally religious poet, in his verse also identifies the language and emotions of sexuality with the language and emotions of religion, so that the elemental sexual energy associated with the blooming flower and destroying worm takes on a virtually sacred if not sacramental quality. His is not the sacramental sense of life and love one finds in Hopkins, the Victorian poet he most nearly echoes, yet it is surely related to the tradition of religious lyrics in which Hopkins clearly belongs, the tradition of pious Herbert but also of passionate Donne —and not to the tradition of romance. In a variety of ways, then, and certainly in their concentration on sexuality as a serious, difficult theme, these poets present a partial contrast to, but also a perceptible kinship with, the Victorians.

The idealizing of sex, however, including woman worship and woman-baiting, by no means died with the last century. We find it not so much in the major modern poets as in the lyric prose of Henry Miller and Norman Mailer and in some minor neo-Romantic verse. Is there any significant difference between the literature of today, prose as well as poetry, and that of the Victorians with respect to idealization and the whole range of possible attitudes toward sexuality, and in particular toward women? An immediate response might be that writing today can be frank and open about sex, whereas a hundred years ago the treatment had to be timid, veiled, and even hypocritical. That response, that impression, would be based in large part on differences in vocabulary. It has not been necessary in this study, as it would be in a comparable study of more recent literature, to use the familiar "four-letter words" of the common sexual language, because serious Victorian writers did not use them. The fact is in one sense trivial and in another significant. Meredith, Patmore, and Browning can deal quite as explicitly with, say, sexual intercourse as Miller or a contemporary poet can. Significantly, the Victorians may very often seem to readers clearer on the subject, because the intense and "dirty" associations readers still have for these words may tend to get in the way of a contemporary writer's specific meaning.[1]

The important differences between Victorian and modern are not mainly differences between prudery and frankness.[2] It may be fair, and it certainly is not ludicrous, to

1. Is a passage in Miller that seems to be about sexual intercourse to be read as a glorifying of mutual joy, as an insult to the woman and perhaps the conventional reader, or simply as a narrative account? Visceral reactions, along with the fact that in ordinary usage "four-letter words" have become as empty of real meaning as "oh!" and "well!" and "you know," may reduce the sense of such a passage to hardly more than that of a noise. In dealing with this problem the Joyce of *Ulysses* is much more successful than the Lawrence of *Lady Chatterley's Lover:* when the words occur in Joyce they occur as elements of believable speech and thought, they mean what they say and are no mere shouts of defiance, and they are not dwelt on relentlessly. The use of "frank" language presents a particularly acute problem to a writer like Mailer whose apparent intention to declare the terrible power and mystery of the sexual is almost fatally compromised by his use of such language. Just as sex has always been closely related to religion, so that chastity, potency, and fecundity may all be matters of sacred import, so there has always been a close parallel between obscenity and blasphemy. In Jewish tradition the name of God may not be uttered; a pious Christian does not often speak the name of Jesus Christ, and never without a mental if not literal bowing of the head. When Mailer uses the sacred words of sex too freely he can seem to his readers to debase what he wants to present seriously and perhaps to exalt.

2. One might, however, raise the question of explicit psychological range. Except for Swinburne, no Victorian writer of note deals directly with homosexual attachments; this aspect of sexuality has become a subject of considerable importance in the literature of our time—especially in the fiction of such European writers as Mann, Gide, and Genet, and the work of Iris Murdoch, Mary Renault, and, in America, James Baldwin. (Forster's posthumously published *Maurice*, on this subject, is a touching and significant novel but not as impressive as his best fiction.) The theme of

argue that we can learn more about human sexual nature
from their literature than from that being written now.
The essential questions of men's and women's sexual freedom are present in their poems about wooings and wed-
dings, isolation and divorce. When Victorian writers were
reactionary, they were often more illuminating and humane than modern sexual reactionaries, with their tendency
to insist on feminine submissiveness and to brutalize women
by regarding them as objects for pleasure or for breeding.
Twentieth-century versions of the male mystique generally lack the religious or romantic belief in marriage of a
Patmore or even a Rossetti; and if it is true that Victorian
husbands used the myth of sacred marriage to keep wives
in bondage, it is also true that they deeply needed to believe the myth for other reasons as well. Kate Millett comments aptly that "in Mill one encounters the realism of
sexual politics, in Ruskin its romance and the benign aspect
of its myth."[3] It might be added that poets and people in
general have always needed myth as well as realism to live
by—myth more in keeping with social realities, however,
than Ruskin's was. The post-Romantic artist and the
thoughtful person must try to humanize and realize their
myths—as the Victorians earnestly tried.

Relevance

Finally, we return to the quality that makes literature
modern in any age—not its specific relevance to the present

---

homosexuality in modern literature suggests an attempt to liberate
and understand the varieties of sexual experience and also implies
profound criticism of, and alternatives to, the great western myth
of marriage.

3. *Sexual Politics* (New York, 1970), p. 89.

situation but its more general relevance to the universal human situation. There are many points of view we could now take toward sexuality as it appears in nineteenth-century literature. A Christian response might be that when religious faith is lost, marriage ceases to be sacred and is debased to the animal level. A Marxist might well point out that pure capitalism inevitably turns marriage into a "cash nexus" exploitation of sex so that it is essentially the same as prostitution, and that Dickens, Browning, and other reflect this situation. A feminist might say that marriage laws and customs have long debased and exploited women and that this truth began to be widely recognized in the nineteenth century.

There is some validity in each of these arguments. But the theme of marriage in Victorian poetry, especially in the poetry of Tennyson and Browning, is richer than any one of these responses indicates. Tennyson, we have seen, is inclined to present the ideal of marriage in relatively personal and direct verse, making wedlock a metaphor, a symbolic union, while he dramatizes—in monologue or dialogue —the frustration of marriage or its failure; more consistently dramatic, Browning is more consistently interested in the immediate experience of sexual love and union or of divorce. Still, these two poets, as well as Meredith, Clough, and Arnold, have a good deal in common. Before Freud, but of the age that nurtured him, before D. H. Lawrence, but of the age that produced him, they were already aware of the creative and the destructive, the repressively self-destructive, aspects of human sexuality. Their poetry, in which the experiences of marriage and divorce, momentary ecstasy and deeply frustrating isolation, are imagined, attempts to present truly, cutting through the polite lies of

society, both the need for a humane idea of a bond between the sexes and the knowledge that sexual relations,
which can be intense but brief, are invested with profound
importance but invite an ambivalent response.

The theme of marriage, then, is a central theme for the
Victorian poets as well as the prophets and novelists of the
age, one that has far-ranging implications for their world
and for ours as well.

Index

SEX AND MARRIAGE IN
VICTORIAN POETRY

Designed by R. E. Rosenbaum.
Composed by York Composition Company, Inc.,
in 11 point linotype Janson, 2 points leaded,
with display lines in monotype Deepdene.
Printed letterpress from type by York Composition Company
on Warren's Number 66 text, 50 pound basis,
with the Cornell University Press watermark.
Bound by Vail-Ballou Press, Inc.